Young at Eighty

The prolific public life of
Michael Young

Young at Eighty

The prolific public life of
Michael Young

Edited by

**Geoff Dench
Tony Flower
Kate Gavron**

CARCANET

First published in 1995 by
Carcanet Press Limited
402-406 Corn Exchange Buildings
Manchester M4 3BY

ISBN 1 85754 243 6

The publisher acknowledges financial assistance
from the Arts Council of England

Typeset by Tony Flower

Back cover photograph courtesy of the *Guardian*

Printed and bound in England by SRP Ltd., Exeter

Funded by
THE
ARTS
COUNCIL
OF ENGLAND

Contents

QUALITIES

IDEAS

Introduction

Michael Young is now eighty. This collection of essays, by some of the people who have been influenced by him during his remarkable public life, is offered to him on his birthday as a tribute to the continuing inspiration which he gives us. He is surely one of the leading citizens of the modern age. Not only has Michael been close to the heart of public life for well over half a century - perhaps ever since his schooldays when he had several discussions with Roosevelt on the build-up towards war in Europe - but he has been actively involved in many of the great issues of our age. At the same time we are conscious that because of his unassuming manner and quiet ways of going about things, there are many people who simply do not realise just how much he has achieved and contributed. Asa Briggs is preparing a biography which will do much to reveal the full extent of Michael's involvement and impact, and to put his role in perspective. In the meantime we hope that this volume will promote wider recognition of the flavour and astonishing range of his activities.

This collection makes no claims to being either comprehensive or perfectly balanced. The decision to produce it was only made a few months ago so, given the tight deadline, a number of people who would have liked to contribute items to it were unable to do so. This means there are, inevitably, some gaps in it. By the same token, we had no time to draw up a master framework before inviting people to write pieces, so there is some degree of overlap in the contributions that we have received. With hindsight this does not seem such a bad thing. For in the event we have been rewarded for our haste with a spontaneity and diversity of approaches and styles which we might well have inhibited if we had taken on a more pro-active editing role.

As a result, the pieces brought together in this volume represent quite a mixture. They include evaluations of Michael's ideas and influence, analyses of his contribution to particular organisations and causes, personal tributes from colleagues, attempts to analyse what it is that makes him tick, and explorations of issues which are close to his heart. This rich variety goes some way towards reflecting the tremendous compass of Michael's interests and the scope of his spirit; and the most commonly repeated refrain among contributors to this collection who have looked at the emerging list of contents has been

i

that they really had no conception of how many different things he is up to. How much more astonished will be readers who have not themselves worked with him.

In spite of the enormous span of his public life, and the variety of angles adopted here for looking at it, certain themes run strongly throughout the whole book. Most of the commentaries refer to Michael's total commitment, and his unquenchable belief in the indomitable character of the human spirit, in the supreme importance of every individual's life, and of the value of people coming together in mutual support; simple but utterly fundamental matters which many of us tend to forget. In terms of this elemental humanism he can have few peers. But this book is not a simple panegyric. Running alongside the celebration of Michael's love of humanity there is a frank recognition that working with him is not easy. Words like irritating, exasperating, badgering and so on pop up regularly to describe his behaviour. His vision is clearly so demanding, his own will so strong, that travelling with him is not for the faint-hearted or self-indulgent.

It is however significant that all of these little expressions of annoyance which occur should be visibly embedded in a solid rock of affection and admiration. We are all generally aware that our complaints about Michael are an aspect of our own failure to keep up with him, and are directed in truth at our own weakness. When the pressure builds up though, and there is stress and pain, we are liable to blame him for it. The frank accounts in this volume contain some valuable material offering insight into what it is like working with someone so creative and industrious, and also perhaps into the psychology of leadership. But this is not an analysis that we are competent to pursue ourselves.

Although any single-dimensional classification is bound to be difficult within such a diverse collection, the essays can be grouped into three broad categories.

First of all there is a group looking at some of the specific organisations and institutions which have been created by Michael since the early fifties when he grasped at a destiny outside of a career with the Labour Party. Then there are a number of contributions which try to evaluate or summarise Michael's activities across a wider range, or to pin down exactly what it is that is so distinctive and remarkable about them. Finally a few discursive pieces examine the analytic content of Michael's thought and writings, or plough a parallel furrow to these, both as a means of understanding more about the man and also of locating Michael's wider position and importance. These three categories, albeit ambiguous and overlapping, have been used to generate the main structure and progression of this book: from activities, to qualities, to analytic ideas.

The chapters open with a discussion by Peter Willmott of Michael's decision to step out of direct employment in the post-war Labour Party into the world of independent research and policy analysis, where most of the contributors to this volume have known him. Peter, who himself made the move with Michael from Transport House, details how the Institute of Community Studies was set up by Michael as a base from which to challenge the giant of statism which had stolen the heart of the Party.

We get a glimpse of the vitality which Michael has brought to this mission in Jeremy Mitchell's account of his involvement with Michael over two decades and in three major organisations. The sunset image of Jeremy sitting, thoroughly drained after a long and probing conversation, while Michael moves off to prepare for a new adventure, is utterly familiar. The contribution of Ann Cartwright illustrates that Michael's empire is constantly evolving, and that one of the most crucial processes is that whereby new institutions are eased to the margin once they become capable of surviving autonomously.

Many new ideas and creations, on the other hand, never become properly established at all, or not in the forms originally intended, as Peter Laslett shows for the Open University and some related projects. This is not the case however with the distance teaching initiatives exported *via* IEC, and Tony Dodds' essay indicates that in this area at any rate Michael has found a number of doors ready to be pushed open all over the world.

Marianne Rigge shows in her outline of the development of the College of Health that Michael is on the look-out for unlocked doors and innovative opportunities almost constantly, and certainly not least when in hospital recovering from an operation. A common factor in this seems to be an almost instinctual capacity for fellow-feeling, and Tessa Blackstone recounts that even as President of Birkbeck College he could not resist becoming a student again himself and marvelling at the commitment and concentration of his fellow-students. This belief in the boundless curiosity and creativity of ordinary people, and the uniqueness of every person's experience and achievements, emerges strongly in the history of Open College of the Arts presented here by David Davies.

It is the impetus too behind a number of recent initiatives undertaken by Michael, and reported by Kirsteen Tait, which represent a revival of his interest in the importance of childhood and of protecting the opportunities for children to develop. Kate Gavron shows how he has also become actively concerned in recent years with the welfare of the Bengali community in and around Bethnal Green. It is fitting that he should now be committed to the people of Tagore, who was such a strong influence and inspiration for Michael himself in his youth. To conclude this section, Wyn Tucker and Sue Chisholm suggest that ICS can now be seen clearly as Michael's home base, from which he has carried out developmental research and set up most of the practical ventures enabling citizens to come together in empowering associations. It is the hub of the empire he has created.

In the first of those pieces which are mainly analytic and evaluative in focus, Peter Marris, who himself contributed much towards developing the ICS research style, looks at how the classic studies carried out in the fifties and sixties can be seen as 'exemplary stories', whose authority rests in the end on the integrity of their research method. Garry Runciman makes a related point by drawing our attention to Michael's incredible facility for communicating easily with people from all sorts of backgrounds. It is this which gives his writing and analysis a directness which is so often absent in sociology. This gift of Michael's must be related to his strong belief in the worth and dignity of every person; and Vincent Brome feels the personal integrity arising out of this to be Michael's strongest and possibly defining characteristic. This contribution takes us further than any of the others across the line dividing private from public life; but Vincent, as the contributor who has known Michael for the longest, is surely entitled to do that.

When it comes to trying to distil the essence of what it is that Michael does, Tony Flower produces a thumbnail guide to some of the processes of institutional invention, casting Michael as a social sentinel, permanently on watch for cases of social distress, and for ways of alleviating them by introducing small, practical changes which have a built-in propensity for maximum growth and leverage. Malcolm Dean defines Michael's method as that of an architect designing solutions to social problems, and declares that Michael will be remembered as more successful at this than Robert Owen. What fascinates Roger Warren Evans is Michael's skill as a draftsman in laying down a constitution for new organisations, and his finesse in retaining just the necessary minimum power for himself. Bob Gavron is impressed by Michael's flair for making money, which could have won him a personal fortune several times over if he had wanted it. But apparently he does not, and prefers to seek out a new cause and challenge than to cash in on past victories. From the other side of what is, to many researchers and activists, an opaque screen, Patricia Thomas reveals that the Trusts sometimes do yearn for some more stimulating and worthwhile applications, and that Michael is usually game for a few.

The American sociologist, Daniel Bell, argues that Michael's whole assembly of talents and interests is in itself extremely unusual, and has no parallel in the USA, but that in the end it is his ability to engage successfully with the instruments of government which truly marks him out. This view is not entirely endorsed by Chelly Halsey, who has sat with Michael near to these instruments, and who points instead to Michael's deep moral concern, for community and fellowship, and his arguable emergence lately as an ethical socialist, in distinguishing his influence. Confirmation for the idea that Michael is only intermittently engaged in direct political action comes from Trevor Smith and Alison Young, who prefer to see Michael as moving periodically between different modes of activity, and perhaps as being somewhat ahead of his time in doing so. Andrew McIntosh expands this by documenting the way in which Michael is not a frequent attender at Westminster, but has a pattern of involvement there which enables him to give consistent support to favoured causes.

Paul Barker opens the section emphasising the theoretical analyses informing Michael's work with a discussion of the meritocracy idea, which he argues we should not make the mistake of failing to treat as a serious prediction just because the story is couched in irony. In a similar vein, Ronald Dore explores what the meritocracy model would have led us to anticipate, and whether any of it is coming to pass. Geoff Dench chases some leads in Michael's thought concerning motherhood, and the mother-daughter bond, to see how far Michael may look on the distaff side for his model of communal and civic virtues.

Next, Naomi Sargant examines the part played by the interests of consumers in Michael's conception of a democratic state, which underpins not just his political vision but also many of his practical ventures. Michael's interlude exploring the rhythms of time, which for a while drew him further away from the political arena than any of his previous interests, and which - significantly perhaps - he spent many years anticipating before initiating, is measured and drawn up here by Tom Schuller. Asa Briggs then reflects on the distinctive nature of Michael's attachment, not just to time, but also to place, and how unusual this is for a sociologist, whose primary focus of interest is necessarily on institutions.

Finally, Mary Douglas considers Michael's recent work on the importance of funerals, both in reaffirming community among the living and also in extending it meaningfully to the dead.

This last chapter might appear to bring us to the end of a natural cycle. But Michael is not so easily contained and pinned down as that. Even as we write he is restoring his interest in the beginning of life and the education of young children, and is busily revisiting the subjects of housing and community, and the new problems which have arisen in the forty years since *Family and Kinship* first appeared. His will to solve yet more problems and overcome further challenges seems to be as strong as ever, and he is certainly not ready yet to have a pattern imposed on it from outside. We have collected a certain amount of information together on his enterprises and writings so far, which we present at the end of the essays. But we have no sense of it being the time to carry out a definitive accounting, as there are many things still to be done. Michael is young at eighty.

Happy birthday, Michael. We all hope to celebrate many more of them with you.

Geoff Dench, Tony Flower & Kate Gavron
9th August 1995

ACTIVITIES

Resolving the Dilemma of Bigness
Peter Willmott

In 1948 the Labour Party published a discussion pamphlet, *Small Man, Big World,* by its then research secretary (Young, 1948f). It was about the defects of large-scale organisations, public and private; its argument was that although democracy requires smallness, efficiency often requires bigness and that this presents one of the 'dilemmas of modern society'. Michael examined three main solutions: 'establishing the right kind of democratic leadership', 'establishing close two-way communication' between top and bottom and 'reducing the size of organisation' wherever possible.

It was, incidentally, this same pamphlet that prompted my first meeting with Michael Young. As a mature student at Ruskin College, Oxford, I had written enthusiastically about it and received in return an invitation to chat over a pub lunch that led subsequently to an enduring relationship as colleague and friend.

Michael was later to write that *Small Man, Big World* belonged to a period in his life when 'I still had faith that one had only to hammer away' to persuade governments to introduce the necessary reforms, adding that as time went on he came to believe that the impetus was more likely to come from outside governments and political parties (Young, 1983c). This perception and his decision to turn his back on a career in party politics and government power - he could certainly have been an MP, and eventually a minister, had he chosen to go down that road - was a crucial step in the development of his life and work.

The Institute of Community Studies

In 1953 Michael established the Institute in Bethnal Green, East London - a tiny institution, intended in its modest way to help combat the formidable array of large ones whose faults he had identified so clearly in the pamphlet. The other founder members were what Michael has recently described as 'the three Peters' - Townsend, Marris and myself (Young, 1995a). Fittingly, our main research focus in the Institute's early years was the smallest institution of all, the family in its nuclear and extended versions.

Michael was able to launch the new institute because he had per-

1

suaded his fellow members of the Elmgrant Trust, the Dartington Hall charity, to put up some initial money. Further funds came from the Nuffield Foundation and from the late Edward Shils of Chicago University, some to begin with from Shils himself and then larger sums from the Ford Foundation on Shils's recommendation. Writing later about the development of sociology in Britain after 1945, Shils described the institute as 'the chief achievement of sociology outside the universities' and paid tribute to its founder as 'the first of those Labour supporters who renounced the tired phrases of inherited socialist doctrine and sought contact with reality by other means' (Shils, 1985).

The original prospectus for the new research centre - a *Draft Proposal for the Establishment of a London Institute of Community Studies* - laid emphasis on two distinctive features (Young, 1953b). The first was the link with policy. The institute's studies would seek to examine the daily lives and needs of the working-class people whose interests had so far been inadequately recognised by those in power; this would enable them to see how effectively existing policies helped such people and to propose new ones where necessary.

The second characteristic of the new institute was to be a concern with readability, the need to 'make social science intelligible to the interested layman'. This was linked to the preoccupation with social policy. There would be little value in reporting policy-oriented studies unless the findings and proposals were, as Michael put it, 'free from the deplorable jargon that afflicts so much of sociology'.

The first result of the new approach was *Family and Kinship in East London* (Young and Willmott, 1957). Part of the reason for selecting Bethnal Green as a base in the 1950s had been because the area contained much poor housing and was therefore a place from which large numbers of families were moving out to the new municipal estates in Essex.

Our initial question had been about how people in Bethnal Green and in the new suburban estate in Essex had been affected by the policy of dispersal from the slums. Those we met in the new housing estate told us, as we had expected them to, about the lack of corner shops and pubs, the inadequacies of the local bus services and the costs in time and money of commuting back to London for work. But they also told us about the relatives left behind and about the gap that left in their lives. These early findings sent us back to Bethnal Green to look more closely at its patterns of kinship and community.

Although kinship now became the central theme, we were more than ever aware that it was critically influenced by housing and planning policies. As we said in our new introduction to the relaunched *Family and Kinship* some 30 years later:

'Because of the importance of the system of kinship - which became the core of our study - the effects of official policy on the family were even greater than we had imagined. When young families were rehoused away from Bethnal Green they were cut off from their relatives, and from the mutual aid thus provided. Contrary to the stereotype, they had not been socially isolated where they lived in the city. But they certainly were after the move.' (Young and Willmott, 1986 edition).

The informal social ties - particularly those of kinship and neighbourhood - that meant so much to so many people were ignored because the common view, among sociologists incidentally as well as politicians, civil servants and journalists, was that they hardly existed in modern, supposedly anonymous, cities. The failure to understand what mattered to people had led to misconceived policies.

In the light of our research findings, *Family and Kinship* advocated a shift to policies that would enable the members of extended families to stay close to each other if they wanted to. This meant both thinking again about ways of rehousing more people inside the cities and devising allocation procedures that would enable those members of social groups who wanted to move together to do that.

The next two books in the institute's series, by our colleagues Peter Townsend and Peter Marris, similarly contained recommendations for making policies more responsive to people's needs. Townsend, in *The Family Life of Old People*, found that most elderly people in Bethnal Green were members of three-generation families, and he showed the ways in which family support augmented - and often far outweighed - that from the official services. His policy suggestions were for ways in which those services could 'support the family' in its task (Townsend, 1957).

In his study of *Widows and Their Families* Marris found, contrary to our expectations, a tendency for widows to withdraw somewhat from kinship relationships, partly as an emotional reaction to their grief and partly because of a desire to maintain their independence. His policy proposals were intended to strengthen that independence by changes in widows' benefits and in particular by abolishing the earnings rule that prevented many of them from securing financial independence by working part-time and complementing their benefit (Marris, 1958).

My reason for going over this ground again after so many years is to demonstrate that, despite our central interest in kinship, we all sought to propose policies that would meet the (often unrecognised) needs of ordinary people. Those first three studies have been followed by a score or more of others, all including recommendations for policy (examples from the next four decades are Willmott, 1966; Young and Willmott, 1973a; Marris, 1982; Young and Schuller, 1991d). Although many of the institute's studies have been in far-off places, including Lagos, Nigeria (Marris, 1961) and American inner cities (Marris and Rein, 1967), through the years it has continued to function as a local 'laboratory' in London's East End, and its current research is largely focused on Tower Hamlets, of which Bethnal Green is a part.

Creation of New Bodies

So for more than four decades policy-oriented research has continued to be one of the main aims of the institute. But research did not remain Michael's sole preoccupation for long, and it is easy to see why he thought it inadequate on its own. Although research can sometimes help to change policy, the process by which it does so is slow and uncertain. Most policy researchers can recognise that the attempt to bring about change through research alone depends upon what Michael described as 'hammering away' to persuade governments. Few saw so clearly that the alternative was to do something about it.

Michael had already indicated in his initial prospectus that he hoped that 'action would follow the research'; he was then thinking mainly of local action in Bethnal Green - 'action by the local community itself to relieve the distress which exists among its members' (Young, 1953b).

The turning point came with the creation of the Consumers' Association in 1957 and the publication of the first *Which?*. The decision to publish the first consumers' journal in Britain was taken by a group of which Michael was a key member. The group had hesitated, partly from fear of libel (a fear largely dispelled when the leading libel lawyer advised that the anxiety was unfounded) and partly because of lack of resources. Pressing the others to take the risk of going ahead with a first issue of *Which?*, Michael typically added an inducement by offering the Institute as a base from which to launch it.

To the surprise of everyone the response from press and public was staggering. It was so large that on the first day and over the next four or five, research had to be set aside as all members of the institute's small staff were called upon to deal with the sacks of mail from which spilled out thousands of letters from people (mainly middle-class, then as now) eager to subscribe to *Which?* and to join the Consumers' Association. A stream of telephone enquiries from press and public added to the atmosphere of frenzied excitement. By the weekend a group of volunteers had been gathered to paint up an empty garage made available by the University House settlement next door, and a few days later the first staff of the Consumers' Association were installed there.

An instant success, *Which?* was soon large and affluent enough to move to bigger offices elsewhere and, as is well known, continued to expand and flourish. Despite all efforts the journal has failed to reach the wider audience it aimed to reach. But, as Naomi Sargant points out in her contribution, there can be little doubt that consumers in general have benefitted from its reports and its campaigning efforts, even though it still benefits mainly middle-class consumers.

It is my belief that the experience of using the institute as a base for *Which?* had a dramatic effect on Michael Young. Seven years earlier, while still Labour's head of research, he had in fact included a proposal for a national consumers' body in the Labour Party's manifesto for the 1950 general election, an election that Labour narrowly scraped through but that was followed 18 months later by another, won decisively by the Conservatives. Commenting later, he said of his proposal '*luckily* (italics added), nothing was done to implement it, leaving the way open for a private initiative' (Young, 1983c - Epilogue).

The wording is important because it indicates a shift in thinking, and chimes with the remark I quoted earlier about Michael coming to believe that the impetus for change was more likely to come from outside than inside government. The launch of *Which?* heightened his awareness that independent bodies, intermediate between the family and the large institutions both public and private, could be crucial in strengthening the power of ordinary people. Michael also saw that in the Institute of Community Studies he had a vital tool: a potential launch pad for further new bodies. From then on the institute's role was not just to carry out policy-oriented research, important though that continued to be; it was also to generate intermediary bodies that could defend people's interests against the might of the state and the great private corporations alike.

The examples are too countless for me to deal with, and I shall mention only a few. The first among these were concerned with education, coinciding with Michael's membership of the Plowden Committee on primary schools (Central Advisory Council for Education, 1967) and a number of research studies that he undertook at about the same time (Young, 1965a; Young and McGeeney, 1968b). The Advisory Centre for Education, with its journal *Where?*, represented the interests of parents and many teachers, while the National Extension College aimed to provide and encourage 'distance teaching' for adults by means of courses by correspondence, radio and television.

It was set up partly to campaign for the Open University, a proposal first put forward by Michael in *Where?* in 1962. Writing later about the Open University, he explained:

> '*I was prompted to push for it partly by the satire, intended
> to be deadly serious as well as funny, embodied in the book,*
> The Rise of the Meritocracy *[Young, 1958]. The meritocratic
> elite of the future was to be open only to those who could as
> children sail through one examination after another. The
> Open University was, and is, open to anyone, with or
> without qualification.*' (Young, 1983c.)

He also commented, echoing the remark I quoted earlier about the
critical importance he attached to independence from the state, that the
Open University was '*unfortunately* [italics again added] too expensive
for anyone but the government to finance'. The implication seemed to
be that had he been able to launch the Open University from Bethnal
Green he would have done that too.

The principle of encouraging distance teaching through an
independent body was later extended to an international scale by the
creation of the International Extension College. This and many
subsequent initiatives are discussed in other contributions here; and
most are included in the list near the end of this volume. As these
discussions show, not all of the new bodies have proved to be equally
successful, although the success rate has certainly been high. Indeed
some have spawned others. An example is the Mutual Aid Centre,
which has itself created a range of self-help groups and bodies,
including the College of Health, Healthline and the MKOK DIY car
repair workshop in Milton Keynes.

Conclusion

I return to Michael's 1949 discussion pamphlet, *Small Man, Big World*.
Despite the limitations he later identified, its theme was an important
one and its title an augury. It was a pointer to what, in default of
effective responses from governments or political parties, he - and
those he was able to inspire or cajole into helping him - were to do
later through a combination of research and innovative action.

Michael's method embraces both social research and social action;
and since the 1950s his life has been a constant restless movement
between the two. He has continued to spend much of his time working
as a researcher and much of the research has been of a basic kind that
adds to understanding about modern society in ways that do not fit
neatly into a dichotomy between research and action. *The Rise of the
Meritocracy*, for instance, was much more than an essay on the
limitations and dangers of selective education, and an argument for

wider educational opportunity. It used a dystopian vision to challenge what Michael saw as a fundamental - and damaging - trend in British society.

The Metronomic Society (Young, 1988b) is on the face of it even further away from detailed issues of policy, ranging as it does over biology, genetics, circadian rhythms and the organisational patterns of modern industry. But the book does end with recommendations intended, as the blurb puts it, to 'resolve the conflicts between the needs of the person and the needs of the organisation' - a phrase that echoes the familiar aspiration of making a large and complex world more accommodating to ordinary people.

Michael Young's strongest commitment has been to the twin tasks of policy research and institutional innovation, both directed to the same end. It would be absurd for me to suggest that his whole professional life has been confined to these preoccupations. As I have noted, three and a half decades after the publication of *Small Man, Big World* he almost dismissed it as the product of a more innocent phase (Young, 1983c). But I would argue that the central theme in his work since he wrote it has been the attempt to resolve in these two ways the dilemma so aptly expressed in its title.

A Triptych of Organisations
CA: SSRC: NCC
Jeremy Mitchell

The phone call came on a Saturday evening. 'Could you meet me for a drink before lunch tomorrow? At the Flask in Highgate? Say, twelve o'clock? There's something I would like to talk to you about.' It was not the first time that I had been propositioned by Michael Young and it would not be the last. As the summer sun filtered through the trees in the courtyard of the Flask, I was given a potted history of the East End garment business - the changeover from hand to mass production, the falling numbers of Jewish tailors, the survivors finding it difficult to market their skills. However, a marvellous opportunity had opened up - the Belgian trouser market. Because of some glitch in international trade, there was a shortage of mens' trousers in Belgium. East End tailors had a comparative advantage. Their twenty - or was it thirty? - minute trouser meant that they would be very price-competitive in Belgium. However, they didn't have the marketing organisation or skills to seize this opportunity. What was needed was someone to set up an export marketing co-operative. He was sure he could get hold of a start-up grant to help get the thing going. I was just the person. Could I start next week?

For perhaps half an hour, the web of words which he span seemed immensely seductive. There would be benefits for everyone. The East End garment business would be resuscitated. The Belgians would no longer be trouserless. Once I had got the thing up and running, I could go on to a more relaxing project - international disarmament, perhaps. It needed a clear head to resist the attractions of the proposition and plead for time to think about it. By Monday morning, my sanity had returned and I phoned to say it was not for me.

This was not my first experience of Michael Young's imaginative and energetic approach to solving problems. For more than two decades, it played an intermittent but powerful part in my own career at Consumers' Association, the Social Science Research Council and the National Consumer Council.

Consumers' Association

Many years before the conversation at the Flask, I had learned to be wary of my own judgment in assessing Michael's new ideas. We first met in 1954, at supper with Peter and Phyllis Willmott in the flat above the newly launched Institute of Community Studies in Victoria Park Square. Over coffee, he produced some copies of a long established American magazine, *Consumer Reports*, published by Consumers Union on a non-profit basis. What did I think of it? What about launching something similar in Britain? I thumbed through the comparative test reports on cars, refrigerators, washing machines, patent medicines - even hunting rifles. 'It would never work here', I said.

Wisely, my view was ignored. With an Anglo-American couple, Ray and Dory Goodman, Michael set out about preparing the launch of *Which?* and the founding of Consumers' Association, described in detail by Eirlys Roberts in *Which? 25 - Consumers' Association 1957-1982*. A year after the launch, well established into what stretched ahead as a lifetime career with ICI, I had taken my first phone call from Michael. *Which?* was up and running, with a growing membership, but the testing and research needed to be properly organised and put on a systematic basis. They were setting up a new post running the research side, working to the Editor. Was I interested? If so, Eirlys Roberts would interview me.

The floor of the *Which?* office had an alarming tilt to it and the first test was to keep my balance walking across the room. I can remember nothing of the interview other than coming away enthused by the prospect of working with Eirlys and Michael.

In the months and years that followed, these two were the driving forces in the development of CA. Eirlys instilled a love of truth, simplicity of expression and attention to detail into her research and editorial team. From the chair, Michael bombarded the organisation with an uninterrupted stream of new ideas, new initiatives - many good, a few terrible. There was no time for consolidation, for steady progress. CA seemed to become the conduit for Michael's pragmatic radicalism. Much time was spent appraising his proposed ventures and clearing up the debris if they failed.

The tensions in this situation disclosed a rare strength in Michael - an unsentimental approach to both people and institutions. Never content to rely solely on the company of people with the same background and outlook as himself, he chose colleagues who offered a wide diversity of experience and attitudes. These choices were often brilliantly successful, but in some cases disastrous. The failures did not survive for long.

The same was true of new institutions. Those that did not click, or were too far ahead of their time, were rapidly discarded. Michael had the unusual ability to move on quickly rather than linger over possible failures. One example was Unit 2, a research organisation set up in October 1960 as a vehicle for his political interpretation of the consumer interest, which he realised could not easily be accommodated within the scope of CA. In *The Chipped White Cups of Dover* (1960a) - a Wilkesian pamphlet with a Wilkesian title - Michael charted the decline of Britain and the failure of the two major parties to tackle the many aspects of national life which shackled the lives of the people. Why should manufacturers be allowed to fix shop prices? Why are shops shut at the only times when working women are free to buy? Why are public services so unresponsive to people's needs? Why are council tenants subject to petty restrictions? Why is higher education available to so few young people? Why is our political system so insular and unwilling to learn from the solutions that other countries have found? The two major parties were dominated by producer interests. What was needed was a new progressive party, which would focus on the needs and interests of individuals.

While Unit 2 did not survive for more than a few weeks, the core ideas put forward in 1960 have had a much longer life. They can be traced through to the formation of the SDP more than twenty years later - and beyond, to the current transformation of the Labour Party. Even the answers to a Gallup Poll question that Michael commissioned for the pamphlet, on likely backing for a new party at a General Election, were remarkably prescient of the SDP's eventual support - 25 per cent said they would vote for a new party.

Social Science Research Council

In 1965, I left CA for the National Economic Development Office, in the mistaken belief that it was nearer to the fulcrum of change in the heady early days of the Labour government. Michael himself had been approached by Tony Crosland, then Secretary of State for Education and Science, to be the first Chairman of the Social Science Research Council. This must have been an irresistable offer. It was an opportunity to bring the techniques of the social sciences to bear on the solution of the now familiar but extremely complex problem - how to transform the institutions of society so that they could better serve the needs of individual people.

Within a year of the SSRC being set up, I received another phone call from Michael. The Scientific Secretary of the SSRC, who had been inherited from the Department of Scientific and Industrial Research, was leaving to take up a chair. The job involved co-ordinating the SSRC's support for research over the whole of the social sciences - economics, sociology, anthropology, social psychology, management, education ... Was I interested? Yes. NEDO was persuaded (with little difficulty) to release me from my contract.

Once again, I was working with Michael, though this time in a publicly funded and accountable body rather than the buccaneering CA. As there had been at CA, there were tensions, but of a different kind. Some academic social scientists, outstanding in their generation, recognised and respected his intellectual quality as well as his entrepreneurial flair. They included T H Marshall, Marie Jahoda, Raymond Firth, A H Halsey, W J M Mackenzie, Edmund Leach and Claus Moser.

There were others, though, who were suspicious of a polymath whose intellect ranged so widely over disciplines in which he had had no formal training. There was resentment at Michael's attempt to build bridges between disciplines - 'multi-disciplinary means non-disciplinary', I was told by a critic. SSRC's Next Thirty Years Committee was looked on with particular scepticism, as a symbol of intellectual charlatanism. Nevertheless, few social scientists could afford to dissociate themselves from such a powerful organisation as the SSRC, which used peer group appraisal to dispense public funds for research grants and studentships.

Michael eventually tired of the inevitable rigours and routines of procedures involved in allocating public money. They must in time have seemed to outweigh the advantages his post as Chairman gave him - especially, access to a diversity of intellectual talent to help him sharpen and refine his ideas. His own aptitude at getting people to distill their life's work in response to twenty minutes or so of interrogation was very evident. I was even on the receiving end of this myself in a bizarre setting. Michael and I were visiting the US to examine the institutional arrangements for the funding of large, permanent social science research centres of a kind which did not then exist in the UK. After an intensive day in New York City, we went at sunset to 666, a cocktail bar at the top of a skyscraper, high above Park Avenue. As a Dartington Trustee, he was much occupied with the economic and social regeneration of South-West England. In discussion, it emerged that - for reasons that are too tedious to explain - I knew a little about the Cornish pilchard fishing industry. After two whisky sours and eighty questions from Michael, he had assimilated everything I knew on the subject and distilled it for his own purposes. I was left exhausted by the process, gazing down at Manhattan with an emptied mind.

Michael handed on the chairmanship of the SSRC to Andrew Shonfield, temperamentally very different but with many similar qualities of intellect. He was subjected to a similar sceptical reaction by many members of the social science community - he was interested in too many things and was too energetic. Pursuing Michael's interest in the future, Andrew had put together a consortium of public and private sector organisations to back the establishment of an Institute of

Forecasting Studies, which would develop methods of social as well as economic forecasting. This proposal polarised opinion on the Council. When it came to the final decision, one of the Council members, David Worswick, who was then Director of NIESR, came to the meeting with a prepared speech, which he read out in a very loud voice, predicting the end of civilisation as we knew it if the proposed Institute of Forecasting Studies was set up. The noes had it, narrowly, and soon the SSRC fell into 'safe' academic hands. Fortunately, though, it survived subsequent assaults from a Conservative government which equated the social sciences with the unsound, left-dominated subject of sociology. After intensive scrutiny, its name was changed to the Economic and Social Research Council. Honour was satisfied on all sides and the SSRC lives on under a new name.

National Consumer Council

At the beginning of 1974, I moved to the newly established Office of Fair Trading, to work with the first Director General of Fair Trading, the late John Methven. The OFT was itself the product of a U-turn in the Conservative approach to consumer policy. One of the early actions of the incoming Conservative government in 1970 had been to abolish the publicly funded Consumer Council along with a number of other quangos - although it was rumoured at the time that the Prime Minister, Edward Heath, was not prepared to accept the Council's choice of a successor to its retiring Director, the late Elizabeth Ackroyd. In 1972, Geoffrey Howe was appointed as Minister for Consumer Affairs at the Board of Trade. His scrutiny of the inadequacies of both competition and consumer policy led to the passing of the Fair Trading Act in the following year and the setting up of the OFT.

In an attempt to seize the initiative in consumer policy, the Labour Party in opposition had in 1972 published a Green Paper on advertising. This criticised the abolition of the old Consumer Council and proposed that a 'national consumers authority' should be set up. Among other functions, this body would test claims made by advertisers, publish the results and implement a statutory code of regulations on advertising. 50 per cent of all advertising and sales promotion expenditure would be disallowed as a tax deductible expense and the revenue raised would be used to finance the new authority.

Alarum bells rang in the advertising industry when the Labour Party came to power in 1974. They rang even more loudly at the subsequent Advertising Association conference in Brighton, when both John Methven and the Secretary of State for Prices and Consumer Protection, Shirley Williams, put the advertising industry on notice that its self-regulatory system was not working effectively. The advertising industry got its act together extremely quickly and a revamped Advertising Standards Authority, financed by a voluntary levy on advertising, was launched.

The proposals for a publicly funded consumer body then changed course, with a reduced emphasis on advertising and a change of name to National Consumer Council. Who should lead it? I accompanied John Methven to a meeting with Shirley Williams and her officials, at which Michael's name emerged as first choice. As I had worked with him at both CA and the SSRC, I was given the job of making the first, off-the-record approach to see whether he might be interested.

It was my turn to make the phone call. When we met and talked about the possibility, Michael made it clear that if he took on the job, he would want the new body to be very different from CA. CA was a great success, but, although everyone had benefited indirectly from its work in terms of the boost it gave to higher quality goods and services, its direct benefits had gone mainly to middle class consumers. They were better placed to assimilate the results of comparative testing. They had the purchasing power to turn *Which?* reports to their own benefit. He would like the new body to emphasise the needs of disadvantaged consumers. Also, its work should not be restricted to the private sector. The consumer implications of public services provided by central and local government, as well as nationalised industries, needed urgent attention. Though funded by government, the new body must have its own public voice and be free to criticise anybody - government included - if criticism was justified.

I carried the message back. The machinery started turning and the National Consumer Council was set up in 1975, with Michael as the first Chairman. As with CA and the SSRC, he gave the NCC a powerful impetus and a distinctive character during its first two years. In quick succession, the NCC produced reports and recommendations on consumer problems with nationalised industries and with paying for fuel. There was also a focus on the problems of council tenants with studies on rent arrears and tenancy agreements.

In 1977, Michael Young handed over the chairmanship of NCC to the late Michael Shanks and I was appointed as Director. Unlike the old Consumer Council, the NCC survived a change in the political complexion of government. In all its twenty years of existence, under a succession of Chairmen who have followed Michael's initial lead, it has continued to emphasise the needs of consumers who are not well placed to look after their own interests. It has also spoken out when the actions of government have seemed to be threatening consumers' interests. It is no easy task to explain to consumers in other countries how a publicly funded body can criticise government policies without fear of having its budget reduced or its powers clipped. The NCC has also been fortunate in having members appointed by government from a broad spectrum of political opinion.

In the three very different organisational contexts of CA, SSRC and NCC, Michael Young has been a highly discontinuous but extremely powerful influence on my life and views. I have drawn from him a deep distrust of both public and private corporate power and an awareness of the extent to which it can become self-serving. On its own, that would be a purely negative attitude. Expressed positively, the principle which for me underlies his thought and action is that the institutions which we create and to which we delegate power should exist to serve the lives of individuals and communities. Political power, radical change and institutional arrangements are important because they can be used to improve the quality of people's lives and to give them the opportunity to fulfil themselves. It is an approach which carries echoes of Victorian social improvement. This is no criticism. For if we do not devote ourselves to enhancing the lives of our fellow human beings, what other conceivable justification is there for our work?

The Exemplary Sacker
Ann Cartwright

I planned to title this: Michael Young - Role model for establishing an Institute, but was told that was too long. And when I thought about putting it succinctly what he did was to sack me from the Institute of Community Studies, although that is not how it felt at the time, and he did it in the nicest and most positive way.

The Institute of Community Studies must surely be one of Michael's most successful and long-lasting innovations. I left a tenured academic post to go and work there in 1960, attracted by its independence, its orientation and the stimulating companionship of Michael himself and of Peter Willmott and Peter Marris. I had already done some work with Michael and Peter Willmott, commenting on the questionnaire and sample for their study of *Family and Kinship*. Other attractions of ICS were its location in the charming Queen Anne house at 18 Victoria Park Square and the possibility of playing a part in the way the organisation developed: the topics it studied, the methods and approach used, and the physical and intellectual environment.

The original purpose of ICS was to study the relationship between social services and working-class family life, and its early studies were done in and around Bethnal Green. I think the idea behind my recruitment was to extend the scope to health services, and also to broaden the geographical cover. The first study I did there was of hospitals and the intention was to look at them from the patients' or consumers' point of view. I broadened this to include the experience and views of both patients and general practitioners, arguing that general practitioners were in some ways consumers of the hospital service. Further studies of other aspects of the health service followed: general practitioner care, family planning and the various services involved in the care of people who died. All these were looked at from the point of view of patients, potential patients and the professionals providing care, and the Medical Care Research Unit was set up within ICS.

During the initial planning for my first study at ICS, *Human relations and hospital care*, Michael was keen that patients should be interviewed while they were still in hospital. I was unhappy about this approach partly because it made it difficult to get a proper sample but also because of the problems of interviewing patients in that situation.

17

I felt they were less likely to criticise the care they were receiving while they were still in hospital and that, in addition, it would be difficult for them to see their care in a reasonable perspective. A pilot study in which some patients were seen in hospital and a separate random sample were identified by a postal questionnaire reinforced my views, and Michael agreed that I should go ahead with a sample selected from the electoral register in twelve randomly chosen parliamentary constituencies in England and Wales. In subsequent studies that I and my colleagues in the Medical Care Research Unit did at ICS Michael played a less active role, although he took a keen interest in the methods we used as well as in the results. One of my contributions, for which I am sure Michael is eternally grateful, was to recruit Wyn Tucker to the staff of the Institute. Initially she came for a week in 1961 and is still there some 34 years later, a vital but unobtrusive support and contributor to many aspects of the Institute's work.

I worked at ICS for ten years, and during that time I learnt a lot about the running of a small independent research institute. Michael himself played a large part in determining the basic structure of the Trustees and the Advisory Committee, and in obtaining funds. The day to day running devolved on the Treasurer, Howard Dickinson, the secretary and the research staff who took responsibility for particular things. It was informal, loosely structured, and generally worked because of the small size and friendly relationships. The staff had a mutual respect for each other and at least some understanding and interest in each other's work.

Michael's interests and concerns were, as ever, widespread and people mostly found them enlivening rather than capricious, engaging rather than alienating. Some of the ventures I remember were the link with local traders (during which time we became unusually well-dressed), and the sadly unsuccessful attempt to persuade people to commit a proportion of their income to poorer countries. There were other diversions from our main work and as such these were regarded with a mixture of welcome and resentment - the lunch time poetry reading, for example, which Peter Willmott said afterwards should be for consenting adults in private. A more successful feature was the annual Christmas party, which put quite a strain on organisational resources, which Michael seemed not to notice, but it brought together both the people involved in the Institute's work and those whom we sought to interest and influence.

Money raising was inevitably a continuing concern although in the 1960s it was easier than to-day. Michael was creative about this and one of the lessons I learnt from him and Howard Dickinson was not to underestimate costs in grant proposals. I benefitted from an underspend on my first project and was generously allowed to use some of it on a trip to the U.S.A. It was the first time I had been there and the strategy paid off as I subsequently got grants for two projects from the US Public Health Service.

It was fund raising that was the immediate cause of my 'sacking'. It turned out that Michael and I were planning to seek funds from the same organisation for different projects. Michael's lateral thinking solved the problem by suggesting that my Medical Care Research Unit, which had been part of ICS, should separate off and become an independent institute. It was not something I had envisaged and initially I was quite taken aback. But Michael facilitated the establishment of the new institute by offering us premises in the basement of 18 Victoria Park Square and by allowing us to share the services of ICS's treasurer, Howard Dickinson.

I would never have dreamt of setting up The Institute for Social Studies in Medical Care without Michael's encouragement and example. Working at ICS for ten years gave me confidence and experience to make use of the opportunity. One reason Michael gave for his action was a belief that small was beautiful. It was a view I shared because I wanted to continue to do research myself and not spend all my time on organisation and management. I had the example of the way ICS was run, and Michael did not overload me with advice; the one bit I remember was to have the minimum number of Trustees.

So, thank you Michael for providing a role model of how to establish and run an independent research institute, for letting me participate in the activities and organisation of ICS, and for giving me the sack when you did and in the way you did it.

Opening Up the University, with a Share to Everyone, Everywhere

Peter Laslett

In no direction was elite domination more complete in Britain when Michael Young began his career of institutional innovation than in education. This was so throughout what we are pleased to call the educational system; though some might say that the only truly systematic feature of our educational practices has been in this very tendency towards exclusiveness and scarcity. So it was in higher education - no satisfactory expression this one either - that the policy of admitting only the few, the fewest possible, was at its most formidable. This can be demonstrated from a single axiom, that which was adopted by those opposed to the foundation of the then new universities during the 1960s: 'More means worse!'

That this should no longer be so, that it could be argued by his 80th birthday that a person living in Britain has as good a chance of some experience of advanced learning and research as any other person living anywhere else, perhaps even a better chance, is Michael's doing more than anyone else's. It is astonishing to recognise that ours is now a country which is looked to for theory, advice and practical models in the matter of communicating university level knowledge and accomplishment to every willing participant.

It was in Britain in the 1970s that a housewife began to be able to have a chemistry set suitable for her honours level science course delivered to her, place it on the draining-board when she had finished the washing up of an evening, do the prescribed experiment for the week, and work out the result on the kitchen table. No matter that she had no previous knowledge of chemistry or any qualification whatever for university studies. It is astonishing also to recognise that it was in Britain in the 1980s that a man of 55, or 65, or even 75 or older began to be able to join a course of his own choice, in Ancient Greek, or Chinese, or Mathematics, or Computer Programming, or all four if he could manage it, and be taught what he felt he needed to learn by a person with the requisite knowledge in his own age range and at a price well within the slender budget of most pensioners. He is now able to do things like this as a member, not as a student, of an organisation which makes it possible for him whatever his educational history had been, with none of this nonsense about qualifications, or a teacher/taught hierarchy, even a professoriate.

21

These examples are drawn of course from the Open University
and the Universities of the Third Age, in the foundation of which, a
first in both cases for Britain of all countries, Michael had a leading
part to play, indeed in the former, the predominant part. At the Silver
Jubilee of the Open University in 1994, it was reported that 25 or more
national universities had been founded on the original British model.
That original body was, as I well remember, engendered by despair
upon impossibility. Who would have thought that the Speaker of the
House of Commons, Betty Boothroyd, the person chosen as the
preferred candidate if ever there was a President of England in place
of a King or a Queen, would be willing to accept its ceremonial
headship after only 25 years of its existence? Or that at her installation
it could be claimed that the Open University has been and remains the
chief source of innovation and experience for the principles of distance
teaching in all parts of the world? And distance teaching, as Michael
well knows, is the wave of the future for all educational purposes.

As for the British Universities of the Third Age, or U3As as most
of them prefer to be called, they are now numbered in their hundreds,
are present all over the country, and represent the most expansive
educational movement we have. They already have as many, or more,
participating members, teaching each other and learning together, as
those present in the organisations with the same title instituted
officially ten or more years earlier by existent universities in France,
Germany, Italy or Spain. There those in the Third Age are taught as
students by the staff of those existent universities. In spite of the
differences, in method and outlook, British U3As are regarded in these
countries themselves as the most interesting and original, perhaps even
as the most effective.

With the U3As at the moment there is in this respect a repetition,
in a much friendlier fashion, of the struggle with the Establishment
which went on in the 1960s inside Britain when we were working at
the other Michael Young educational experiments, as well as the Open
University. These other organisations were and are ACE, the Advisory
Centre for Education; NEC, the National Extension College; and IEC,
the International Extension College. It is not perhaps generally known
that Michael and others founded the NEC to *become* the Open
University, but that Jennie Lee rejected it in favour of the more
traditionally ordered body which has made such remarkable progress.

Some of the flavour of these original controversies, and of the
instinctive attitude towards them of the dons in whose midst all these
experiments were going on, can be gathered from a statement made by
a very eminent and quite elderly Fellow of the august establishment to
which I belong myself, Trinity College, Cambridge. After I had
introduced my brother to him as a guest at High Table dinner, this

pillar of the Establishment said to him, 'So you are Peter Laslett's brother? I hope you do not spend your time as he does, tilting at windmills!'

It will be noticed that all the Michael Young institutions which I have named so far were originally set up at Cambridge and two of them, the OU and the U3A, at one of the largest and best-known of the colleges. At the very heart of the Establishment itself, it will be readily recognised, and not in a working-class borough like Bethnal Green where the tens, or dozens (or is it scores?) of other Michael Young enterprises came into being. Not all of these ventures survive, of course, and many of the ideal models, at least of the educational organs which he thought up, never got off the ground in any form. This is a point of some importance because it is the first principle of innovation in any field that you have to be prepared for failure and never to be discouraged by failure from trying again, at that or at something else.

In fact the failure of ideas for a new institution becomes so familiar to the innovator that he or she is more surprised by the successful parturition, nurturance and growth to promise of permanence of an idea than by its abortion, still birth, neo-natal death or extinction in infancy. It is abundantly evident that Michael Young understands this principle, and the further and more encouraging one which predicts that something tried once, and miscarrying, will frequently, if by no means always, have to be tried again if, after considering what happened to it, it looks worth making a further attempt in the original or a modified form.

I was myself mixed up with two of the innovatory ventures in higher education which Michael mounted, or joined in mounting, at Cambridge during the 1960s, which came to nothing at the time. One was the notion of founding a second university on the same site as that which had been occupied for seven centuries by the present University of Cambridge, a second university which would be in session for that half of the year when the members of the existent institution were on vacation. As a Teaching Fellow for some years in that decade at the then newest Cambridge college, Churchill College, and as a University Lecturer in Sociology, he had noticed that the installations provided at Cambridge, huge in size and immensely costly, lay idle for six months out of every twelve. And this at a time when the country was so much behind its compeers in higher educational provision and was actually showing signs of being conscious of the fact. But nothing came of it, then, as Michael admits in a recent article (1994c)[1].

---

1. This piece, which was originally given as an address in Cambridge on the occasion of the 25th anniversary of the Open University in April 1994, prop-

He states there that I was myself the only person outside Churchill College who supported that extremely bold proposal. This support was not very effective, however, because I was under a particularly opaque cloud in Cambridge at that time. This was for having proposed that Oxford and Cambridge should become the central edifice of a University of England, exclusively postgraduate and using their premises and endowments for giving access to all university teachers in the country who needed the academic infrastructure which these two institutions possessed in such abundance and which were so meagre on other university campuses[2]. Once more, without any effect at the time apart from a bluster of controversy. But significant in the long-term? Significant not only to the handful of academic reformers who have been at large in our country, but finally to the multitudes of the educationally excluded who would in the end crowd into the Open University, the NEC, the IEC and its sisters in other countries, especially developing countries, and the U3As?

The same comment might be made about the other experiment in higher educational reform, with a negative outcome at the time which Michael and a few others of us set on foot during the interlude when the University of the Air was working its way up into the NEC, so leading to the establishment of the Open University itself[3]. It is not widely remembered that when the first experiments were being made in Cambridge in the use of electronic communication for teaching and

oses a research foundation for open learning, the feasibility study for which has now been financed by the Leverhulme Trust.

2. See 'The University in High Industrial Society' in *Essays in Reform*, 1967, edited by Bernard Crick, Oxford, 1967. The piece had originally been given as a talk on the much-lamented Third Programme some years before, and had been published in the much-lamented *Listener*, with a photograph of Trinity College Great Gate on the cover. Not ingratiating to the academic establishment, and perhaps uppermost in the mind of the don who talked of tilting at windmills.

3. Because the NEC never itself became the national open access, university-level institution, it has never used broadcast television or radio as its main medium for teaching. But it has developed and is beginning to perfect all the other ingredients of what we originally called the English recipe for opening up university teaching to everyone everywhere - correspondence, tailor-made programmed courses, telephone consulations, brief residential courses and so on. Everyone in the business now knows that these have turned out to be collectively more apt, especially in their recent form (videos, tapes and so on) than the open circuit broadcasting which was to have been the grand instrument of the University of the Air.

learning, we also had a programme for the third element of the specific university type, research. As well as setting up the first broadcast university lectures in the famous *Sunrise Semesters*, we arranged to link universities together, first for the exchange of closed-circuit, not broadcast, teaching occasions, and second for joint research seminars. We wanted to share scarce resources and enable fledgling universities to be fed for the time being by their already grown-up companions. We wanted, in fact, to integrate the system as far as we could, to expand its resources by co-ordinating them so as to be better able to meet the demand for higher education as it was opened up to everyone. This experimental programme failed, and I know of this only too well because I took responsibility for chairing the committee conducting the research on behalf of five, then nine universities which took part in the programme.

Electronic university intercommunication came to nothing, therefore, at the time, but did so with some prospect of a distant echo forwards to the present decade of breakneck change in higher education, when such interchange may become common. But the notable feature of that first attempt, and one which is significant in my view for its bearing on innovation in this arena, is that the programme went on for months, even years after we should have realised that it just would not fly. We, I should have said they, the other members of the project, had come to believe in the notion and no matter how often the Committee was told there was no sign of effective demand, it was pressed relentlessly forward. It must succeed, so the converts kept telling themselves, because it was such a splendid idea and so obviously necessary. After all, our other splendid idea, the University of the Air/Open University was going like a train.

This experience impels me to shrink away every time a U3A enthusiast waxes eloquent on that institution simply because it was such a marvellous idea. Having the original idea is never, never enough. But we must ask ourselves what these experiences, these moments of insight, these flashes of inspiration, these false starts and ill-advised persistencies have to tell us about Michael Young as an innovator in the more advanced types of teaching and learning, or about innovation generally in this field.

We should not perhaps expect it to tell us a very great deal, certainly not on a theoretical level. This is because what we are trying to understand is to all intents and purposes a unique case. (An elaborate comparative investigation into the resemblance shall we say between Michael Young and Michael Faraday, or St Ignatius Loyola, or even Clive Sinclair might conceivably reveal something we ought to know about the personality who founded or helped to found the Open University, the U3As, and so much more). All that we can expect to gather will be in the way of description; at its best description with insight.

Because the concern is with higher learning, we have to begin with the obvious point that to be an innovator here it is highly desirable, if not essential, to be learned yourself, an authority in the accepted vocabulary. Michael's case certainly confirms this point. His scholarly standing is of the highest, as has very recently been recognised by his election as an Honorary Fellow of the British Academy, an extremely rare distinction because so very seldom awarded. It is true of course that his achievements as an academic innovator must have played a part in such highly conspicuous successes. But the list of scholarly book titles attached to his name must have counted for much more.

When we were beginning to get down to it in the 1950s, 60s and 70s, that list was itself only starting. *Family and Kinship in East London* was already in print, *The Rise of the Meritocracy* appeared early in our operations, but *The Symmetrical Family* and the books on time and on ageing and so forth were only just appearing and have gone on doing so as creative institutional efforts have succeeded each other. These publications have given Michael a standing in the academic world which could never have been occupied by an outsider. Even a powerful politician out for change, change which he as a politician could threaten to carry out by compulsion, could not have had such a purchase over those whose minds had to be influenced.

Nevertheless it has certainly not been a disadvantage for those purposes that Michael has a pronounced political identity himself, nor does it in this country do him any harm that he is a Peer of the Realm. Nothing could be more deceptive than the sight of the House of Lords on television as an arrangement of empty benches alongside a great gilded tabernacle of anachronism, benches studded here and there by a recumbent Lord or Lady of advanced age, with one of them standing, if not exactly erect, and making a halting speech. The acquaintances and alliances, the links of support and opposition, the *chuchoteries* which go on in such a place, and even more in the unending corridors of offices, offices of the conventional and of the euphemistic description, must be of colossal importance in a world whose effectiveness consists so largely in personal influence and persuasion. These circumstances are particularly significant in relation to the field of higher education which is seldom an object of conspicuous and declared political conflict, but much more of rival opinions and contrasting policies, if often highly ill-informed policies. Even a personal history of changing party allegiance might help in such an arena. Like divorce and re-marriage, such a hiatus enlarges your connections.

What goes for political connections goes for academic and intellectual connections as well, and here to the possession of skills and experience has to be added the true imponderable, the element of personality. In spite of what Michael has said and what has been said here of the extreme rarity of university teachers and researchers, in Cambridge or anywhere else, with any concrete notion of institutional change or sympathy with university reform, it was never true that the academic world was a homogeneous whole, consistently hostile to suggestions for opening up the little world they live in to society at large. There were always potential allies, even in the least likely places, in this case at the Cambridge High Tables, and Michael was, and is, just the person to attract, interest and even finally to convert and enlist them.

Academics are all interested in ideas on the one hand, and nearly all interested in techniques on the other, the most recent and intriguing techniques above all because it is technical knowledge and advance which make possible the testing, the development, the operationalisation of ideas. It has been of considerable advantage to Michael Young and those around him engaged in this set of causes that the universalisation of access to the academy could be accomplished by electronic communication and intercommunication. The years of the opening up of universities have also been, after all, the years of the introduction and spread of computerisation in academic life as well as of television, radio, tapes, videos and CDs, and this recital ends by the two sources of technical innovation flowing into one. There is and has been sufficient sympathy in enough of the academically-minded intent on engaging what they outrageously call 'the outside world' for there to be widespread interest in the idea of making use of technical advance to invite the outside in. All this is true in spite of the fact that open circuit broadcast television, with which it all began, did not turn out to be able to do all the things that we expected of it.

To my mind the demonstration of this can be seen in what happened when the Open University did get established and started to recruit a staff. There was an inrush of talent and promise such as I should think has never been seen in modern university history. These brilliant younger academics gave the impression of having waited for the chance. The phenomenal success of the idea, so largely Michael's idea, of the Open University has perhaps been due as much, or more, to the outstanding quality of those members of its staff as to the original notions themselves, together with the hard labour and persistence against opposition of those who collaborated with him to push these notions forward. This has been true to a considerable extent of the Extension Colleges. In these directions Michael, to use the commonplace phrase, caught the imagination of his generation of

British academics, perhaps not one generation but two or three; all those who set out to enter the academy after the 1950s.

At this point the traditional account of how change came about would have to take over, and a full citation made of the personal qualities required: originality; insight; flair; unyielding persistence and determination when policy demands it; imagination; sympathy; the common touch; the ability to play on hopes and ambitions, as well as on the frustration and resentment of large numbers of people; the knowledge of when *not* to persist. No associate of Michael's is in any doubt that he has an immoderate share of all these attributes and has them also in a peculiar mixture which is very hard to analyse, but quite evidently supremely effective.

This mosaic of qualities is a combination which places him firmly in that category we are so fond of alluding to, the category of genius. I have myself, I believe, always judged that Michael had this supreme attribute. He is the only genuine genius whom I know, or know well. What his superlative talent exactly consists of, and how it is that he manages to sustain its effectiveness after so many decades with no overt sign of diminution, continues to baffle me. The influence which it gives him over friends, officials, political notables, university authorities, students and ordinary folk, whilst all the while lacking what is usually thought of as personal charisma, just the quality which one might perhaps expect to find in such a person, I cannot begin to figure out. Working with Michael, as very many who have done so will confirm, is not an experience without irritation, even sometimes exasperation.

I make this last remark from observation and not out of the long years of personal association between us. I have never known him except as an undemanding friend, collaborator and ally, though a friend at a distance, a distance which is not simply physical, confined to the mileage between Bethnal Green and Cambridge. It is as a loyal and affectionate friend, as I hope I may describe myself, a sincere and convinced convert to his aims and achievements - what an amazing extensive list is here alluded to! - that I offer my personal tribute to Young at eighty.

A Vision of Development: Education in Seven-League Boots
Tony Dodds

Where did it all come from?

On one of my first overseas trips for the International Extension College, which Michael founded in 1971, I went to Calcutta at the invitation of the Bangladesh Government-in-exile. My task was to discuss ways of using distance education to stimulate educational activities among the 10 million refugees around that town from East Pakistan (as Bangladesh was still called). In Calcutta I met a powerful West Bengali woman committed to promoting Bangladeshi independence, culture and education. When she heard of the origins of the organisation I represented (the IEC) she said "You are the great-grandson of my movement: your founder, who inspired your Open University, got his inspiration from Rabindranath Tagore and his Shantiniketan, our Open Air University". Whether her claim of great-grand-parenthood is justified or not I have never been able to establish. But two facts are correct: Michael was greatly influenced by Leonard Elmhirst who, with his wife, Dorothy, founded Dartington; and Leonard Elmhirst, as secretary to Rabindranath Tagore, was deeply influenced by that great Bengali poet and educator.

More mundanely, the International Extension College grew out of the lively international interest shown in the National Extension College experiment, especially from developing countries in Africa. People about to set up correspondence education programmes in, for example, Kenya, Uganda and Malawi, visited the new Cambridge-based NEC and asked for help, advice and access to its courses. They received a warm but hesitant reply. NEC had, to some extent, grown out of reaction to commercial correspondence colleges' failure to take the interests and circumstances of its students into account. An alternative response was to set up an international information exchange and support agency to promote innovation in this new combination of educational approaches which we first called "three-way teaching" – correspondence courses in print, educational broadcasting, and occasional face-to-face tuition.

There is a story that the idea of creating the IEC came from a chance meeting, on a plane, of Michael, Donald Chesworth, who was to be one of IEC's founding Trustees and Bishop Trevor Huddleston.

The last comes into this story again at the end of this article – but whether this story is apocryphal or accurate I have been unable to verify. It is certainly characteristic of Michael and his opportunism. My own first meeting with Michael, and with the idea of an IEC, was in Tanzania where I was working as an adult education radio tutor, in 1970 – the year President Julius Nyerere declared 'Adult Education Year'. Michael's vision seemed like an opportunity to merge this Tanzanian inspiration and experience, and that of several other developing countries, at least in Africa, with the experience of the UK, through the NEC and new Open University.

What was the philosophy behind this international venture? The venture itself (or at least the institution) has remained small and modest. The philosophy was and is large-scale and ambitious: everybody has a right to education; education is about life and every individual's opportunity for self-fulfilment; only an approach which breaks down the barriers created by formal and institutionalised schooling, and uses the modern as well as the traditional media of human communication can make this possible. For only in this way can it reach adults who missed out on formal schooling, who live in isolated and deprived communities, and who will otherwise continue to be bypassed by development. More than this: in Michael's eyes there were distinct advantages in moving outside the restrictions which are imposed by the formal and institutionalised structures of schools and colleges. To achieve this vision no one – not developed countries, not the Open University, not the NEC or the IEC – has a monopoly of ideas. Many experiments were happening in many countries and in many cultures at that time, and would continue to emerge. The IEC set out to capture, to learn from and to exchange information about such innovations wherever they occurred and to do so in the interest of developing countries.

The IEC ideal – an unfinished search

In the 24 years since it was set up, the IEC has been closely involved, over varying periods of time, but for at least two years each, with 20 different distance education programmes in developing countries. Many it has helped to devise and establish. Others it has supported through new developments and expansion. They have varied from university degree programmes through out-of-school secondary courses and teacher in-service training to adult basic and non-formal education projects. The first four, in Mauritius, Botswana, Lesotho and Nigeria came about as a direct result of Michael's personal initiatives, as have several in South Africa in recent years. Others have grown out of Michael's ideas but not his own involvement. Almost all, through their link with IEC, have been touched by his style and his thinking.

Firstly, they have all followed the path of pragmatism. As an organisation without guaranteed funds, the IEC has had to respond to invitations for support from almost wherever they came – so long as we could convince ourselves that the project stood a reasonable chance of extending educational opportunity to people deprived of it by traditional and formal structures of education. Most of the resulting programmes have themselves, like IEC, tried to use the methods of distance education to reach varied groups of students at different educational levels.

Secondly most have been inspired by the spirit of innovation. There have been common approaches: most have used the three ways of teaching with which IEC identified from the outset. There has, perhaps, been too much uncritical loyalty to this combination. But most have experimented with the ways in which they were used, especially the balance between the media and the face-to-face contact. Such experiments have tried to discover which mixture was most effective with particular student groups.

Thirdly, in doing so they have illustrated the limitations of the phrase, distance education, which for the time being at least has gained international acceptance as the generic description of this kind of education. For they have stressed the importance of individual or small group human contact rather than the technology with which distance education is so often associated. They have emphasised the purpose of the approach – to widen access to learning – rather than the methodology.

Fourthly they have been outside school, starting from the belief that the mass media can break the institutional barriers of the formal education system. Indeed Michael has sometimes argued that in this way distance education is ahead of conventional schooling. It is not constrained physically by time or space or intellectually by the confinement to a single institution.

A fifth and perhaps the most important common theme in many, though by no means all, has been the attempt to use distance education for adult basic and non-formal education. Distance education has at least two clear lines of descent. First it is related to attempts to give students who have started schooling but, for whatever reasons, been unable to complete their qualifications in school, a chance to continue and complete them out of school by correspondence. A second tradition has been the drive, through educational broadcasting, to improve and enrich the quality of what goes on in schools, especially in schools in socially deprived areas. But can those two traditions give birth to an effective way of reaching out with education to those millions of adults – often a majority of the population – in developing countries, who have never had the opportunity to go to school at all?

Projects with which the IEC has worked have consistently tried to find ways of harnessing the media and approaches of distance education to this purpose. In several cases such attempts have related to adult literacy: in Lesotho, for herd-boys; in Pakistan for young women in villages whose social circumstances severely restrict their chances to attend normal classes; in Somalia for refugees; in Ghana as part of a national campaign; and in South Africa as part of the new government's commitment to compensate for the effects of apartheid. In most cases they have also concerned themselves with non-formal education, related directly to the improvement of the quality of life: health education and child care, community education and the establishment of cooperatives, agricultural education and food production.

In 1980 the IEC produced a book based on its experiences so far, called *Distance Education for the Third World* (Young *et al.* 1980). In it an argument was made for the establishment of radio colleges as the bases of a network of adult learning centres in developing countries where radio lessons, supported by appropriate printed materials, would be studied in learning groups under a trained group leader (who need not be a teacher). In this proposal we were strongly influenced by what we had learned of the radiophonic schools of Colombia and other Latin American countries and by the radio study-group campaigns of Tanzania and Botswana. At the end of the book Michael summed up this ambitious, and possibly naive, proposal as follow:

> *'If you have the technology without the face-to-face groups then in educational terms nothing much may happen. If you have the groups without the technology something will happen, but it will often happen better with the support of broadcasting. For there is technical knowledge available... which can raise the quality of life for millions of people and increase the control they have over their own lives, if the knowledge is made more freely available'...*
>
> *The new distance learning belongs to a world-wide movement. The barefoot technologist of education is partner to the barefoot manager and the barefoot doctor.'*

Since then the world, and especially the developing countries of Africa, has gone through an extended period of severe economic recession. Resources for grand ideas of educational expansion and innovation have not been available: governments have struggled to maintain what they have and know – the formal schools – rather than to invest in the unknown and unproven. Those schools have themselves, in many cases, deteriorated for lack of resources. As economic disasters and political conflict have flourished in that and other continents, the need for new approaches to education and new ways of delivering it to growing numbers of illiterate or barely literate adults and young adults has nevertheless increased. While IEC's dream of radio colleges, or something similar, has not turned into large-scale reality anywhere, the idea and the ambition have survived. This is illustrated by two examples of IEC's work in the last fifteen years. Both were directly inspired by Michael.

Education for refugees, that nation without a country

IEC's commitment to the methods of distance education is based on an ideological principle: the right of all people to continuing education. At a very early stage IEC was involved in drawing up plans for an education project for Bangladeshi refugees in West Bengal. The project never happened because, after a war between India and Pakistan, Bangladesh became independent and the refugees went home. More than ten years later the IEC helped to set up an emergency programme of education for a sudden influx into Botswana of South African refugees from the 1976/77 Soweto uprising. By the early 1980s it was clear that the phenomenon of mass refugee settlements in developing countries was a growing and long term problem. Most of the governments concerned, and the relief agencies, saw shelter, medical care, and food and water supplies as the most pressing needs of such communities. The refugees themselves recognised also the urgency of providing education to children and adults, as a means to retain a degree of control over their lives and to keep alive hope for the future.

If ever there was a community for whom distance education was an appropriate, perhaps the only, means of providing education, it was the huge community of refugees in the Horn of Africa and the front-line states who were South Africa's and Namibia's neighbours. At Michael's inspiration the IEC put forward in 1983 the idea of a World Refugee College which would both draw attention to the educational needs of refugees and, with any governments and national or international agencies interested, including those of the refugees themselves, experiment with ways of using distance education to meet those needs. For the next ten years, and more, we have worked in particular with four such projects – with Namibians in exile through the Namibian Extension Unit based in Zambia, with Ethiopians and Eritreans in exile in Sudan through the Sudan Open Learning Unit, with South African exiles in several front line states through the South African Extension Unit in Tanzania, and with Somali refugees from the

Ogaden with the Institute of In-Service Teacher Training in Somalia. Programmes of in-service primary teacher education, of out-of-school secondary education, of vocational or para-professional training and of literacy and non-formal education have been developed and run with some success – though not without problems. All have now either moved back with the refugees to changed political circumstances at home (in South Africa and Namibia) or have changed or are changing into local institutions meeting the needs of deprived local communities in the host country (Somalia and Sudan).

We never managed to set up the World Refugee College, though the concept and the outcomes of the idea have drawn attention to the educational needs and possibilities. As the refugee crises of the 1980s deepen into those of the 1990s in Rwanda and Burundi, and the former Yugoslavia, there are perhaps signs that the proposals contained in the World Refugee College are at last gaining credence. The first is that education has a crucial role to play in refugee emergencies, and refugees themselves, the world over, see education as one of several top priorities. Second, therefore, it is necessary for educationalists to be included in international teams which assess the emergency needs for relief and rehabilitation when such crises occur. Third, education must be rapidly made available, must be flexible, and must be built on a minimum of institutional resources: the methods of distance education have crucial roles to play in providing education to these, the most deprived of all communities.

South Africa turns

Michael's involvement with and commitment to education for the victims of apartheid in South Africa predates the IEC. He was a founding sponsor of the South African Committee for Higher Education (SACHED) in 1958. This was an agency established to struggle to provide black South Africans with continuing access to education of equal quality to that available to whites in spite of Bantu education. SACHED grew into and has remained one of South Africa's major educational NGOs committed to the overthrow of apartheid and its effects. In the process it has carried out many experiments in the use of distance education in that country. In IEC's early years, while involved in setting up the Botswana Extension College (now the Department of Non-formal Education's Distance Education Department) and the Lesotho Distance Teaching Centre, Michael maintained contact with people at SACHED. On one occasion he used his newly acquired peerage to put pressure on the South African administration to grant an exit visa to study in the UK (or to go into exile) to one of SACHED's senior administrators who had recently been served with a banning order for his part in a SACHED venture which ran foul of the state security services.

This, together with IEC's active involvement with the South African Extension Unit and through that with the ANC's education department in exile, meant that IEC and Michael were well-placed to respond to requests to help the ANC to prepare plans for the reform and expansion of distance education services for the new South Africa. As so often Michael sensed the dramatic changes that were coming to that country before they happened – and while most people were looking on in incredulity. Michael, while theoretically on holiday with Sasha in 1990, made informal contacts with John Samuel, SACHED's Director at the time and ANC's first Head of Education in South Africa after it was unbanned. These led to requests for a series of consultancies from IEC, in which Michael played the lead role, on potential developments for distance education as that country moved towards freedom.

Three new institutions or programmes grew rapidly out of these consultancies. An out-of-school secondary experiment, linked to SACHED, called A Secondary Education Curriculum for Adults (ASECA) was launched to try to provide remedial and relevant secondary education to people whose education had been disrupted during the years of struggle. A small experimental Adult Basic Education Programme (ABEP) was set up in Fort Hare University in the Eastern Cape to explore ways whereby the University could make its services directly available to the people in the community where it was based. A South African Institute of Distance Education (SAIDE) was created to act as advocate, supporter and professional developer for new and changing distance education initiatives, wherever they may occur, during South Africa's transition from repression to freedom.

A fourth proposal was never implemented. Consistent with Michael's vision – and, symbiotically, IEC's – this was for a much more ambitious experiment to make the media of distance education immediately available for adult literatcy and non-formal education. A Foundation for Basic Education was to be set up to attract and channel both internal and external funds to the many non-government agencies which were spearheading progressive adult literacy programmes all over the country but were operating on a very small scale. It would also provide these programmes with access to and expertise in using the media of distance education, and, in the process, would serve not only as an innovator but also as a coordinating and quality controlling agency. It was a first national implementation blue-print for a radio colleges network built on the enthusiasm and commitment for change of the incoming authorities and the experience, infrastructures and personnel of existing NGO's and other agencies involved at this level.

But it was an idea before its time – possibly only by a few months.

At the time of writing, the idea has re-emerged, this time with what seems to be a better chance of success. Michael has combined and redesigned the proposal with an earlier suggestion, which also failed to gain support in 1991 but which was discussed with and gained the support of Archbishop Trevor Huddleston, perhaps this time on a flight of imagination and hope for the new South Africa. This was for an Open University on Robben Island, the famous political prison for so long of many of ANC's leaders, now in positions of national or local authority. In Michael's own words, in the new proposal presented to the South African Ministry of Education in 1995:

'One option [for the transformation of Robben Island] would be to revive the prisoners' university' in a new form, the main reason being the inspirational effect which Robben Island could have for future African students ...

'The nature of the Island requires that if anything is done on any scale, reliance will have to be placed on distance education ...

'The most crucial decision is... about the nature of the student body. Where is the most grievous educational gap at present? ... Many millions of people lost out on their education in the years since 1976 ... Basic education – including political education and education designed to improve earning power – surely has the strongest claim.'

It appears that the proposal this time round has caught the imagination of many of South Africa's new leaders, and now stands a reasonable chance of progressing at least to a serious feasibility study. Whether or not it succeeds it captures many of the themes and much of the flavour of Michael's international education initiatives; that is:

- The concept is launched with an idea or title which is likely to catch the political imagination and spark the enthusiasm of potential supporters.

- It is a radical and imaginative proposal suggesting new ways of attacking problems of educational deprivation which the conventional education services cannot reach.

- It builds on ideas, initiatives and experiences from other places and other times, but re-interprets them in ways which

address new needs of particular people in a particular place.

- It addresses inequalities of power, opening access to education in ways which increase people's control over their own lives.

- It plans to start small, seeking ways to minimise the need for extra resources, but it has a grand vision and the potential to work on a scale commensurate with the educational needs it addresses.

- And, finally, it demonstrates that neither prison nor school walls need to be a barrier to education.

Self-help and Empowerment in Health
Marianne Rigge

The creation of the College of Health exemplifies very clearly a number of Michael's qualities: his abiding interest in the ways that people can help one another at the same time as themselves, by coming together to meet their needs; and his talent for being in tune with popular sentiments and inspiring people to action through the institutions he invents.

The idea of the College came to Michael when he was in Guy's Hospital with cancer. While he was there, being the archetypal consumer that he is, he saw that there were many things that could be improved. But also there was this rather interesting practice of Ian McColl, who was the professor of surgery looking after Michael there, and who subsequently played a valuable part in the work of the College. He had a way of sitting his patients around a table, offering them cups of tea and biscuits, and asking them what had been wrong with the care they received while they were there. In the nature of these things, they all said 'Oh no, Doctor, it's been absolutely wonderful; the doctors and nurses were marvellous.'

This helped Michael to see that there was a need for an organisation to encourage and enable patients to discuss openly and fully their experiences as consumers of health care, and which could have some impact on the the way that the health service functioned and communicated with patients. He came up with the notion of something to be called the Association of Trained Patients, which was obviously too negative and went down rather badly with the doctors he discussed it with. So then I was offered the task of scouting around to see what organisations already existed in this field, and whether we would be in any danger of treading on other people's toes if we moved in.

I had first met Michael when I was at the Consumers' Association, then worked with him at the National Consumer Council, and for the last five years had been closely involved with him in the Mutual Aid Centre. The new idea fitted in closely with the general concept informing all of these bodies.

Also I had grown up as a GP's daughter in the days before there were general practice health centres, and so I was very familiar with patients' problems from the other side. So the notion of giving people help and information in order to make more effective use of what is there for them, in this case the NHS, appealed to me very strongly.

Over the next few months, in the spaces left within what proved to be a very demanding programme of lobbying and discussions with professional interests and organisations, we made some visits to hospitals to witness consultation processes at first hand. What struck us was how little opportunity patients were given in formal discussions with doctors, compared with casual chat to nurses, to talk about their own experiences and feelings. It seemed to us that communication was much more effective, not just for providing patients with pastoral care, but even more so in finding out how they felt about things, in those contexts that were less formal.

This proved very influential for us. All of the consumer audit work which is now a large part of what the college does arose out of the awareness that formal situations are inhibiting. You didn't need to talk to large numbers of people; and you didn't need tick-in-the-box satisfaction surveys which were the only research that was being done at that time. These will mostly tell you that ninety-nine per cent of people think that everything is wonderful, or *say* that it is. But that's because they are feeling both vulnerable and grateful. You can actually learn a lot more about a service, and what is good and bad in it, and about what could be done to make it better, without necessarily spending a lot of money, through talking to relatively few people, but letting *them* set the agenda, and not having everything too structured. All of our subsequent research has grown out of that realisation.

We spent seven or eight months working up the College before it was launched properly in October 1983. Money of course was a struggle at first. Then Malcolm Dean did a splendid write-up of what we were doing in the *Guardian*, and there was quite a good report in the *Sunday Times*, and out of these we got our first paying members, at ten pounds per year. Membership increased substantially a little later, after the CA put a flyer about the college in *Which?*

So there was no need on this occasion for Michael to carry out any of his heroic feats to secure resources. He can be amazing. His performance, for example, when we were trying to get the OK stations going - as part of the Mutual Aid Centre - will stick in my mind forever. This was an idea that came from Sweden of a motorists' co-operative, and we were trying to raise about three-quarters of a million pounds, if not more, from oil companies in order to get it started. Michael sat down with some people from one of the big oil companies, and he gave them a 'vision' of how when they were grandfathers they would be sitting down with little children on their knees saying 'You know these stations all around the country called OK, actually I was one of the people who started it.' We didn't have anything like that with the College.

After we had got going properly, in the Autumn of 1984, HRH The Prince of Wales, who had been taking a keen interest in our progress, came to Bethnal Green for an informal visit to meet the college staff and to enrol as the ten-thousandth member. The visit was preceded by Col. Jack Stenhouse's 'walking the course', to time everything and brief everyone. Then on the day itself we all had to be in the building by 1.00pm, so that no-one else should arrive after it had been inspected by Chief Inspector Gritty and his black Labrador. The Prince, who joked about an envelope pinned on the notice-board addressed to the Royal College of Health, and was photographed with Michael and myself, asked a lot of pertinent questions and stayed longer than planned; when he left he chatted with the large group of small children who had gathered outside. The College was established.

More than ten years on, Michael plays a less central role, though he still attends executive committee meetings. But his ideals and methods are wholly embodied in the organisation, which is dedicated to informing and empowering ordinary people in their dealings with the health services and to changing the hearts and minds of health professionals towards a more patient-centred pattern of care. It is very much of a piece with the Young tradition.

Bringing Out the Artist in Everyone
David Davies

An artist is not a special kind of man, but every man is a special kind of artist.

This phrase of Ananda Coomaraswamy, the Hindu philosopher, was used so often by Eric Gill, the artist-craftsman, that everyone assumed Gill had invented it. It is a phrase that would appeal to Michael too, representing not just his own view of the arts, but also a rallying cry for his initiatives to make the arts more available. This chapter is not about Michael's own artistic background (his father was a musician and his mother a writer) nor about painting (though he is an enthusiastic painter), writing and poetry; it is the story of how in characteristic way he converted his own personal interests and observations into yet another institution, the Open College of the Arts.

The arts in Western society have become something that is done to or for you rather than by you. The very word 'amateur' is often used as a term of mild contempt, discounting the enormous personal pleasure that people get by doing things themselves rather than by having things done to them. The primary-school child will, if lucky, do all sorts of creative things; but then the secondary-school child will discover that the arts are certainly not at the centre of the curriculum. And by the time a young person emerges from full-time education into the light of common day, the arts will for most be something to go to, to buy, or to admire from a distance.

It is, for instance, a matter of regular comment that for the westerner music is, by and large, a commodity that is presented to them, at a price, whereas in many other cultures, music is a shared experience that everyone partakes in.

It was not always so. Michael once wrote to me: 'In the seventeenth century, the ability to hold a part in domestic music-making was rated by Pepys as an indispensable quality in a new serving maid; and down to that time music was composed mainly for the voice, addressed to the singers rather than the listeners. Could we have a little essay in next year's brochure on how the arts permeated medieval society?' (Though if Michael had read a few pages further in Pepys' diaries he would have found Mrs Pepys tartly observing that her husband had never taken pains to teach his own wife to sing in the way he devoted effort to teaching Mary Mercer, the maid.)

Our current situation is not irretrievable. Deep down, almost everyone wishes they could participate in some artistic or creative activity. Ironically they may be put off by the very quality of what they see and hear professionals doing. But if they can be convinced that everyone has something special to say, and that it is worth investing time, energy and a little money to find one's own voice, good things can emerge.

Of course, well before Michael turned his mind in early 1986 to the question of education in the arts, there was already a very rich tradition of evening classes, choirs, drama groups, photographic and art societies and so on. He observed much of this himself at Dartington and described it in detail in *The Elmhirsts of Dartington* (Young, 1982a). He even, in that book, allowed himself to make a fleeting appearance on the subject of the arts: '[The Elmhirsts] always believed with Coleridge that "deep thinking is attainable only by a man of deep feeling" - their criticism of Bill Curry [head of Dartington Hall School], and of me, was that we were too much men of the head - and that the arts could bring about creative action only by marrying feeling and thought.' The perspective that Michael added to what he saw around him came from his long experience of open learning - that lots of people were inhibited from self-development by the inaccessibility, both mental and physical, of conventional education and of arts facilities.

There were undoubtedly other influences in his mind. The uppermost could well have been his recent experience of establishing the University of the Third Age. This had revealed large numbers of older people not just willing to explore new things, but also keen to share their own lifetime of experience with others. It is interesting that many of the people crucial to the enterprise of the Open College of the Arts had already had one career, but were willing, in their third age, to have another career sharing their experience. As if to underline this point, OCA has just published an entertaining and comprehensive course on singing written by and summarising the distinguished life work of an eighty-six year old.

I have never known Michael knowingly undersell any of his organisations in its title, and so the first discussion paper put together on the subject of open-learning in the arts, in conjunction with his long-term collaborator in open-learning, Hilary Perraton, was called 'The Idea of a European Open University for the Arts and Crafts'. The paper disarmingly begins: 'It seems laughable that you could learn to sharpen a chisel, paint a picture or make music by watching a television programme or listening to a cassette tape.' It then ranges against this statement arguments based on experience and on ideology (access, concern for the quality of life). It sets out a long-term vision: to widen opportunities for creativity at the highest level. And it identifies four audiences - those with no experience, those with some experience, those wanting to understand and appreciate without doing, and school children.

There was as yet no clear idea of how to start and with what, but a list of ideas included Afro-Caribbean music; peripatetic painting tutors for the housebound; courses for children in schools without specialist teachers; ceramics; courses transferring skills internationally such as 'bookbinding to Portugal in exchange for traditional tilemaking'; and starter courses in various arts.

Armed with this paper, Michael toured the country, often accompanied by Sasha. He went to education authorities and noted that one chief adviser thought that art lent itself to distance teaching much better than other subjects. He went to the Open University and was told of the growing interest in continuing education there and the strength of art history in the OU degree programme. He went to the Crafts Council and learnt about knitting and pottery. All of this in two weeks of January 1986. There were also people prepared to say that it couldn't be done, but they wisely didn't commit their views to paper, and Michael saw no point in recording the doubts.

What Michael really needed was someone to become the first Director, to consider the ideas (there were no shortage of them, and every visit brought up more) and to decide which to run with. And before even a director could be appointed there would need to be money.

Amongst the people he visited - did they know they were being interviewed? - the one who came over best was Ian Tregarthen Jenkin; retired Principal at Camberwell and Curator of the Royal Academy Schools. Michael noted he 'was keener on the concept than anyone I'd met so far ... had had many common room discussions about a really good correspondence course in painting and about how much one could do over the 'phone to encourage students to look carefully and draw.' And crucially 'would be prepared to be mentioned in grant applications as someone ready to convene a working group to prepare a course in painting/drawing.'

For at the same time he had to find money - perhaps £100,000 - to see this emerging institution into existence. Michael had already learnt from the Open University that it cost them £1million to launch a Foundation Course, but all his experience told him that if he was not going to get substantial government funding for this venture (and I suspect he didn't really want it) a lot could be done for far less, provided he could inspire people who either had another income, such as a pension, or who relished the challenge.

Michael wrote Ian a characteristic letter using, for the first time, a phrase that was to recur, 'a marriage between British excellence in distance-learning and the equally marked excellence in the arts and the crafts.' 'There are, in our post-industrial society,' he continued, 'growing numbers of people whose lives would be enriched if they were able to express themselves creatively; for this to be realised they need stimulus and encouragement at the highest possible standard of quality.' Then the question was delicately put: 'I think you would be the ideal person to lead this venture ... I imagine there may not be a real chance of this ... but could I ask you to think it over and let me know if, after all, there is a chance that you might be able to take on this pioneering job.'

Within days Ian had been charmed into becoming Director and, even before taking up his job in September 1986, into convening advisory group meetings to which a plan for the first year would be put. For his part Ian Jenkin introduced to the project Ralph Jeffery, formerly in charge of the Art and Design school inspectors. The paper for the advisory meetings of what was now envisaged as the *European University for the Arts and Design* spoke of two major areas for development.

The first was 'to start soon on a draft masterplan for the first distance teaching degree on OU lines in art and design.' It was envisaged that this would be a six-year degree requiring 20 hours study a week, with a first period devoted to general and taster courses, and in later years specialisation. A large question, the paper asked, was whether to aim at a parallel music course, and a not-quite-so-large question was 'how might gardening fit in?' The second area of development was to prepare a course for the teachers of primary children, also to be launched in September 1987.

As if this were not enough of an agenda for an organisation which did not yet have a full-time Director, let alone any staff, and only a few thousand pounds in the bank, 'we need to try ourselves out on a range of other courses such as: music for beginners, knitting, running a crafts business; dance/fitness; ceramics. Mini-gardening is another strong possibility.'

By the time Ian started officially the institution had become the *Eurocollege for Arts, Design and Crafts*; Michael had spotted a piece in a magazine about bogus degrees, and decided that the title of university was perhaps imprudent. The Open University had also indicated to Ian and Michael that it could not at that stage get involved in any practical way.

A new statement of intent began to look at the importance of tutors providing occasional support in colleges or in their own studios; it was also becoming clearer that the scale of activities would have to be much more modest in the first year or two; two or three courses (including a primary teachers' course) would be piloted in limited parts of England though there still remained a statement that 'we shall be seeking to develop similar opportunities elsewhere within the EEC' and there still remained a clear ambition eventually to make a degree possible through the college.

The next year was to prove frantic for both Ian and Michael. They had to set up a charitable trust, they had to go on finding money, and Ian had less than twelve months to create a course from scratch. But Michael was not to be limited; if the introductory art course was to be the main objective for a launch in September 1987, he was still yearning for diversity. He had for some time been hoping to produce some form of kit that people could buy and so learn by themselves. He hoped that the new college, by November 1986 the *Open College for Art, Design and Crafts*, could produce one to help people be better gardeners. He even listed the contents that a kit-in-a-box might contain: an illustrated manual, a pop-up suburban garden complete with moveable shrubs and trees; 3-D glasses to look at various cut-out schemes; a kitlet on how to use photographs; a soil analysis kit plus rain gauge; a happy families card game; possible selection of garden poetry to hang up in the kitchen. I have to add, somewhat regretfully, that this kit was never made.

But he also wrote to a friend at almost the same time, 'I'd like it if we could pilot some sort of basic course in skills needed in a variety of industrial crafts, e.g. plumbing and metalwork. This could be financed by the new College of the Air.' This was a reference to what eventually became the Open College. The Open College had been as strongly supported by Lord Young of Graffham, the Cabinet Minister, as had the Open College of the Arts by Lord Young of Dartington. Both went public in September 1987. But there the similarities ended. The Open College was able to draw down £32 million from the government and pay its Chief Executive a salary four times what the *Open College of the Arts* (as it eventually became known) could afford.

By April 1987, Ian and Michael had visited the fledgling Open College, and a number of industrialists, and the basic craft skills suggested above had been transmuted into a Design in Business course which the OCA was trying to interest the Open College in. Eventually nothing came of this.

This was probably a good thing; the most important thing for OCA was not to acquire more ideas to work on, but for Ian Jenkin to be able to launch the Foundation for Art and Design course, which was increasingly seen as the main breadwinner for the first year. Ian had to contend with a team of ten authors (never since have we had more than three!) and an editor.

As the first chapter came off the stocks it was whisked off to Bideford in North Devon. This was my own introduction to OCA. I had been working with and for Michael in North Devon for some years and had already helped to get a thriving University of the Third Age branch going. Michael asked, in one of those early Sunday morning phone calls that his collaborators get used to, if I could put together a small group of Third-Agers plus a tutor to try out this new idea. It was not a question expecting the answer no. In fact I don't ever recall having a phone call from Michael expecting the answer no.

As the foundation course began to take shape and be piloted, the network of tutorial centres began to be put together - in the first year (beginning January 1988) the course was only to be available in six counties and with tutorial support at about thirty centres, mostly colleges but also including art centres and individual artists' studios. The tutors had to be briefed, the publicity generated, a system handling enquiries and enrolments created, and a way found of packing and distributing the materials, all in four months. The heroic staff of 18 Victoria Park Square suddenly found themselves dragooned into help, with Tony Flower designing the course books and arranging their printing, and Wyn Tucker and Sue Chisholm opening and dealing with a voluminous mail and responding to incessant telephone calls. OCA had struck a responsive chord with the public; over 1,200 people signed up for the first year. There were to be countless problems ahead, but at least the show was on the road, and by the end of January 1988 students were busily working at the course.

It had been two years since the idea first began to be put about; two years in which Michael simply followed his instinct that the country needed such an institution. There is no evidence in the early papers of OCA that Michael ever asked an accountant to pronounce on the possible viability of the venture; why bother if you are going to be told that it couldn't work? I once asked him, when he was pressing me to do some market research, on what basis he had launched OCA, and the reply was simply 'hunch'. And, of course, he has an extraordinary ability to listen to a very wide range of people from professionals to people he is sitting next to on the train.

Michael's involvement in OCA thereafter was characteristic; he gave a lot of his time and effort for a year or so, but was all the time looking for people to take over the burden. Fundraising continued to be very important: in 1988 he was still regularly firing off requests for £10,000, and occasionally landing money; OCA was not going to be able to survive on the £99 fee that 1,200 students had paid and there was no other income for many months.

He was also very concerned that by the time OCA entered its second year it had a wider range of courses to offer - painting, sculpture, textiles, photography, garden design and creative writing were all mentioned in a three-page memo to Ian Jenkin and Jane Brown, the production director, in February 1988 that began, 'Do forgive me for writing and from such a distance. 7,000 miles away I may be, but in spirit I am in the next room and thinking about OCA.' And finished 'Best of luck!' Sasha took on a much more active role in editing course manuals and OCA acutely acquired the part-time services of Ian Simpson, recently retired Principal of St Martin's.

By early 1989, it was clear that although OCA was going to have teething troubles for the foreseeable future, the organisation was growing (never remotely as fast as Michael hoped for) and was totally overburdening the staff at Bethnal Green. By now I was working on another dream of both Michael and myself - that the Elmhirst family home, Houndhill in Barnsley, should be some sort of miniature Dartington of the North.

Alfred and Gwen Elmhirst, dearest of friends of Michael for over fifty years and great supporters of the arts and education, willingly invited us in. It seemed - and still seems - a good idea that OCA should move out of London to somewhere where space, such as farm buildings, would be available for expansion, and where an enthusiastic and dedicated team of staff might be created. Ian Jenkin passed over the directorship to me with the grace that has made him so many friends, and he has continued to work for OCA in many practical ways ever since.

But the move to Barnsley, although it removed Michael from immediate contact with OCA, hardly reduced the flow of ideas that now came in phone calls and letters (Michael curiously doesn't seem to use the fax). His first letter to me as director proposed eight new lines of activity, each with a price tag to the nearest £10,000. Just one of these eight included the suggestion that we have small local groups for 'pottery, glass-blowing, cabinet-making, jewellery, paper-making, leather work, patchwork, quilting, antique restoration, frame-making, tapestry, basket-making, dance, music, etc.'

The next letter began 'I've had an idea ... that the OCA should sponsor the building of a cathedral ... we could recruit a volunteer labour force in their fifties who would undertake to stay with the work into their seventies, learn some of the skills, e.g. masonry, by distance methods but after that would need to spend a good deal of each year at the site. Perhaps the original Fountains Abbey or Rievaulx or Conisbrough Castle could be built not too far away from the present ruins.' Despite OCA's failure to achieve progress on almost all of these fronts, by January 1991 Michael felt able to pass the chairmanship over to his long-time friend Bob Gavron and gradually to relinquish the reins.

There has continued to be a flow of suggestions, based on his own ideas and his encounters with others. He has always hoped that there could be closer interlocking with the Open University, and still dreams of OCA students being awarded qualifications in collaboration with OU which cross some of the traditional subject frontiers.

And the idea that the arts is for everyone burns as bright as ever. A year ago I asked Michael to write a new letter to go with our publicity pack. This is what he wrote: 'My own interest and hobby is painting and I have got more pleasure out of it than anything else I have ever done. It is an eye-opener, literally, and can even be spiritually uplifting. It can be the same with any of the arts. They can show all of us what depths and gifts there are in ourselves which we normally do not tap at all.' The manifesto could not be put more clearly.

The Birkbeck Presidency
Tessa Blackstone

No social reformer since George Birkbeck in the 1820s and 1830s has done more to advance the cause of the education of adults than Michael Young. The Open University, though associated in the public mind with Jennie Lee and Harold Wilson, was his idea. The International Extension College for Africa and elsewhere in the third world was his idea. More recently, the Open College of the Arts was invented by Michael. His passionate belief, way before the idea of life-long learning became fashionable, that adults should have access to education throughout their lives, has helped to create many new opportunities for mature students. These opportunities were created because when Michael Young believes in something he campaigns for it, fights to make it happen, badgers people, bores people, irritates people and goads them into action. Some no doubt take action only to get rid of Michael; others do so because his powers of persuasion have hooked them to the cause.

Others will be writing about Michael's role in the founding of the Open University and his work in promoting distance learning in Africa. I want to concentrate on his Presidency of Birkbeck College and in doing so to give a personal and anecdotal account of how he played this role.

Most, but perhaps not all, of the readers of this collection will be aware of Birkbeck's unique position in British higher education. It is the only university dedicated to taking part-time mature students, who study in the evening. George Birkbeck founded it in 1823 as the London Mechanics' Institution for men who worked by day and studied by night.

Over the last 175 years it has remained faithful to George Birkbeck's original mission. Women students, incidentally, were admitted from as early as the 1830s. Of our current students 92 per cent are studying part-time; the full-timers are mainly graduate students doing research degrees. Our youngest students are in their early twenties; our oldest current student is eighty. The average age of study at Birkbeck for undergraduates is 28, for postgraduates it is 32. Degrees are available in the sciences, the arts and the social sciences and there is a huge range of diploma and certificate courses available in Birkbeck's Centre for Extra-Mural Studies. Just under 6,000 students are studying for degrees and a further 22,000 on extra-mural courses all over London.

The President of the College is an honorary appointment and is the equivalent of the Chancellor in most universities. When I arrived in 1987, there had only been ten previous Presidents since 1823. They included George Birkbeck himself, Viscount Haldane, the Duke of York before he became George VI, William Temple - the Archbishop of Canterbury, Field Marshall Earl Wavell and Lord Denning. A year or so later when the then incumbent wished to stand down, Michael seemed to me the obvious candidate for the post. His great distinction as a social reformer and as an academic, and his genius as an inventor of new institutions - above all institutions designed to support and protect people without the benefits of privilege - made him a President of whom we would be immensely proud. It was, however, for his passion for creating opportunities for adults to continue their education that I really wanted him to become Birkbeck's President.

When I approached him he was at first reluctant. Unimpressed by titles, with an active dislike of pomp and ceremony, and concerned to conserve his precious time for the various projects he was pursuing at the time, he needed to be persuaded. I promised him that it would not be time-consuming and appealed to his sense of duty, particularly to adult students. In the end he gave in. Everyone at Birkbeck was delighted.

Having been told it would not be time-consuming, in his inimitable way he set about making it just that. At the age of 74 he became a student again, enrolling for an MA in Philosophy. Apparently he chose Philosophy because he was interested in exploring the links between philosophical thought and sociology, his own discipline. He later claimed to have found some links 'but not too many' between sociology and 'the ethics of Hume and the scepticism of A J Ayer.' Whilst impressed by the ethics of Hume, he was in his own words 'amazed by his fellow students.' Indeed so fascinated was he by these remarkable people that his sociological curiosity took over, leaving his drive for philosophical insight behind. He became, as he put it, 'more interested in the students than Hume and Ayer.'

This first became apparent at the College's Founder's Day Dinner soon after he had embarked on the MA. In replying to the Guest Speaker, Sir Robin Butler, on behalf of the College, he entertained us with a delightful account of what it was like to be a student at Birkbeck. Just before 6 pm the College corridors filled with people rushing in from all over London, trying to get to the first of the evening's lectures on time. They streamed into the lecture theatre, still wearing their overcoats, some with smart briefcases, others with plastic bags and motor cycle helmets, falling over each other to get a seat. He described the middle-aged male student who always sat in the front row with a large tape recorder to record the lecture. He later became friendly with this man and asked him what he did with the tapes. He turned out to be a taxi-driver who played and replayed the lectures as he drove round London in his cab and in doing so managed to get a grip on Hume and Ayer. Then there was the man who worked in the rag-trade, who decided to do the same and tape the lectures, so that he could listen to them as he drove between the East End and Great Portland Street.

Michael observed at first hand the thirst for learning, the enthusiasm for their course, the incredible motivation of his fellow students, all in the face of considerable sacrifices to study in the evening after work. This experience seemed to strengthen his own commitment to the cause of expanding opportunities for adults, who had missed out earlier, to have a second chance. His studies at Birkbeck more or less coincided with the setting up of the Open College of the Arts, which he established against the odds with his usual determination.

The idea of taking on Michael as a student might not appeal to everyone. Argumentative and sometimes obstinate, some might find him a little tricky in the classroom. All Birkbeck academics become accustomed to the special challenge of mature students who expect high standards from their teachers, and do not let them get away with sloppy thinking or inadequate evidence. But a tutorial with Michael would intimidate all but the super-confident. When he became a philosophy student there were two professors in the Department: the flamboyant and controversial right-winger, Roger Scruton, and the scholarly and absent-minded David Wiggins, who has subsequently returned to Oxford to the Wykeham Chair of Logic there. Putting Michael together with Roger Scruton would have been interesting but a trifle risky, so David Wiggins became his tutor.

David remembers their first meeting in the Philosophy Department at 12 Gower Street vividly. This is how he describes it:

'He was a pale, modest, most diffident figure. He explained that his thoughts about time and the part that time plays in human routine had made him curious again about philosophy. He gave me a copy of his book about time, designating one or two passages for my attention. We discussed these two or three weeks later, though the discussion didn't (I fear) hit the spot, so far as he was concerned.'

David goes on to describe Michael's participation in lectures, 'where he looked (more or less happily) puzzled, rapt or disconcerted at our philosophical goings on'; in seminars, where he particularly remembers one Michael introduced on Kant's essay *Perpetual Peace*; and at Cumberland Lodge in Windsor Great Park at the Department's biennial philosophical weekend, 'where he was as effective as he was apparently diffident in communicating with students 20, 30 or 40 years younger than himself.'

I asked another Birkbeck philosopher, Barry Smith, whose classes he attended, what it was like to have Michael as a student. 'Jolly hard' was the immediate reply. Whilst apparently very interested in what Barry Smith had to say, he kept interrupting with quasi-anthropological remarks. He appeared to be as interested in the sociology of philosophers as in the philosophical ideas themselves, if not more interested. When any idea was introduced he wanted to know who the perpetrators were, what were their backgrounds, and life-styles, how were they rooted in a cultural sense. What was this strange network of intellectuals peddling philosophy?

Smith talked about knowledge and belief exploring the difference between really knowing something and merely having good evidence for it. Searching for an illustration of certain kinds of knowledge he posed the question, 'Where can Chateau Margaux be bought at a reasonable price?' Michael, constantly seeking information that might be of some practical use; stopped the class in its tracks with the question, 'Do you actually know where you can get it at a good price?'

To give a flavour of Michael's extraordinary intellectual curiosity I can do no better than quote another tutor at Birkbeck, Geoffrey Thomas, who also supervised Michael during the 1989-90 session.

> *'As a former social scientist I already knew him, of course, as the author of* The Rise of the Meritocracy *(1958), and I wondered exactly what as a sociologist and political theorist his interest in philosophy amounted to. I put the point to him. The answer came in two parts. 'When I was a child,' he told me, ' I often crossed the Atlantic Ocean. Liners, large and imposing, emblazoned with mysterious lights, would pass by. I was intrigued; I wondered what went on in them. That really is how I have always regarded philosophy - as a mysterious passing vessel. Well, this course is my opportunity to come on board.'*

> *'The second part of the answer came more slowly. Lately, I think, as a result of attending David Wiggins's lectures, Michael showed great interest in the moral philosophies of Kant and Hume. Kant particularly appealed to the world*

citizen in him. The Kantian moral community is the world community of vulnerable, rational beings; and this kind of universalistic ethics slid neatly into place as the moral basis for an ideal which Michael had long cherished and never abandoned, that of world government.

'Our weekly supervisions, for which Michael usually drove over from Bethnal Green in the worst of the evening rush hour, were an increasing pleasure to me. (In daylight the supervision always began with an aesthetic interlude in which Michael gazed through the window admiringly at the trees in the gardens behind 14 Gower Street.) I was struck by Michael's creative intellectual energy and by his philosophical outsider's ability to spot things I had simply overlooked. He once remarked, for instance, on the absence from political philosophy, in the era of European integration, of any serious, developed concern with political units larger than the nation state.

'We learned from each other. I remember one lively exchange in which Michael sat back reflectively and said: 'This really is odd. You're arguing like a sociologist and I'm arguing like a philosopher.'

'Towards the end of the session Michael opened a supervision by saying, 'I have a statement to make.' I wondered just what was coming. The statement was that he felt a formal degree course to be an unsuitable medium for his philosophical interests. 'If I were half my age...' he said. 'But you are, Michael, you are,' was all I could reply.'

When illness and other pressures forced Michael to give up being a student at Birkbeck, he was missed by both staff and fellow students. As David Wiggins put it, 'Long may there be sufficient *Spielraum* for it to be possible for us to admit such memorable persons for them to work on the margins between this or that and philosophy.'

As President of the College, Michael did not confine his interest in what was going on at Birkbeck to the Philosophy Department. He asked Christine Mabey, the College Secretary, herself a social scientist whose PhD was on the attainment of black pupils in London schools, to take him to meet academics and students in departments where neither he nor she had any expertise. She was struck on these visits by the lateral thinking behind his questions and by his attention to detail. This was as true of his discussions with crystallographers as with art historians and modern linguists. In the Art History Department, housed in 46 Gordon Square, he reminisced about a earlier visit. 'I remember,' he said, 'coming to see Keynes here when he was ill just after the war.'

Reminiscences about this period entertained Birkbeck students and their friends and families when Michael was made a Fellow of the College at a degree ceremony in Autumn 1994. He received his Fellowship from Lord Healey of Riddlesden, better known to most of us as Denis Healey, and Michael's successor as President of the College. They had worked together at Transport House during the 1945 Labour Government. Their banter on the platform not only amused a large Birkbeck audience, it also provided it with a little bit of Labour history many of them will not forget. Although Michael's period as President of the College was all too short, and although he believes occupying such positions is without much merit, he brought to it his own special approach to give it some point. Small though his contribution may have been in this role compared with his many other achievements over the last eighty years, he left an indelible impression on those who met him at Birkbeck, and his name lent lustre to the College and the ideals it represents.

A Baptism in Grand Designs
Kirsteen Tait

Some of Michael Young's most recent ventures in education have tackled educational disadvantage and individual underachievement, and have involved the establishment of two new charitable bodies, Open School and the National Association for the Education of Sick Children. They form only one part of Michael's working life over the last five years. But as if this wasn't enough, there have been other Michael Young education initiatives in Victoria Park Square during that time, including Education Extra and the Tower Hamlets Summer University - as well as many more in other places, directly or indirectly influenced by him, for example, Birmingham Education Authority's new University of the First Age.

The two I deal with here and have been involved with myself look at things in an entirely new way and question orthodox thinking, unpopular as that is to the establishment and exhausting for those working with and for Michael. But otherwise obstacles will not be bulldozed away and the children not helped. Michael has focussed on them only intermittently - yet often more intensively than I could easily sustain. His head around the door, apologetic yet insistent; 'I think it's time we went to the DFE and told them what's going wrong'. 'Do you think we might now set up a *new national agency?*' or, 'Have you been able to write the paper describing how *we could take it over and do it better*' and 'Oh, I don't think the press will take an interest unless we give them a map showing *how it would work for the whole country*'.

This sort of thing is familiar to those who have worked with Michael. But I was a late starter and it has been dramatic for me. I was on leave briefly from Abu Dhabi in September 1989 when a friend telephoned: 'If you are looking for work when you get back, you might just go and see Michael Young about a new project of his'. The conversation I then had was meant to be about the recently established Open School, not going quite as he wanted. In the event it ranged over the whole education system, underachievement, Tower Hamlets, the ICS and the fate of today's children. 'Are you interested in it then? Oh well, go back to Abu Dhabi and write a paper on it.'

If the task appeared both difficult and vague in a Bedouin city on the shores of the Arabian Gulf, it was to be neither clearer nor easier round the table at 18 Victoria Park Square on January 2nd 1990. I was now being interviewed for the same organisation, but to do something entirely different. A lot had happened since September. 'But what shall I be doing exactly? What shall I tell my children my new job is?' I asked plaintively, sensing all too clearly the inappropriateness of the questions.

Open School had been set up to adapt the principles of the Open University to the needs of school-aged children and to help a range of children who might otherwise underachieve. It was from the outset about open and individual learning generally and about specific strategies for children who needed help to make use of their educational opportunities - sick children, traveller children, children in small schools with limited curricula, ethnic minority children who needed a way in to mainstream schooling, children who couldn't get started because they were hungry or distracted by breaking-up homes. Open School has done things to help all of them.

But it cast its net rather wide. Its aims and objectives have encompassed most of what is missing in the education system and involved creating new attitudes as well as strategies. It takes a long time to change attitudes and Open School is still pioneering ways of encapsulating and selling its ideas. It has had a difficult five years. Over that period I have regularly attended sometimes dispiriting discussions, under Michael's chairmanship and since, about what really is its essential mission, its main purpose. It has not yet fulfilled its potential, in spite of work and commitment all round.

I suspect that Open School, like others of Michael's creations, was at the same time a bold grand idea and an umbrella for tackling a number of more manageable things that needed to be done. The only fixed point was children. The lack of fit between what was provided by the education system and what was needed irked him. Driving to Dartington in 1990 for a meeting, we stopped at Weston-super-Mare for a cup of tea and he described a speech he was going to give somewhere. Would it be alright, he wondered, to say that compulsory education should end at eleven (or maybe it was twelve) and children be free to go out and work because the household needed money, or the father needed help, or because that was what was timely and exciting? And they would all have coupons for another five years of education which could be cashed in at any stage of life.

Ideas something like that were behind the birth of Open School. Education should be available in more flexible form going more than halfway to meet children who for circumstances beyond their control might otherwise underachieve or be unable to make the best of their opportunities. It was typical of Michael to see that for some children the best way to promote education in the long run might be to relieve them of it in the short run. I believe the ideas behind Open School are some of his grandest and most wide-ranging, even among the distinguished company described in this book. But unlike the Open University, Open School has not had millions of pounds of government money invested in it. And it has been struggling to survive in a much less congenial climate.

In the period I am describing; 1990 to 1995, money has been increasingly difficult to find, and the education system exhausted and constrained by change. The introduction of the National Curriculum, local management of budgets by schools and legislation prescribing arrangements for children with special needs, however valuable, have all meant that schools and teachers are only interested in things that solve prescribed problems and relieve immediate burdens. Open School's life has coincided with hard times for vision. What has eluded it has been one overriding mainline application of its ideas. Instead it has presented a series of interlocking ideas and too many possibilities - in a way the perfect setting for Michael's own brand of the visionary and the operator. Open School Trustee meetings have been stage sets for a remarkable range of Michael Young *tours d'horizons* and ingenuity, ideas for next steps, for the way to secure the elusive funding. These have been produced, sometimes discursively but always elegantly, like conjuring tricks, without apparently reading the papers. Originating in chance meetings, and built, like cardcastles, on small foundations.

Once he asked me to think about schools as after-hours refuges for children whose parents' marriages were breaking up or who were needing a break from other serious family problems. This was inspired by a project in Ayrshire and we could apply it to Tower Hamlets. I have always regretted that I was too exhausted at the time to take up the challenge, but I like to think it was part of the process that gave birth to the now flourishing Education Extra. A bit of it may also have crept into the Family Covenant Assocation. Another time the tiny Open School team in London gave him Christmas lunch in a local cafe. We talked about the Tower Hamlets children who again go to school hungry - as they did a hundred years ago. Could we set up a Breakfast Club at the local primary school, did we think? This time it was the other way round. Determined that this should not be lost to Open School, I bundled it under its umbrella, putting 'Books and Breakfast' first into some Poplar schools, and then doggedly transferring it, under Language 2000, to Bethnal Green. And trustees quite reasonably asked why Open School was doing it.

His interjection of new visions could be exhausting at times, and for the sake of survival we would sometimes conspire to divert him from the more predictable ones. Sitting round my kitchen table in

Camden Town one evening in the autumn of 1992 the Open School staff prepared for his arrival. 'For goodness sake keep Michael off sick children. It'll go on all night and we've got too much to do already.'

But he, of course, turned to me almost at once. 'What are we doing about sick children?' I was all prepared. 'I've looked into it, done the research,' I said, 'There's a real need for professional development for hospital teachers. No question. They want it. They're isolated and they're not properly supported. No one's doing anything about it. I've consulted HMI etc. *But it's no good*, Michael, *everyone* says that now is the wrong moment. The whole future of sick children's education is in the balance. Hospital teachers are worried about their very survival.' There was only the briefest surprised pause. 'But that's when you get things done, when things are in a state of flux. That's your best chance to change things'.

In the end there was no more to be said. He'd convinced me that something had to be done. But it was more important for me than that. It was a lasting lesson about grasping opportunities and one of those moments that permanently change the way you look at things. In practical terms I had fallen straight into a trap. It meant long hours of assembling the groundwork for a campaign, and the familiar struggle to raise the money to cover costs that we had anxiously already incurred.

Sick children had to be squeezed into the purview of the National Commission on Education, papers written and the issues perceived - to an absurdly tight deadline. In these circumstances, Michael is a curious combination of the supportive and impossibly demanding. I have never known anyone else make you feel you ought to be doing so much better and quicker. It is only recently that I have stopped creeping past the door to his office on the ground floor of the ICS for fear of a new task or impossible challenge. Lately I have had even a little success in reversing the process, pinning him down with a little of the sort of ruthlessness which he may himself have taught me. 'Look, Michael, I really need your help about that submission to the DFE. It won't be any good unless you ...' 'You really can't go on holiday. I need you to come to ...'.

The National Association for the Education of Sick Children was conceived that evening in Camden Town and Open School gave birth to it. It was formally set up in July 1993 to improve the educational opportunities for sick children and to make them available to all of them, wherever they lived or went to hospital. We have sometimes been chided with taking away from Open School one of its client groups and the one that would be easiest to raise money for. I am unrepentant about this - more unrepentant probably than Michael, because sick children were so much part of his early vision of Open

School. As I see it, to do what had to be done for such children within Open School would have risked unbalancing the ideas that inspired it, while at the same time lessening the chances of tackling the problem single-mindedly. Perhaps that's Michael's influence.

The NAESC started with an advantage Open School never had - a clearly defined focus. But that does not mean that its intentions were moderate or limited. It too planned to change the world. In the summer of 1993, when it started work, Michael said what we are saying now, two years and volumes of research later, that section 298 of the Education Act 1993, which put a new statutory duty on LEAs to provide suitable education for sick children, would actually make things worse for them. This was because it lumped them together with 'excluded' children whose needs, though great, are different and will often be met at the expense of sick children because their profile is higher. It has happened just as he predicted. He said then that hospital teaching could not safely be left to LEAs, whom the government were denuding of responsibilities. This was unpopular because, away from LEAs, although we were in favour of them, we wanted to take hospital schools and services and set them up as grant-maintained schools, which in *principle* we were against. This may have cost us the success of an amendment in the House of Lords, but again Michael was right. Many LEAs are not doing it properly. They are rationing sick children's entitlement to teaching and putting excluded children first. This is because there is not enough money for both and because it is health matters and health policies which dictate what needs to be done.

Now Michael says that hospitals themselves should employ the teachers because they recognise the need for the education as part of child-centred provision and may have the money to pay for it, unlike LEAs. There has been a great deal of opposition to this idea, from, amongst others, teachers, who say that it will threaten their professional status, and from me. But he may be right about this too. In some states in America children's hospitals regard continuity of education as a marketing benefit and so pay for education co-ordinators and teachers, which the state should, but does not, provide in sufficient numbers.

I have thought about little but the education of sick children since the summer of 1993 and regularly dream about it. Michael gave it the full blast of his creative energy and relentless determination when we first took on the subject. This was all the more remarkable because it happened in the months when Sasha was dying. He fought the Education Bill in the House of Lords; we took some sick children and their parents to 10 Downing Street; and we wrote applications for start-up funds and launched the National Association. He drove all this along and then he unfaithfully gave his attention to new things. He travelled when I wanted his help, and he put his head round the door and demanded new ventures when I wanted to be left in peace to consolidate.

'Have you come round to the idea of a new national agency yet?' 'Michael, in this political climate? When quangos are discredited? It would require a change in the law and the new duty only came in in September'.

'Well. I think we have to really. It won't be any good suggesting anything else.'

Another thing I've learnt from him is that it is no good starting off with a compromise, just because people will not agree with what you really think should be done. You are there to have a vision that will really make a difference, and if you don't get agreement, which you probably won't, you'll at least end up with something.

'Dear Michael' said last Thursday's letter from the Permanent Secretary of the DFE, '*We do not find the idea of an agency attractive* ... (New paragraph) 'I should, however, be willing to look more closely at your idea of a study *to consider how we address the issues that you raised.* The first step would be ...'

I don't know if we will transform education for sick children but we will certainly prevent the worst of what would have happened in today's crabbed and penniless education culture if it had continued to be a hidden and neglected subject. And that is because of the daring scope of Michael's intentions for the Association. Open School is pioneering teletutoring and FAXtutoring for children with Special Educational Needs, children sick in hospital and at home, excluded children, children in care and children in detention centres. It is extending what is available for children in very small schools on islands in Scotland. Teletutoring and FAXtutoring could transform education in and out of school and open learning is beginning to be accepted within schools. Open School may not get the credit but it has nurtured a series of ideas which are more than ever needed in today's hard educational times.

Embracing New Communities
Kate Gavron

I have a favourite private image of Michael. He is a large and ever-vigilant spider in the middle of his web. We, the mere flies and other insignificant insects, are caught on his web and gradually become entangled beyond escape. If we are unwise enough to struggle, perhaps to move away from his web to work in other fields, or we begin to become engaged in some project with which Michael is not interested, along he comes and binds us more tightly with the silken ropes of a new Young invention.

I remember a conversation in Provence when we discussed the length of time it might be before I finished writing up my PhD thesis and could devote myself full-time to the next (several) research projects that Michael had in mind for me. This conversation carried on as we got into Michael's car for a short journey between two houses, and then it took (to me) an unexpected turn. Suddenly Michael, behind the wheel of his new car, shot off down the road at a reckless speed. I took this to be Michael's suicidal revenge for my stubborn refusal to agree that I would write my thesis in less than three months. In fact, the truth was different, but characteristic. As many of Michael's friends will know, he has a surprising ability to carry on a lengthy conversation about cars. Not just about the sociological aspect of cars and their effect upon individualism, families and communities, but about the characteristics of particular models of particular makes. As we shot along a twisting country road and I gripped the edge of the seat and tried to conjure up a pacifying remark, Michael suddenly announced:

> *'You see, I wanted to show you that this has very good acceleration even though it has a diesel engine. Citroën have been doing an enormous amount to improve the performance of diesels for their medium-range cars.'*

Michael first suggested that I should join him at the ICS when I was half way through a late degree in Social Anthropology at the LSE. He said that he was interested in doing research again in Bethnal Green, forty years after he and Peter Willmott had worked on *Family and Kinship*. As they noted in the Introduction to a recent edition of *Family and Kinship* (1986, p.xii), the most important change in Bethnal Green since the mid 1950s has been the arrival of a large Bangladeshi community. If Bangladeshi men were present in Bethnal Green when they were doing their first research (as in fact they were, although in very small numbers at that time), they were invisible in the research and in the pages of *Family and Kinship*. Michael persuaded me (with no difficulty at all) that I should combine research in Bethnal Green for the Institute with research for my own PhD.

At a very early stage in the research I remember being taken one evening, with Michael and a few other colleagues, around a part of Spitalfields, in the western end of Bethnal Green, to visit some Bangladeshi families. This was, I believe, the first time Michael had visited a Bangladeshi household and here he showed his extraordinary ability to engage with anybody he meets. To Michael any stranger is a source of interest and new knowledge. He was enchanted by the small shy children who hovered in the background in the houses we visited, and by the hospitality we received. He was struck during this visit by the decoration in the Bangladeshis' houses, especially by the pictures of Mecca and the Taj Mahal we saw in one house, illuminated by many tiny light bulbs acting as stars.

I remember in particular going that evening to visit a small supplementary school for Bangladeshi children, who were learning written Bengali as well as studying the Qu'ran and having extra lessons in some of the subjects covered at their primary schools. The school was buzzing with the sound of small children at work, and the walls of the pre-fab in which the school was housed were covered with pieces of their work and samples of script for the children to copy. The teachers were all giving their time for free. Naturally, for Michael this was an inspiring visit; here around the corner in Bethnal Green was an organisation that he might easily have created himself; surviving in straightened circumstances, staffed by volunteers and filling a special need in a special place.

In September 1993, there was a local council by-election in the Millwall ward of the Isle of Dogs which was won by Derek Beackon, who was representing the British National Party on generally racist and specifically anti-Bangladeshi policies. The by-election was followed by an increase in both low-level racism and overt racial attacks. Just as worrying was the prospect of the full council elections taking place only a few months later, in May 1994, with the BNP putting forward a number of candidates in Tower Hamlets and with a perceived chance of winning control of the Isle of Dogs Neighbourhood and its £27m budget. For Michael, needless to say, this was an opportunity for action. Following the by-election there had been a great number of reports in the media, in newspapers especially but also on radio and television, covering the results of the election and the situation in

Tower Hamlets. Many of the details in these reports had been inaccurate, in particular those concerning local housing availability and council housing allocation, subjects of great concern to the whole local population, white and Bangladeshi. In several places the misleading impression had been given that Bangladeshi families had been given priority in the allocation of good new housing at the expense of 'local', i.e. white, people. In their pre-election campaign, the BNP had used to good effect some incorrect figures about the allocation of houses on an attractive new Thames-side council estate on the Isle of Dogs itself.

As a long-standing daytime resident of Bethnal Green, Michael was, like most other residents, distressed that the borough of Tower Hamlets was becoming notorious for the election of a fascist councillor, more than fifty years after Bethnal Green had proved such a successful recruiting ground for Mosley's British Union of Fascists. Michael knew that, as was the case in the 1930s, extremists and racists are in a minority, but they were becoming a vocal minority who were quickly poisoning the atmosphere.

As usual in answer to a crisis, Michael decided to act. There were several reasons for this. One was that he had developed an affection for the Bangladeshi families he had met and for the Bangladeshis working as researchers in the Institute. He appreciated the way in which the Bengali community had enhanced the district; their food and clothing shops, their restaurants, and the vivid expanding commerce of the Whitechapel Road market. He recognised in the large Bangladeshi households of extended families an echo of the extended families sharing a few 'turnings' and popping in and out of each other's houses in the pre-redevelopment 'golden' past of Bethnal Green. The 'family values' which are increasingly neglected in wider British society are alive and well in their full glory (and, I would add, with some of their attendant *dis*advantages) in the Bangladeshi community in Tower Hamlets. But a more important reason was Michael's love of Bethnal Green itself, as it had been and still is, and his abiding affection for the old 'Bethnal Greeners', the 1990s grandparents who had been parents with young children when he was researching *Family and Kinship*. These were the people who were being vilified by the national media as throwbacks to pre-war fascist mobs. The newspapers in particular seemed to be glorying in the primitive antagonisms which seemed to be emerging once again in the grimier parts of the capital.

Michael has always talked to people he meets in local cafes, queueing in sandwich shops, waiting for trains. He had also recently been visiting elderly ex-Bethnal Greeners living in the 'Greenleigh' of *Family and Kinship*, and to some of the elderly long-time residents who remembered the Bethnal Green of the 1950s. However much Michael himself deplored the intolerance and racism of those who had been tempted to vote BNP, he understood a feeling of dispossession and alienation felt by some of the older people who compared today with the myth-misted security and 'community' of their remembered youth. He is not one for blindly taking sides and condemning, because he will always understand different ways of seeing things; his solution is to teach people to see things in another way.

As in many other situations, Michael's proposed solution was therefore a programme of education. For this, he needed to create a new short-lived organisation. We settled on the full name of Tower Hamlets Independent News Service, shortened to a more pithy and dictatorial THINK - at one point Michael became keen that we should perfect the acronym and call it the Tower Hamlets Independent News and Knowledge, but we settled for the imperfect but more honest original. With his habitual energy and persistence and with the help of Robin Richardson of the Runnymede Trust, Michael gathered together a group of people either living or working in Tower Hamlets, who were all prepared to help campaign in whatever way was feasible for the defeat of the BNP in the May 1994 elections.

Showing his usual passion for a fight in a just cause, Michael had raised the money to conduct a survey in the Isle of Dogs to try to ascertain voting intentions. The other strand of THINK's activity was that Michael decided that we should produce for the press, and anyone else expressing interest, a series of bulletins covering various aspects of local affairs, for example housing funding and allocation, in order to try to counteract the off-the-street gossip that was feeding newspaper columns. The hope was that we could replace some of this misinformation with more accurate, disinterested, non-party political facts about sources of funding, and about both the possibilities and limits of local government policy and practice. This resulted in an extended campaign in the local government offices as Michael cajoled them into co-operating by feeding THINK with papers, figures and reports. In extremis he even once or twice let slip a normally unused 'Lord Young' in an urgent request for a particular report or speedy response to some arcane question about Housing Association funding. He invited editors and journalists from the local newspapers to attend some of the famously frugal Victoria Park Square lunches in order that he should persuade them of the correct and judicious line to take in their leader columns addressed to the electorate.

The survey was carried out (by ICM) in a very few weeks. Before the results were ready, Michael had already arranged to see both the leader of the Liberal Democrats and the Labour party's main London campaigners in the House of Commons. His idea was that if the survey showed that the vote seemed to be evenly spread between Labour, the LibDems and the BNP, both the Labour and LibDem leaders should be persuaded to enter some sort of pact to try to ensure that a split vote should not open the door to the BNP, as seemed to have happened in the by-election. Slightly to my disappointment, as I was relishing the prospect of seeing Michael argue the case for a pact in his uniquely persistent style, the survey predicted (with great accuracy, as it turned out) a large Labour majority and a much reduced LibDem vote. At the pre-arranged meetings this news was greeted with delight by Labour and with very gracious disappointment by Paddy Ashdown.

There was still a chance, however, that the poll might be wrong, given the probable reluctance of the extremist vote to reveal itself, despite a carefully thought-out response method for the questions about voting intentions. Michael had heard that a special pre-election free news-sheet was to be distributed to all the residents on the Isle of Dogs. He decided he would write a letter, to be signed by a sympathetic local resident, discouraging a BNP vote. This was a good example of how Michael sometimes draws mercilessly on the skills of those around him. Having written a draft of a letter, he suggested we should send it to his journalist son, Toby, to get his reaction. The result was that Toby, having found out the exact purpose of the letter, completely rewrote it and produced the inspired and moving final version which was used in the news-sheet.

As it turned out, on election day the voting turn-out was high and the BNP, far from gaining further seats, actually lost their one existing seat. Though I personally doubt it, it is just possible of course that none of Michael's endeavours and ideas made any difference: many people besides Michael were fighting to keep the BNP out of the Tower Hamlets council; the local churches, for example, did an enormous amount of work and supplied escorts and vehicles on election day to encourage the elderly or nervous to go and vote. However, despite all the other work undertaken elsewhere, what happened with THINK was that Michael's passion for a good cause and his determination to put wrongs right mobilised some action that would not have taken place without him.

Since the May 1994 elections, Michael has not relaxed: he remains vigilant in a continuing situation of potential conflict. As problems which usually occur on the street or in other public places tend to be exacerbated in the summer, when street life is more active and young teenagers do not have the formal structure of school life to discipline them, Michael (with Tony Flower) has been working alongside other organisations in Tower Hamlets on trying to establish yet another new project, a Tower Hamlets 'Summer University', specifically designed to encourage young Asians and whites to integrate with each other on shared activities, both educational and recreational. He is also embarking on new research at the Institute into good practice in race relations, looking at ways of minimising mutual distrust between groups who see themselves as competing for limited resources, of which housing and employment are the most obvious in Tower Hamlets. So, as in the 1950s and 1960s, research and action are again bound up together in the activities of the Institute of Community Studies in the 1990s, as Michael returns to one set of his own personal roots, in this case the roots in *Family and Kinship*.

Michael's response to the approach of the local elections of May 1994 did not take place, I hardly need say, when Michael was searching idly in his 79th year for something to do. He was already fully occupied, with a book he was finishing and a multitude of other organisations demanding his time and participation. But Michael never turns away from something that he believes needs doing, and one of his qualities is his ability to take others, argued into enthusiastic participation, with him along his various yellow brick roads. The journey is always inspiring, and always worthwhile.

The House that Michael Built
Wyn Tucker & Sue Chisholm

The elegant and surprisingly roomy Queen Anne house two minutes walk from Bethnal Green underground station has been the location for the Institute of Community Studies and the centre of Michael's creative activity for more than forty years. Understanding his relationship with the Institute is essential to any appreciation of how he has managed to achieve so much.

Firstly, it is important to realise that Michael has come to feel very strongly attached to the Bethnal Green area, and perhaps even to consider it his real home. In many ways the grand medieval estate of Dartington has always been more like a parental home for Michael. He derived his basic philosophy from Dartington, went on to become a Trustee there for half a century, and has often called on Dartington resources to help new organisations to get started. Dartington became the territorial designation for his peerage; and this recognition of where he came from paid some of his debt. But it is in Bethnal Green, at the Institute, that he has chosen to work out his own interpretations and practices, and plant his own intellectual and political seeds. This is where he has built his own base.

The early research studies with Peter Willmott brought him into very close touch with local life, and for a period he opted to live in the flat above the Institute (as did Peter and Phyll Willmott for a while, and also Peter Marris and Tony Flower later on) in order to get a better feel for the place. In addition, he lived for some years in a house just down the road from the Institute, and altogether felt much more at home in the area than the people who merely came to work in the borough during the day.

Having chosen Bethnal Green as his working base, Michael then collected around him people he could rely on to keep things going. Anchor people. In many ways he is a good person to work with. For example, he doesn't bear a grudge, or labour points. He gets things over with and if he's got something to say, if he doesn't like what you've done, he says it and then it's forgotten. And you're back to where you were before it happened. However, he has his faults too. He doesn't realise the effort that has to go into keeping a place like the Institute going. Not at all. For him it just happens. Because nobody presents much of a problem to him he thinks that things happen by magic. He has never really learned how to use things like photocopiers and fax or franking machines, and leaves it all to you. Sometimes he drives you mad and you get totally exasperated. And then you remember the wonderful things that he does and you think, 'Oh, well!'. You couldn't do it if you didn't admire him.

If people can't get on with him then they soon leave. But if you stay then Michael knows that he can rely on you. So the Institute has always had some dedicated staff, like Daphne Piccinelli who was his secretary for many years, who are able to keep things running smoothly.

This has been very important for Michael, because it was the knowledge that the Institute was in safe hands which enabled him to become involved in and start up so many projects elsewhere. Peter Willmott was crucial here, because he was active in all levels and dimensions of the Institute's work - including many projects of his own - so that even when there was a great deal going on in Bethnal Green it was still possible for Michael to spend long periods away. He had the freedom to go and be in Cambridge or Mauritius or Nigeria or America because there was always Peter keeping the Institute itself going.

The Institute was always there to come back to: each time that Michael has gone off to and then come back from adventures elsewhere it has become ever more knitted into a web of overlapping and often mutually-supportive enterprises and organisations, of which it is clearly the centre and heart. Over time this has helped to change the character of the place. In the early days most of the space at the Institute was taken up by people engaged in social survey work. We were buzzing with the coming and going of interviewers. Michael and Peter used to go out themselves quite often to do some of the interviewing. Maybe Michael didn't always follow the questionnaire but at least he was directly involved and got the feel of it. Sometimes we were very busy, and during the late sixties, when Ann Cartwright and the Medical Care unit had a lot of research on the go too, we were so crowded that some of us moved to Hampstead for eighteen months, in a sort of overspill. But then, as Michael spent less time on research and more in setting up new organisations, the Institute tended to become more of a centre for planning groups and committees to meet, or from where organisations which were operating elsewhere were administered, and where fledgling institutions could spend their infancy until they became established and independent.

In this way, most of the many organisations and projects initiated by Michael have spent some time at Bethnal Green. This is detailed at the end of this volume. Some of these ventures failed early on and never got any further, like Bethnal Green Exports which was perhaps rather too different from all the other organisations to fit in with them, and Support the United Nations. SUN probably never was going to succeed, because of how its creators went about it: they just took a sample of names from the electoral register and asked these people to donate a percentage of their income to help the UN. We had a lot of people who were quite badly off phoning in to say that they paid their taxes and didn't have any money to spare. So that idea never really left the ground. But many others did well, and took off as they developed the resources to expand.

Even organisations which have never been based in Bethnal Green, like NEC and IEC and their various offshoots, have had administrative links with us, and Howard Dickinson, for example, commuted for many years between London and Cambridge to look after the accounts of both the ICS and Cambridge based bodies. As time has passed, the movement of Michael between other organisations and ICS has tied the Institute into an ever growing number of external activites; but at the same time it has highlighted the Institute as the common factor in this complicated web, and as the heartland of the Young empire. This has made it extremely hard to separate out the Institute from the person of Michael. In the course of creating a far-flung empire he has built himself an identity and public personality which for many practical purposes is the Institute itself. And it is still growing.

QUALITIES

Knowledge and Persuasion: Research at ICS
Peter Marris

In 1954, Michael Young, Peter Willmott and Peter Townsend came together, under Michael's direction, to found the Institute of Community Studies. I joined them a year later, extricating myself from the moral dilemmas of a district officer in Kenya. None of us had the academic background in sociological theory and method that would now be the expected preparation for a career in social research, although Michael Young had recently completed a doctorate in sociology at London University under Edward Shils' guidance, and Peter Townsend had read anthropology at Cambridge. Both of the original studies - Michael Young and Peter Willmott's *Family and Kinship in East London* and Peter Townsend's *The Family Life of Old People* (both 1957) - pioneered their own technique out of a blend of direct observation, random sampling and long, open-ended interviews. They derived their understanding of patterns of behaviour mostly from listening to what people said about their relationships, and then confirmed the representativeness of these patterns by analysing the responses to each question in the sample interviewed. The life stories and vivid quotations carried most of the interpretive argument. The tables, many of them relegated to an appendix, provided numbers in support.

This method merged two distinct British traditions of social enquiry. It was influenced by Charles Booth's monumental study of London life and labour, the work of Rowntree and the Webbs - the systematic documentation of social conditions for the purpose of informing policy - and at the same time, as the dust jacket of *Adolescent Boys of East London* (Willmott, 1966) put it, 'In its research methods, the Institute tries to bring some of the strengths of anthropology to sociology, combining personal observation and illustration with statistical analysis'. Much of the interviews in the early studies were taken up with drawing wide ranging kinship charts; and I remember the dogged persistence with which we would insist on pinning down where our informant's mother's brother lived, and how often he was seen. The early studies, then, were written with two distinct frames of reference in mind. They set the strength and hardships of working class east London life in the context of social policies such as slum clearance and housing, retirement pensions and widows' benefits; and they set family relationships in the context of the structural-functional schema of comparative studies of kinship systems. As Michael and Peter wrote in 1961, their aim was 'to study the relationship between the social services and working class family life. The assumption was that the policy makers and administrators were (to use a somewhat elusive term) *insufficiently* aware of the needs or views of the working-class people who formed the bulk of the users of social services, and we hoped that social research might provide a more realistic basis for policy ... we had, as well as the desire to derive practical suggestions about policy, some broader interests. We wanted to find out more about the structure and functioning of the family in industrial society, and about working-class patterns of life.' (Young, 1961b.)

The method was brilliantly successful for its purpose. The first of the Institute's books were widely reported in the more intellectual daily papers on the day of publication. Excerpts were printed in the *Observer*, and *Manchester Guardian*. Even the tabloid *Daily Mirror* published a series of articles derived from my study of widows in its *Women's Mirror* supplement. Most reviews were enthusiastic. 'Vivid picture of the actual nature and quality of kinship ties in Bethnal Green and their significance in the social affairs of a settled working class community', wrote *The Times* of *Family and Kinship in East London*; and the *Financial Times*: 'This shrewd - and in places extremely amusing - book combines warmth and feeling with careful sociological method'. Kingsley Amis wrote in the *Spectator*, 'Observant, tactful, sympathetic, humorous ... I really feel that nobody who wants to know how our society is changing can afford not to read Young and Willmott.' *The Family Life of Old People* was equally well received, as a penetrating sociological study in the tradition of Booth and Rowntree. Almost everyone agreed that these books were highly readable, compassionate, and at the same time models of how social research could be used to throw light on issues of social policy. Everyone, that is, except sociologists.

Academic sociologists were characteristically much more critical of the Institute's work. They complained that the samples were too narrowly drawn, that there was too little comparative data, and that the method of argument was fundamentally flawed, because interpretations drawn from informants' life stories could not properly be grafted onto patterns derived from statistical analysis. That is, you can show that the majority of women in your sample see their mothers many times a week, and you can quote from an interview a woman's words about her warm attachment to her mother, but you cannot properly infer that therefore all the other women who see their mothers frequently are also warmly attached to them. Michael Young, Peter Willmott, Peter

Townsend and myself all used the storyteller's art to bring the people of the East End to life, with their wit, warmth, hardships and endurance, and in terms of the ideas of social science then in fashion this was illegitimate. But above all, the Institute's work was dismissed or patronised by academic sociologists as lacking any satisfactory context of theory.

The theoretical ideals behind this attack arose from ambitions at odds with the influences which lay behind the founding of the Institute. Many sociology departments in Britain had come into being only after the Second World War: Oxford and Cambridge still refused to recognize it as a respectable discipline. Academic sociologists were defensive about their credentials, determined to establish their field as an intellectual discipline distinct from economics, psychology, anthropology or politics (and therefore entitled to the autonomy of a university department with its own faculty, students, degree and budget). They were especially concerned to dissociate sociology proper from vocational departments like social work or social administration, which lacked the prestige of a pure academic discipline. So when the Institute's work drew on ideas from social anthropology, psychology and history, as well as sociology, to explain behaviour, and justified this eclecticism by its relevance to understanding policy, it seemed to undercut academic sociologists' essential claims to be developing a separate discipline with its own distinct subject matter, methodology, and theoretical framework, whose justification as knowledge no more rested on its application to policy than did biology or physics.

This antagonism was aggravated by the paradigm of sociological theory then in fashion. In the United States in the 1950s, where sociology had been longer established in universities, and more readily accepted, the work of Talcott Parsons was generally acknowledged as the foundation for a comprehensive, universal theory of social behaviour. Naturally enough, therefore, many British sociologists latched on to Parsons' work as the starting point of their theoretical enterprise. Parsons' convoluted jargon, which only the initiated could hope to understand or appreciate, helped to reinforce the claim that sociology was indeed an exacting discipline, beyond the competence of the lay reader. The very clarity and readability of the Institute's style was therefore suspect, as evidence of superficiality. And there was also a subtle, less easily recognized ideological disparity. Parsons' work was intended to develop a universally applicable classificatory schema, through which to codify patterns of human relationship. It relied heavily on roles and norms as the descriptive elements of a social system, combining the classificatory principles of biology with a structural-functional characterization of relationships derived from the

comparative anthropology of Radcliffe Brown. To this Parsons added
an emphasis on socialization derived from Durkheim and Freud. This
placed great importance on normative consensus as the basis of society.
In the context of the cold war, and the anti-communist hysteria of
McCarthyism, the theory seemed to imply that the values of an
American middle-class "Judeo-Christian" consensus were essential to
the survival of democratic society. But the Institute's work implied just
the opposite - that there were important differences between middle
class and working class value and norms of behaviour, and respect for
both was compatible with, and necessary for social integration. So
while the Institute's work sought to be relevant, eclectic, readable,
empirical and respectful of cultural diversity, academic sociology in
Britain was trying to become more abstract, pure, exclusive and formal,
and so was indifferent, if not hostile, to the Institute's central concerns.

The Institute's work has survived much better than the theoretical
ambitions which inspired its critics. About ten years after the Institute's
first publications, Parsonian sociology fell into disrepute because of its
implied ideological agenda. When Alvin Gouldner published *The
Coming Crisis of Western Sociology* in 1970 - the most thorough
critique of the moral and intellectual shortcomings of Parsons'
theoretical work - the crisis had already arrived. Students all over
America and Britain were protesting against the Vietnam war and the
military-industrial complex. In the anti-imperialist, liberating and
experimental excitement of those times, Parsons' concerns with
socialisation and consensus seemed to represent the very conformity
and cultural homogeneity against which they were rebelling. Marxist
theories began to come into fashion again, refreshed by the rediscovery
of Marx's earlier writings and dissociated from the stodgy,
anachronistic Communist parties of Western Europe and the United
States. But Marxism was not inherently antagonistic to the spirit of the
Institute's work. It, too, ranged across conventional academic
disciplines, and set its intellectual agenda in terms of social action,
even if Marxists sometimes patronized the Institute's work for being
merely empirical and reformist. And partly for these reasons, Marxism
has never become established as the theoretical orthodoxy of sociology
in the way that Parsonian sociology was accepted in the 1950s.
Sociologists have tended, for the most part, to give up on "grand
theory", retreating into sub-specialties, each with its own jargon and
theoretical concerns. In this more open, heterogeneous conception of
sociology, the Institute's work could finally be accepted.

So the controversies over the Institute's early work arose largely
from the incompatibility of the values, ambitions and ideological
assumptions which separated the members of the Institute from their
academic critics, rather than from differences of theory and method,

through which the attacks were expressed. In practice, although critics like Jennifer Platt might argue about sample size or comparison groups, the Institute's methods were not fundamentally different from more self-consciously academic research. And its contributions to theory generally fitted the structural-functional way of explaining persistent, generalisable patterns of behaviour which Parsonian theory indicated. In the Institute's work, crucial relationships like the mother-daughter tie were seen functionally in terms of exchange: mother took care of grandchildren after school, while her daughter might do her heavy shopping or escort her to the doctor. The relationship linked the daughter to her mother's kinship network, providing a broad base of support in a society where a husband's earnings had for generations been vulnerable to sickness, unemployment and the temptations of heavy drinking. The kinship structure was sustained by functional reciprocity and evolved as needs and circumstances changed. In both *Family and Kinship* and *The Family Life of Old People*, the importance of these functions is used to explain substitutions. For instance, if a woman had no daughters of her own, Young and Willmott found, then a daughter-in-law was more likely to be drawn into a close relationship with her husband's mother and family. A substitute filled the function of the missing daughter, just as old people, as Peter Townsend found, would establish kin-like ties with non-relatives when they lacked family of their own. Not that any of us self-consciously adopted a structural-functional model. As an explanatory principle, structural functionalism becomes notoriously circular when applied to social systems as a whole. The middle level theorizing that came out of the Institute's research left the explanation of larger social forces open.

The most fundamental difference between the Institute's work and more academic research lay not in theory, method or ideology, but in the way we understood the relationship between knowledge and social action. Michael Young and Peter Willmott had been in charge of research for the Labour Party before they started the Institute, and all of us broadly shared the Party's ideals of an increasingly egalitarian society, with social services, planning and housing ensuring the highest possible quality of life for everyone. Richard Titmuss, who chaired the Institute's advisory committee, and Peter Townsend, especially, saw the findings of research as a moral witness to society's success or failure in achieving these ideals. Research showed what had been accomplished, how far we had to go to realize our ideals, and most of all, perhaps, how past policies has been misconceived. The power of research to influence policy rested on the assumption that there was a widely shared consensus amongst civil servants, administrators, Labour politicians, and the educated public about the kind of society we all wanted to create, and the role of government in creating it. This consensus represented, so to speak, the court before which policies could be brought to trial, and the evidence of research presented. Academic sociologists, by contrast, tended to frame the relationship between research and policy by a very different analogy. They referred the findings of research to theory; and it was the theory, rather than the findings themselves, which should guide policy. In this view, applied social research was more like engineering than giving evidence - the adaptation of laws of relationship to the design of tools, structures and mechanisms.

This analogy strongly influenced United States policy makers when they turned to social scientists in the 1960s to help design programmes of action against poverty. Research was a means of selecting, in each location, the relevant theoretical understanding; the theory would then suggest suitable interventions; and further research would then track the experiment, confirming or refuting the validity of the design and the hypothesis which underlay it. For instance, research would suggest that dropping out of school early was associated with poverty. This drew attention to the factors which influenced educational attainment. Theory placed great emphasis on the early childhood development of cognitive skills and the influence of parental involvement. This suggested that early childhood development programmes were a critical intervention against poverty. Then, by measuring the performance of children in these programmes against a control group, the validity of these assumptions could be tested.

This conception of applied research was inherently more ambitious than the Institute's. Michael Young and Peter Willmott tried to reshape housing policies, Peter Townsend worked with Brian Abel Smith and Richard Crossman to reform the structure of retirement benefits; but none of them, I think, believed that in this they were acting simply as social scientists. Research provided a powerful political rhetoric, because it showed what was wrong by systematic evidence that was hard to ignore or refute. But reforming policy also involved the priorities of political constituents, economic constraints, ideological prejudices and legislative finesse. Social engineering, by contrast, seemed to pre-empt the political process by a more rigorous and detached method. In practice, American social scientists soon discovered that political leaders were not ready to step aside while theory and research shaped a strategy of experimental intervention.

Enthusiasm for social engineering waned as it became entangled in the realities of politics. In practice, the choice of interventions against poverty had as much to do with power and money as social theory. Pre-school programmes, for instance, did not challenge any institution, nor raise uncomfortable questions about the ability of the economy to provide jobs, but treated poverty as a problem of individual competence. Even the use of research to evaluate a programme proved to be more controversial and ambiguous than the analogy with scientific experiment suggested. Depending on the questions asked, the outcomes taken into account, the length of time over which effects were measured, and what the researcher chose to explore, the same programme could appear a success or a failure. The pre-school programmes for poor children seemed at first a success, as their first grade performance measured higher than the control group; then a failure when that gain disappeared a few years later; and a success again as the children grew into adult life and turned out to be less likely to drop out of school, or get into trouble with the law if they had been to pre-school. These findings do not fit any preconceived theory or evaluative framework. To interpret them, you need the empathy and open ended, discursive questioning of experience that characterized the Institute's method.

But if the analogy with engineering has been largely discredited, the analogy with giving evidence is misleading too, because it implies an artificial separation between fact and value. The Institute's reports never presented our findings simply as matters of fact, from which conclusions would be drawn in the final chapter on policy implications, although this is what we sometimes pretended. 'How a society distributes its resources is, of course, a political question,' I wrote towards the end of *Widows and Their Families* (1958). 'It need accept no responsibility for widows at all, and can choose just how far it will help them ...' as if this were really an open question. I then went on, 'But it is certain that National Insurance seemed to the widows I interviewed neither just nor adequate. It did not meet even their subsistence needs, nor did it seem to them a fair return for the contributions their husbands had paid. They felt victimized by the earnings rule, and humiliated if they had to appeal to the National Assistance Board. National Insurance, therefore, fell far short of protecting them against hardship and the sense of being degraded by their misfortune.' The paragraph as a whole clearly does not mean to leave society's choices open. The findings of the study - expressed as how National Insurance seemed to the widows - are presented as morally compelling in their own right. The gesture towards the separation of research findings from policy prescription at the beginning of the paragraph is blatantly insincere. At the time, I thought such a disclaimer was necessary to protect the credentials of my argument as social science. But I believe now that it is neither realistic nor necessary to pretend that we can describe human relationships without raising moral and evaluative issues, whatever words we use. Even a deliberately distancing and objective language, by its unnatural lack of feeling, makes us uncomfortably aware of the moral issues it refuses to acknowledge. But this does not mean that social research cannot find lasting and generalisable truths, only that we cannot use these truths in the same way that we use the truths of physical science.

The Institute's work, like most sociological accounts, deals with complex patterns of relationship at a particular moment in time. Neither the circumstances which gave rise to them, nor the context in which we interpreted them, remains stable for long. The Bethnal Green of *Family and Kinship* was already changing as the first books were published, and exploring those changes became a theme of later Institute studies - especially Michael Young and Peter Willmott's *The Symmetrical Family* (Young, 1973a). So the patterns of relationship that the books revealed, and the implications that we drew from them, do not represent simple, invariable relationships, but rather exemplary stories about complex happenings. That is, the stories are told to develop an understanding of human experience whose insights can be used to frame the way we look at other situations, even though these situations are never quite the same. What *Family and Kinship* told about the effect of slum clearance on ties of kinship became the starting point for my study of slum clearance in Lagos, Nigeria. One insight provides the key which opens the way to exploring others, not in a process of confirming hypotheses or establishing laws of behaviour, but by constantly setting stories we know beside events we do not yet understand, to see how they fit. In this, the stories research tells are like proverbs, which also present general truths about human affairs, in the form of highly abbreviated stories. Like proverbs, the truths of social enquiry can contradict without invalidating each other. 'Many hands make light work' and 'too many cooks spoil the broth' are both stories with a moral worth taking seriously. Both alert us to characteristics of human interaction that can help us foresee consequences and avoid mistakes. Proverbs encode the wisdom of society, and if we no longer make much serious use of them, I think it is only because in literate societies there are many more differentiated and elaborated ways of recording and retrieving exemplary stories. When the Kikuyu debated public issues, before most people had learned to read or write, they referred constantly to proverbs, of which they had a rich oral tradition, very much as a contemporary argument would quote the findings of research. Like proverbs, the stories sociologists tell strip away the incidental and irrelevant to reveal the essential qualities of relationships and explain their consequences. And for that very reason, it may be possible to tell a different story, even from the same events, which also represents a true insight. But this ambiguity, or conflict, does not invalidate sociological understanding. It makes it more complex and probing, as we search out the comparisons that seem to link what we know and understand to what we now confront.

The trouble for sociologists, as tellers of exemplary stories, is not their lack of scientific rigour, but rather the opposite - that policy makers are constantly influenced by other kinds of stories, usually less carefully grounded. The findings of applied research have to compete for attention in a public debate already filled with compelling anecdotes, journalistic exposes, highly dramatised television documentaries, and the rhetoric of manipulated statistics. The qualities which give research its authority - careful analysis of systematic observation and measurement, the laying out of the methods of enquiry and testing of received ideas - are at once its claim to attention and a constraint upon its dramatic range. Applied research can be powerfully influential only when it can tell compelling stories without compromising the integrity of its method.

Michael understood this when he and Peter Willmott and Peter Townsend created the Institute's style. He has, I think, always known the stories he wanted to tell, with a feeling for when and how to launch them into the public debate. In Peter Willmott he found a collaborator with a corresponding feeling for the integrity of research - not simply a respect for method, but a sense of when the selection and emphasis which makes a story begins to turn into distortion. Together they created a style of sociological storytelling whose liveliness and contribution to our understanding has outlasted the politics which inspired it and the scientism which sought to disparage it.

Hearing What They Say, Knowing What They Mean
W G Runciman

One day in 1961, when I was at the Institute of Community Studies working on the pilot study for the sample survey whose results were in due course published in my book *Relative Deprivation and Social Justice*, Michael and I went out together for lunch in a Bethnal Green pub. We found ourselves sharing a small table with a man in, I suppose, his mid-thirties whom Michael immediately engaged in conversation. The man described himself, when asked his politics, as a 'socialist'. But he immediately qualified this by saying that he would have voted for Churchill. Asked why, he said, 'You know what he'd have done to the Germans after the war don't you?'. No, we said, we didn't know. 'Cut their cocks off', was the reply. I was so nonplussed by this that I dropped out of the conversation entirely. But Michael carried on without a flicker and was soon being treated to an unflattering account of the habits and life-style of West Indian immigrants, culminating in a reasoned peroration to the effect that it was all very well for people who presumably lived in comfortable all-white middle-class suburbs to take a different view, but if we had some of those families as neighbours we'd soon agree with him.

It was the first of many occasions on which I have envied Michael's gift for talking to people - old friends, chance acquaintances, and survey interviewees alike - in a way which elicits the maximum forthcomingness with the minimum offence. Anyone less gifted who has knocked on doors selected from the electoral register with a ten-page questionnaire in the hand, an uncomfortable smile on the face, and a slight sinking feeling in the pit of the stomach knows just how difficult it can be to draw out of uncertain or hostile strangers the responses on which a successful sample survey depends. But what exactly does the gift consist in? What is lost if the interviewer lacks it? And what is the guarantee that even the most experienced interviewer has got it right?

These questions have a particular relevance in the context of the Institute's own early studies, whose method explicitly embodied the aspiration of an 'alliance with anthropology' (Young and Willmott 1973a, p.1). The approach has not been without its critics. 'Anthropology', it can be said, involves sustained participant-observation by an ethnographer so far integrated into a face-to-face community that his or her presence does not affect the behaviour being studied one way or the other. But to supplement the answers to the straightforwardly factual questions in an interview schedule by prompting a few additional subjective comments can hardly be equated with two or three years of intensive fieldwork, even though the interviewer starts with the advantage of common membership of the same society and culture as the interviewees. Yet there is more to open-ended interviews than chat and cliché. Properly conducted, they can not only add a subjective, or if you prefer phenomenological, dimension to the researcher's eventual account of 'their' lives, but also qualify or even correct a potentially misleading impression which might otherwise be left by answers to questions of fact which may not be by any means as straightforward as they appear. So I am not seeking to dismiss the aim of supplementing survey research with anthropology of a kind, but only to consider briefly how far the difficulties which the method poses can best be overcome.

The difficulties I have in mind are neither technical on the one side nor philosophical on the other. That is to say, I am not concerned with such problems as that a sample may be biased by non-responses, or that respondents may be genuinely unable to remember such things as their father's occupation at the time of their birth or adolescence, or that a question in an interview schedule may be capable of an unintended interpretation not detected in the pilot study. But nor am I concerned with problems about the inherent ambiguity of language, or the historical and cultural relativity of personal identity, or the indeterminacy of translation between sub-cultural speech-codes. I am concerned only with the problem familiar to every interviewer who goes beyond questions about education, car ownership, housing tenure, vote at last general election and suchlike into questions about attitudes, feelings, and beliefs - the problem, that is, of justifying to the reader an authorial confidence in having, in the words of my title, bridged the gap between hearing what they say and knowing what they mean.

Not the least of these problems is the respondent who is only too keen to be helpful. It is explicitly recognised in the Introduction to *Family and Kinship in East London*, where the reader is warned that informants who may not be representative nevertheless 'bulk larger in our account' for precisely the reason that in their interviews they were 'more friendly, more frank, and more full' (Young and Willmott 1957, p.xix). But frankness, or what looks and sounds like frankness, is no more a guarantee of authenticity than friendliness or fullness. Even where the informant is genuinely trying to be helpful, it does not follow that the full and friendly response which goes into the blank half-page in the interview schedule can be wholly relied on as it stands. Here, for example, are two long-standing residents of Bethnal Green quoted in support of the claim that 'there is a sense of community, that is a feeling of solidarity between people who occupy the common territory, which springs from the fact that people and their families have lived there a long time':

> *'Well, you're born into it, aren't you. You grow up here. I don't think I'd like to live anywhere else! Both my husband and me were born here and have lived here all our lives.'*

> *'You asking me what I think of Bethnal Green is like asking a countryman what he thinks of the country. You understand what I mean? Well, I've always lived here, I'm contented. I suppose when you've always lived here you like it.' (p.89)*

There is nothing ambiguous or hesitant about these responses. But do 'they' really mean to convey 'a feeling of solidarity between people who occupy a common territory'? I am not at all sure. You can, after all, live in the same place all your life and be content to have done so without feeling any sense of community at all with others who have done likewise. What is more, people who say they are happy where they are may, whether consciously or not, be concerned to ward off the criticism which they might invite if they admitted to *not* being all that happy but lacking the initiative to move to somewhere else.

At the other end of the spectrum is the respondent who is so ready with a stock response, and so unwilling to enlarge on it, that the interviewer can hardly help wondering whether the respondent really means what he or she is, however unambiguously, saying. There is not merely the possibility that the respondent has something to hide, or merely wishes to get the interviewer out of the door in the shortest possible time, but that a misleadingly conventional response is given unreflectively rather than dishonestly. Indeed, this may happen even when the respondent is persuaded to go on talking at some length. A good example is to be found in Hannah Gavron's *The Captive Wife.* She records that 'In conversation the working class mothers sounded very like the middle class in their attitudes to their children. In practice, however, they appeared more aggressive, and less in control, than their words suggested' (Gavron 1966, p.76). The implication is not that the working-class mothers didn't mean what they said when they said it. On the contrary, the interviews were deliberately designed in such a way to obtain answers about, among other things, methods of bringing up children 'without any direct demand' (p.155). The point is rather that on topics like these many people do genuinely think of themselves as adhering to what they sense to be the appropriate convention. But they (or should I say 'we'?) are seldom the best judges of how far an attitude sincerely held will find consistent expression in the pattern of behaviour which ought to follow from it; and that is one of the things that the quasi-anthropological researcher is, presumably, wanting to find out.

The difficulty posed by this kind of stock response needs to be distinguished in turn from the difficulty which arises from responses which appear, at first sight, either incoherent in themselves or in contradiction with something else which the respondent has said in another part of the interview. The topic on which this difficulty is most familiar to sociologists who use sample surveys is so-called 'self-rated class'. It has, I think fairly, been said of studies of 'images of society' that 'Generally speaking, a very small amount of data from each respondent has served as the basis from which whole complexes of meaning have been inferred' (Hiller 1975, p.256). This does not entail a denial that the terms 'middle-class' and 'working-class' have *a* meaning for the overwhelming majority of respondents to whom questions about self-rated class are put. But what do people 'really' mean when they assign themselves to the 'middle' or 'working' class as the case may be? It is, of course, possible to ask them what they mean in a follow-up question. I did so myself in the *Relative Deprivation and Social Justice* survey (Runciman 1966, p.188). But I cannot pretend that the answers entitled me to claim that I therefore knew precisely what my respondents *did* 'really' mean. The authors of a much more up-to-date study than that one are entirely convincing (to me, at any rate) when they say that 'in so far as it is possible to generalise on the basis of our investigation, we should say that the 'class consciousness' of the majority of our sample is characterised by its complexity, ambivalence, and occasional contradictions' (Marshall *et al.* 1988, p.187).

One possible inference to draw from this is that on topics like these, only a depth interview will do. This, in effect, is the argument of David Lockwood (1992, p.341): such interviews, Lockwood says, 'show that the 'average man' has a remarkably coherent set of beliefs', but show also that 'eliciting the reasoning that connects them takes inordinately more time than the door-step or on-street pollster can conceivably afford'. I wonder, however, whether the conclusion to be drawn is necessarily what Lockwood implies. In the first place, the depth interview may shape as much as it reflects the attitudes and feelings now more amply expounded by the respondent: although there is a sense in which none of us know quite what we think until we have heard ourselves say it, we may be left with the suspicion that it isn't quite what we 'really' thought before we were encouraged by the depth interviewer to think it in terms not entirely our own. And in the second place, a gifted interviewer may be able to elucidate a respondent's attitudes and feelings just as effectively by a few short but skilful prompts on the door-step as by an hour-long discussion in the living-room. The fact that the interviewers in many sample surveys are *dis*couraged, and for good reasons, from prompting on their own initiative in terms of their own choosing is not an argument for saying that a team of Michael Youngs would not be capable of getting closer to what the respondents' attitude 'really' is than either the pollster with a multiple-choice questionnaire or the depth interviewer with a tape-recorder.

But there remains a further problem - a problem, moreover, as familiar to social researchers in the era of Booth and Rowntree as in the era of Young and Willmott. Conversations between interviewers and their respondents are artificial in two ways. Not only is the interview as such a constructed event which imposes its own conventions of discourse, but the relationship between interviewer and respondent is itself an unequal one. The testimony of Margaret Loane, who wrote extensively about the poor of Edwardian London on the strength of her experiences as a district nurse, is very illuminating on this. Thanks to her role, she had ready access to the homes of working-class families to whom she could talk in much the same way as Hannah Gavron about their circumstances and attitudes, and she was at pains to convey to her middle-class readers just how unfitted *they* were to understand what the lives of the urban working class were really like. But she herself was one of 'them', her middle-class readers, not one of 'them' the working-class people whom she was seeking to describe. Indeed, she was very well aware of it - so much so as to doubt whether 'real conversation' is possible at all between the members of different classes (1908, p.231). But then, as Ross McKibbin has commented (1990, p.196), she has by her own argument undermined her claim to 'know' the working class as well as she thinks she does.

In theory, there are three strategies which might make it possible to gain authoritative access to 'their' attitudes and beliefs without running up against Nurse Loane's dilemma. But each has its own in-built disadvantage of a different kind. The first strategy is actually to live like 'them' - not, that is, like George Orwell visiting Wigan, but like Helen Forrester, the daughter of an upper-middle-class bankrupt who was compelled to bring up his seven children on the dole in Liverpool in the 1930s; but her autobiographical reminiscences (Forrester, 1979) are as vivid and illuminating as they are precisely because as the daughter of upper-middle-class parents she, like Orwell, is struck by the awfulness, by *her* standards, of the lives of the people among whom she finds herself and her siblings compelled to grow up. The second strategy is the 'fly-on-the-wall' approach of the Mass

Observation researchers, who went anonymously about the streets and
pubs keeping their eyes and ears open and noting down what they
heard and saw; but their descriptions, like for example one of a street
bookmaker in Bolton with 'the usual cigar and a very prominent
display of gold rings on his fingers', can hardly fail to invite the
comment that 'the observer who was probably middle-class, as were
most people working for Mass. Observation, was probably looking for
such a character to justify his perceptions of working-class life'
(Clapson, 1992, p.170). The third strategy is to go and live among
'them' with a genuinely acceptable cover, like Mark Hudson, the son
of a mining family, going back to the pit village of Horden in search
of reminiscences of what the lives of his father's contemporaries had
'really' been like; but in that role he was, and was conscious that he
was, the recipient of sentiments and recollections doubtfully authentic
in themselves and habitually exaggerated for the benefit of the listener:

> *'The story was the primary mode of discourse in County*
> *Durham. There was no point that could not be better made*
> *by means of some tale or anecdote. Stories that elbowed and*
> *jostled each other, each man vying with his fellows in the*
> *humour and bravura of his stories. They hardly seemed to*
> *listen to each other as they stood, waiting to dive in with*
> *their next tale - bursting with their narratives'* (1994, p.178.)

The conclusion to which all this might seem to lead is that nobody is
competent to interview anybody who is not indistinguishable from
themselves. Indeed, a version of this argument is currently fashionable
in anthropology itself, where a reaction against what is now seen as the
ethnocentric and colonialist bias of much of the earlier fieldwork has
led some anthropologists to argue that only, so to speak, a Trobriander
could be qualified to write Malinowski's *Argonauts of the Western
Pacific*, or, more temperately, that even after extensive fieldwork the
anthropologist will be less reliable than a native interviewer (Aunger,
1995). But whatever the answer to the epistemological question
whether anyone can understand anyone else's experience in the same
sense as that in which we can all be said to understand our own, the
claim that only Trobrianders are competent to describe the lives of
Trobrianders (or women women, or Blacks Blacks, or Evangelical
Christians Evangelical Christians, or Durham coalminers Durham
coalminers) is methodologically self-defeating. It depends on the
presupposition that the Trobrianders can demonstrate the inadequacies
of Malinowski's account of their attitudes and beliefs and the
superiority of their own account of them; but that demonstration
requires them to be able to understand Malinowski's account

sufficiently well for it to be meaningfully contrasted with theirs, which by their own admission they are unable to do. The radical sceptics, accordingly, are left with an inescapable choice: either their criticisms can claim no more validity than the assertions of those against whom they are directed (in which case there is no point in making them) or these assertions are capable of being amended in response to their criticisms (in which case their scepticism is too radical by half).

In actual practice (as opposed, that is, to a philosophy seminar) it is only the second alternative that needs to be taken seriously. No practising anthropologist, however strongly influenced by post-modernism, deconstructionism, relativism, or any other doctrine subversive of the belief that what goes on 'inside the natives' heads' is unproblematically factual (a belief to which no practising anthropologist or sociologist known to me has ever subscribed in the first place) sets out to do research in the conviction of being bound to get it wrong. On the contrary, anthropologists all set out determined not to get it wrong in the way that they regard their predecessors as having done. This does not imply that they suppose, and still less that they would be right to suppose, that theirs will be 'the' absolutely definitive account of the beliefs, attitudes, and sentiments which they want to explore and then convey to their readers. But it does imply that they suppose, and are right to suppose, that there are mistakes which can and should be avoided in getting from hearing what their informants say to knowing what their informants mean, and that if these mistakes *are* successfully avoided the resulting account of their informants' beliefs, attitudes and sentiments will indeed be more nearly authentic than if they had not been.

This applies just as much to the survey interviewer in Bethnal Green or Woodford as it does to Malinowski in the Trobriand Islands or to a latter-day post-modernist anthropologist deconstructing the discourse of members of his or her own community of origin. It is not a matter of following the manual, as it were: there is no check-list of mistakes such that if the interviewer can tick the 'avoided' box for all of them the interview will be as good as it could possibly be. It is, rather, a matter of recognising that, as I have said elsewhere in an extended discussion of what is involved in description of what the aspects of 'their' lives in which the researcher is interested are like for *them* (Runciman, 1983, p.231), 'it is likely to be more rewarding to analyse what makes descriptions bad than what makes them good'. This recognition need not involve a continuous exercise in self-criticism so much as a consistent sensitivity to what is going on in the interaction with the respondent. Michael, to come back to him, is so successful in this not because he has an encyclopaedic familiarity with the methodological literature - in fact, he is probably the better for *not* having it - but because of an exceptional innate ability to get what he's after out of his interlocutors without putting words into their mouths, let alone thoughts into their minds. This does not immunise him any more than anyone else against drawing inferences from what his respondents have both said and meant which his readers may want to question. But it does mean that he can escape Nurse Loane's dilemma unscathed: his example shows precisely that you *don't* have to be indistinguishable from 'them' to be entitled to claim both to have heard what they say and to know what they mean.

If there is any single answer to the question what exactly this gift consists in, it is, I think, in an implicit but profound respect for the individual respondent whose beliefs, attitudes, and sentiments are being explored. This sounds rather pompous, and whatever else Michael may be he is not that. But I don't mean 'respect' in any high moral sense. Sociologists aren't moralists, and have no business setting themselves up as such. As sociologists, their duty is not to be virtuous human beings, and still less to propound their own conception of virtue, whatever it is, but on the contrary to treat their personal values as no more privileged than those of the respondents who are being asked about theirs, and their personal beliefs as no more (or less) 'rational' (Runciman 1991). There is more to this than just the obligation incumbent on all practitioners of either science or scholarship to defer to the evidence, not dictate to it. It involves a recognition that although, when it is a matter of explaining what causes people to behave as they do, the researcher may well be privileged over the respondent, when it comes to describing what it is like to be the person behaving in that way, the respondent is privileged over the observer. Such a recognition will not guarantee that even the most skilful interviewer has got it right: as my chosen examples have shown, the difficulties in the way of knowing what 'they' *really* mean will often require the researcher *not* to be so respectful of 'them' as to accept what they say at face value without eliciting some additional evidence which will either establish or disconfirm that they do mean it, and mean by it what the researcher understands them to mean. But although it is not a sufficient condition, it is a very necessary one; and it is a pleasure to be able to testify from personal knowledge that Michael meets it with, as they say, flying colours.

Practising What You Preach
Vincent Brome

Everyone is familiar with Michael Young's capacity to translate theory into action creating a row of non-profit making organisations which enrich the social services. Lord Annan (1990, p.257) wrote of him: 'Whatever field he tilled he sowed dragon's teeth and armed men seemed to spring from the soil to form an organisation and correct the abuses or stimulate the virtues he had discovered'. That he also translated this remarkable characteristic into his private life, is less well known.

More years ago than I care to remember, in the 1940s, I visited him in his small Soho flat and quickly discovered that it could overnight become a high class doss house. 'We can't use that room tonight, [So and so] is sleeping there'. So and so might be an artist or media man fallen on hard times who had nowhere else to sleep or even (but this was rare) a casual down-and-out.

Actively embattled as Research Secretary of the Labour Party, he had to cope with the wayward secretary of the Party, Morgan Phillips, and those storms alone were sufficient to exhaust him. Hovering over the scene was his formidable mother, already aging but prepared to do battle in any demonstration and constantly saying to me, 'If Michael is as good as you say, why isn't he better known?'.

It was part of his commitment to many of the people he met that he expressed the remains of a bohemian streak in his character by visiting, on the rare occasions when time permitted, the Gargoyle Club, where a mixture of artists, radicals and beautiful women foregathered every night. There he encountered the famous, infamous and occasionally the drifting and the needy. It presented many a 'case' for help or rehabilitation, and he had a remarkable facility for dropping everything and concentrating on their troubles.

We were leaving the Gargoyle Club one night when we saw a man and woman arguing ferociously on the kerb, teetering on the verge of death from the traffic with every threatening gesture. Finally the man struck the woman and strode away leaving her weeping. Michael at once accosted her and discovered the hidden story: the man was a brute who had thrown her out of the home. Giving her all the money that he had in his pockets, he told her to spend it on herself and offered to find her accommodation but she strode away. His wife later

found herself unable to pay, temporarily, the household bills because
he had given the necessary money away to a total stranger.

A much more sustained example ran on for several years. A
refugee from Czechoslovakia - call him Boris - had failed to adjust to
the English way of life and turned to crime. He was the professional
recidivist. No sooner had he served one sentence than he went out and
committed another crime. After spending no less than 35 years in
prison he was regarded as a hopeless case, but the Governor of
Blundeston prison allowed him access to books on the most unexpected
subjects, sociology being one. Among them was *Family and Kinship
in East London*. It lit a spark in Boris' mind. He wrote to Young
saying that he, Michael, was clearly capable of understanding his
somewhat original cast of character and could he meet him. Michael
made contact with the Governor of Blundeston and discovered that
Boris was coming up for possible parole. He had also written a lengthy
manuscript about his life. He telephoned me to ask whether I would
drive up to Blundeston (the return journey 180 miles) to meet Boris in
order to help assess his character and possibly his book.

We set out one beautiful Sunday morning in what was an ordinary
Austin Mini but it turned out to be very 'souped up' and fitted with a
special engine which could drive the frail frame at over ninety miles
an hour. A strong streak of outrageous fantasy beyond normal humour
sometimes enlivened Michael's talk, and now it delighted us both to
see and feel this member of the car proletariat shooting past aristocratic
Rovers and Mercedes at the risk of shattering its vibrating body. To see
him crouched over a wheel travelling at ninety and simultaneously
discussing the solipsistic principles of metaphysics left an indelible
imprint on my mind. It enshrined the intellectual man of action with an
inexhaustible zest for living. We made the 180 mile journey twice. My
memory for conversations on both occasions is dim but tantalising
fragments of an argument about altruism insist on association with the
second journey. Were the satisfactions of altruism so deep that they far
out-reached those of selfishness and if so, didn't that put Michael in a
very ambiguous position? A selfish man? Impossible.

Our first encounter with Boris in the Governor's office was
unexpected. Stereotypically, the governor was a big man behind a big
desk and Boris when he entered the room was a small man in prison
clothes. As Michael (Young, 1971f) later wrote: 'But he, not the
Governor filled the room by his presence and dominated the
conversation from the start'.

He did it by marrying energetic, not to say aggressive self-
assertion, to high, if erratic, intelligence. I can still feel the pain his
gripping hand-shake gave me and the force of his personality. He also
had wit. 'After fifty years in my profession I hope to retire'. It was

time. He had spent fifty of his sixty-five years in a long chain of prisons and emerged indomitable. Inevitably his childhood had been disruptive, with a violent father who beat up his wife.

I read Boris' manuscript, an original but flamboyant document, and realised at once that it needed severe editing. It also had style: 'It all started on *that* train ... Mother was on her way to present me to her everloving family, but I could not wait, so out I came bawling and shouting ... as I have done so many times since'. (Carasov, 1971, p.9.)

The book was a shattering account of one misunderstanding leading to another crime and one prison sentence to another, but he had poured his vitality into the writing and made it - in its disjointed way - gripping.

Agonising editing was followed by his release on parole, publication of the book by Gollancz, and bitter complaints from Boris that we had mishandled the American edition. A single phrase recurred in chapter after chapter - 'Two Gentlemen To See You Sir'. Spelt out it meant - one prison sentence completed, another crime committed and the landlady knocking on his door to say, 'Two Gentlemen to See You Sir', meaning the police had arrived to re-arrest him.

Michael wrote the preface to the book where he compared Boris' childhood to that of Chekhov, quoting Chekhov's poignant question repeated every morning: 'Will I be whipped today?' 'Such a childhood', Michael (Young, 1971f) commented, '*should* have led to such a life and has. Such a life should have petered out in continued misery and has not'. At the time the preface was written Boris had broken away from his crime - misery - prison syndrome and was leading a relatively normal life. How, Michael asked, did he achieve it?

The clue lay revealed, he felt, in that first meeting we had with Boris and the Governor. 'He was no more tamed by authority after spending fifty out of sixty years of his life in prison, than he had been when he was consigned as a small boy to the German ship which was the first of them. By countering external authority with inner authority he had kept his integrity! He had even kept his youth'. (Young, 1971f).

There were other reasons. When Boris returned to one prison after another he observed that some regimes had become a little more liberal and less brutal. Finally, when we met him, he had arrived at a type of prison which reformers had been struggling for years to create - Blundeston. That was the luck of the game. Given the preservation of what he regarded as his integrity in these new surroundings he had qualified in the end for release on parole.

Six months after publication, my telephone rang one day. It was Boris. With some attempts at apology he explained that he had just eaten lunch at the Savoy and could not pay the bill. Would I kindly oblige? In the end of course it was Michael who obliged.

Take another example. Michael became interested one day while visiting his *alma-mater* Dartington, in a prisoner working in nearby Dartmoor prison. He persuaded Leonard Elmhirst, the proprietor of Dartington, to give the man a temporary respite and job, sorting a mass of papers and documents in Elmhirst's Library. The following morning a number of files marked confidential were missing. Challenged about their disappearance the 'prisoner' said: 'Yes - that's right. I saw it said Confidential and I thought they must be interesting. I took them back with me to read them. Here they are'. The episode was absorbed ironically.

There are too many stories of this kind to recall in detail. Others of a more conventional character are written in the records. When the talented young MP Wilfred Fienburgh, who was heading for high places, drove into a tree one night and killed himself, he left a wife with several children unsupported. It was Michael who leapt in at once, and with the skills of a financier conjured a Trust Fund of considerable proportions out of what seemed thin air, since he had no money or banking experience himself. There lay another of the tumult of his talents - he could have master-minded big businesses, he had such a flair for originating business.

About the time I first knew him - 1944-45 - I had launched into a biography of H G Wells and found myself penniless halfway through the book. The resolution of that situation becomes boringly familiar. Michael recommended a grant from the Elmgrant Trust. This was remarkable because I was an autodidact unattached to any university and without a degree of any kind to back my claims.

Economic support is one thing; emotional and psychological support quite another. I would intrude on the privacy of several people involved if I revealed the tower of strength he has been to person after person in distress.

Inspiration. Yes, he has inspired book after book under the auspices of the Institute of Community Studies and in the process launched one young man or woman after another into distinguished careers.

Biographies will be written about him but the biographers will get little help from Michael if it concerns his personal life. Modesty has created an impenetrable wall around such matters. Indeed, I feel a sense of guilty intrusion at revealing even these few anecdotes.

The Art of the Possible
Tony Flower

'What's wrong with the world' says a character in Julian Barnes' *A History of the World in 10½ Chapters*, is that 'we've given up having lookouts. We don't think about saving other people, we just sail on by relying on our machines.' Yet Michael Young is still up there, in a crow's nest in Bethnal Green, scanning the horizon like a social sentinel for those in peril. He doesn't set much store by navigational machines - cars, perhaps, or telephones - but he's never got the hang of computers, faxes or photocopiers, still less the machinery of bureaucracy and convention. While most of us live our lives below deck, autopiloted by the ship of state, Michael has always preferred to be out in the wind and the rain, relying on some kind of natural radar to spot eddies and icebergs in a sea of social copelessness, launching liferafts for the drowning.

Launching new organisations is his speciality. Sometimes they are only partially inflated, sometimes the peril is more imagined than real, and sometimes other rescuers have got there first. But much more often than not Michael's ideas are of the 'why didn't someone think of that before' variety. Often someone *has* thought of it before, but hasn't done anything about it. Each of us carry the genes of creativity, but it is extremely rare to make such creative use of a creative bent as Michael has done, or to use ideas to accelerate social evolution in so many different fields. The question is, how does he do it and, indeed, why?

The 'how' is deceptively easy. Starting so many organisations begins to look, if not simple, at least *possible* once you've been involved with Michael in the birth of, say, a half-dozen or so new institutions. He himself admits that the process can be rather repetitive: you don't in fact have to do anything new, he says, you just do the same thing over and over again.

So here's what you do: you spot a problem, imagine a solution and give it a working title. Then you write to everyone who might conceivably have an interest in it, and many who don't; produce a paper taking in the resulting comments without once losing sight of the original notion; form a steering committee; set up a charitable trust or a company limited by guarantee (preferably both); meet someone by chance on a train outside Basingstoke and invite him or her to become

97

the unpaid director of the new organisation; launch the new body at a press conference, couple this with an article in the *Guardian*, carpetbomb the charitable foundations with grant applications, stick with the fledgling organisation for precisely as long as is necessary, and then push it out of the crow's nest to make room for the other six institutions which you are waiting to hatch that week.

Simple. Except that most people don't get past the first post; the good idea one's had in the bath usually evaporates with the soapsuds. Sheer dogged persistence, even a kind of benign ruthlessness, is what sets Michael apart. He will hang on to an idea sometimes beyond the bitter end, always taking 'no' as a question; assuming the *purpose* of clouds is to have silver linings, and never, ever, giving up.

But no amount of persistence will preserve a soapsud. The idea itself has to have substance, or has quickly to be seen to have form and purpose to stand any chance of becoming a reality. The trick is to look for small changes that have potentially big leverage; to look out for ideas which individuals or small groups can get moving, but which have a built-in potential for growth.

Like Peter Pan, Michael knows that with imagination you can create anything, but he also knows that to fix an image in the mind's eye, and then to bring it to life in other people's imaginations, you have to apply a special kind of propositional intelligence: you have to ask the 'what if' question, thinking through a chain of thought to its likely outcome, visualising its results and then finding ways of locking those possibilities into the world of other people's perception and language.

That's why the process of writing is so important to him, and why he attaches so much value to that skill in others. He's only recently stopped subjecting new arrivals at the Institute to a standard 'writing test', and still prefers to commission people to write an essay or two before taking them on. His own writing is part of the process of invention; it gives him complete creative control over an idea, and a good deal of creative control over the way that idea is perceived.

Like any craftsman, he knows how to get the best out of the raw materials of his trade, and will also make his own tools if necessary. Thus he will often use a *lingua-franca* which delivers a difficult academic or political concept in a journalistic tone - peppering stretches of analysis with startling straplines like 'Love Thy Neighbourhood' or 'Tiffin in Bournemouth' - and, of course, he gives us whole new words, highly successfully with 'meritocracy', not yet quite so successfully with new-found uses for words like 'metronomic'.

His handwriting is quite another matter, requiring as much perseverance for others to decipher as for him to produce. But the first spidery drafts, with their web of amendments, additions and crossings-out, are both a record of an idea in the making, and the making of it. It is quite remarkable how closely most of Michael's finished 'products' adhere to such early manifestos; how nearly right he gets it the first time.

One of the secrets is in getting the name right. An apt, or at least a memorable title is as good as an organising principle, and even a bad one can still do the trick. The Tawney Society is a case in point. Helping to start this body, the SDP's equivalent of the Fabian Society, was my first job with Michael, and my first lesson in how to grab a headline. Naming the Society after the great Labour philosopher was either a very good idea or an extremely bad one, depending on which Party you were in at the time. But in putting the Society on the map it was a stroke of genius. *Samizdat*, a centre-left magazine on which Michael and I collaborated some years later, was perhaps not such a good title, since practically nobody knew what it meant, and if they did, realised that it was hardly the underground forum for dissident writing that the name implied. It did, however, plug a gap that Michael had spotted, and was as welcomed and timely in the dog-days of Thatcherism as the Tawney Society had been until the SDP self-immolated in 1987.

Finding and inspiring willing helpers is the next secret. Emric Pressburger, the filmmaker, once said that the world runs on kindness, not money, which has to be true in Michael's case since financial inducement is rarely part of the package. Working with him would 'save me from affluence', he said, with his customary prophetic accuracy. But he is a kind man, assuming for the most part, sometimes to his own detriment and surprise, that everyone else is basically benign. In fact, he lies somewhere along the line between those who champion the individual and those who champion the state to protect us from our less benign, irrational selves. He is therefore neither a saint nor a psychopath, realising that while we are not perfectible, neither are we irredeemably defective. He does, though, mostly err on the side of giving individuals the benefit of the doubt. Thus he assumes (rightly) that a typist can get a university degree, but (wrongly) that the average Oxbridge graduate can type.

Waifs and strays therefore abound, and many fail to stay the course. Those who do find it an enriching experience, providing they are content to cash their cheques in heaven. A vital person creates vitality around them, and Michael breathes life into people and ideas to a greater degree than anyone else I have ever known. His energy continues to outstrip that of many people half his age (he still has the loudest taxi-hailing voice in London) and while a combination of inspired bolshiness and constant moving-of-goalposts can wear you out, it's all worth it in the end.

It's worth it because, like playing in an orchestra, there is a built-in probability of fulfilment. It's not just the fact that you are working on real projects in front of live audiences, rather than rehearsing policy behind some ivory-towered safety curtain. Nor is it just the privilege of working with a famous conductor, especially one for whom fame has never been part of a personal agenda. It's because the sum is greater than the parts; Michael's vision can reveal glimpses of redemption in which, as Alan Bennett said of the Yorkshire Symphony Orchestra in the 1940s, ordinary middle-aged men in raincoats can be instruments of the sublime. The point is to transcend the individual for the individual's own sake; even, perhaps particularly, the individuality of a leader, since the best of mankind's creations are always beyond anyone's conscious plan.

It certainly wasn't my conscious plan, when I first met Michael in 1981, to stay with him for so long - nearly fifteen years so far. He had invited me to lunch to discuss the setting-up of the Tawney Society - not, as I had vainly hoped, in some grand cranny of the House of Lords, but in the little kitchen at the top of Victoria Park Square.

We had tomato soup. In fact, we always have tomato soup. Everyone has a theory about the man: about his only-childhood; about his mother and grandmother; about Dartington. Personally, I think it's the soup.

Age certainly has nothing to do with it. It was a lifechance new beginning for me, but only one of hundreds of new beginnings for him. The general idea is that you begin to slow down at retirement age. For Michael the opposite is the case. Just in my neck of his woods I've been swept along through what would be anyone else's dotage working on new forms of health education, the creation of the Open College of the Arts, alternative baptism ceremonies, the championing of village schools, a Summer University (bringing together different ethnic groups of young people in Tower Hamlets), myriad political ruses and gambits - including *Samizdat*, the hundred-odd pamphlets which the Tawney Society produced and various reincarnations of tactical voting campaigns - and, er, intergalactic colonisation.

This was the Argo Venture. At the height of Reagan's Star Wars reverie, Michael gave a speech to the British Association for the Advancement of Science about the need to consider and promote the counter argument for the peaceful, even commercial use of space. One of the things we'd need to consider was how ordinary non-astronauts would behave in closed-in space colonies. Michael therefore sought out a whole new group of collaborators: captains of science, including the Plumian Professor of Astronomy at Cambridge and the now legendary James Lovelock; former astronauts, a rich assortment of nutters and about a thousand members of the public who wrote in to offer themselves as volunteers in a simulated space station that was going to be built either on an island in the Severn estuary or in a converted warehouse in London's Docklands.

We nearly made it. The enterprise evolved into a plan for a National Space Museum: a celebration of the objective of mankind's peaceful colonisation of space, which would follow the initial terraforming of planets like Mars by bombarding them with all the CFCs we no longer wanted in our refrigerators. Actually, this might work - as greenhouse gases, chlorofluorocarbons are bad for us, but good for Mars. I can't remember whether the Museum itself was my idea or Michael's. It's always hard to tell these things. But the driving force was certainly his: we formed a partnership with a major property developer, secured the backing of the Science Museum, and struck a gentlemans' agreement to buy the Bankside Power Station and develop the site, at a cost of £70m, before the owner, the CEGB, was inconveniently privatised, and the long spiral of the recession eventually disgorged our site for the proposed extension of the Tate Gallery.

But, anything is possible. Setting up the first national Aids helpline is another example of doing-something-about-it, in this case much closer to home. Here, Michael spotted a problem long before most people had woken up to its awful consequences. One of the main challenges was how to handle the mass fear and worry that people would have about this major new disease. They would need, above all, information. But how could one deliver that information, and do so with the utmost discretion? Michael's idea was a confidential telephone helpline, bolted on to the already pioneering Healthline service provided by another of his creations, the College of Health. Telephone helplines are two a penny now, but they were revolutionary in the early 1980s. Nonetheless, Michael managed to extract several hundred thousand pounds from the DHSS to set up the new service, and badgered the chairman of BT to install, almost overnight, over a hundred of the then very new Linklines (offering national calls at local rates) in our fragile 17th Century building. I shaved off my moustache and flew to San Francisco to get a preview of what might happen here, returning to edit dozens of tapes about a new world of fisting and rimming, golden rain, intravenous drug use and needle exchange schemes - all of which were played on request for many thousands of callers by a dedicated band of operators who manned our switchboard day and night.

We wrote a draft constitution for what was to become the National Aids Trust and eventually, and inevitably, moved on once the government had started its own information service. All the answering machines have now gone, although our venerable building remains largely held together by redundant BT wiring, and my office - the ex-Healthline room - still has more power-points than Sizewell B.

The Institute has itself been a kind of generating station throughout my fifteen-year stint. Other contributors to this book have tracked the evolution of the Institute from being a platform for sociological research and action into an almost wholly action-based nursery of applied sociology - applied humanity, really - which has operated as far more than just Michael's exoskeleton. The Institute became the embodiment of Michael's social inventiveness long before I arrived, and even though there is now a deliberate return to a more objective, free-standing approach founded once more in the durability of research - research that can outlive the researcher - the heart for me has always been Michael's heart. From it has sprung a collectivity of innovation, generically the Institute of Community Studies, but including the Mutual Aid Centre and all the satellites of invention from the Open College of the Arts to the Family Covenant Association. It's the variety that appeals, and the profoundly liberating realisation that expertise need not reside in any given subject, but in securing the object of an enterprise. Not knowing anything about a subject has never stopped Michael apprehending its consequences, although he quickly becomes sufficiently expert to do something about them, and trusts and inspires others to follow suit.

Last, and by no means least, is the question of funding all these bodies. In looking for financial backers Michael doesn't have the usual commercial problems of having to protect intellectual property or applying for patents, since the whole point is to encourage other people to take up the idea - providing sufficient control is retained in the early stages. But he still has to use commercial wiles to gather his seed capital; selling and persuading with as much skill as any business entrepreneur.

To be a Michael Young you have to be benevolently obstinate, charmingly persistent and generously parsimonious, as well as being not a little mischievous and competitive - all useful qualities for a fundraiser as well as a mover and shaker. He's not personally a wealthy man, and is ascetic by nature - believing, I'm sure, that unhappiness is caused by wanting pleasure; that enlightenment is non-attachment. But he knows precisely what money can do, perhaps ever since his early contact at Dartington with Leonard and Dorothy Elmhirst. Money may or may not bring pleasure, but combined with vision and unremitting effort, it certainly helps make things happen - whether it's the creation of the Elmhirst's experimental public school in Devon or the propogation of so many national, indeed international, organisations from a modest base in the East End of London.

The equivalent of a personal fortune for Michael is the world of charitable trusts and government grants (though the latter are only sought *in extremis*). There can't be a Trust in the land that hasn't at some time had an application from him, and several have had more than one at the same time. It's rumoured that on the day Barings' crashed, the bank's charitable foundation had eight separate Michael Young applications on its desk.

But Michael is not just a serial applicant. He's a very successful one. It's easy to forget how effective his fundraising has been over the years, and easier still to assume that raising a few thousand here and a few thousand there is anything less than extremely hard work. His considerable trackrecord helps, of course, but it can also militate against him if it is thought that he's already had his fair share. For the most part, the process of securing grants is a cycle of hard labour, with the high success rate masking the number of well-argued and hard-fought applications which nevertheless fail. It also masks a cycle of assiduous financial management which has enabled the 'mother ship' of the Institute of Community Studies to survive a number of extremely lean patches. By using the core facilities of the Institute, sometimes taking forgiveable advantage of its staff's immense personal loyalty, and pushing his own considerable reserves of midnight oil to the limit, Michael has managed to support countless numbers of his intellectual progeny until they've grown big enough to fend for themselves. But they are then expected to start repaying the parent Institute in the form of rent and service charges which are not necessarily linked, either way, to market prices.

So that's how he does it - or at least a tiny bit of the methodology of invention. To ask *why* he does it, and why he doesn't stop doing it at such an ever-increasing pace, is some kind of an impertinence. But perhaps it's simply because he found out long ago that he *can* do it, and that the only limit to the art of the possible is time.

People who are really good at being human beings are really bad at knowing what to do with their lives. So they try everything, and in Michael's case assume that anybody else can do more or less anything too - provided that they have the opportunity. Providing the opportunity is the key. One of Brian Redhead's obituaries quoted his old tutor at Cambridge, R J White, as saying: 'Life is not about the problems you solve, because that's for crossword fanatics or mathematicians. It's about overcoming difficulties, and while overcoming them, discovering there are others lurking, and then still others which you create by trying to overcome them. That's what politics is all about. It's no use having ideology in politics. All ideologies are damaging. What we want is people who can cope.' Well, Michael can cope. He understands that less morality means more law, unless you can create institutions on the edge of politics which articulate the need for goodness rather than truth, and thus enable other people to cope too. He thinks that humanity's saving grace is its affinity for itself, and that its evil is its affinity for particular prejudices. Above all, I think he's interested in breaking down those prejudices: the barriers to mutuality and the evolution of society erected by poor education, poor access to health care and the atomisation of community. Just as conversation is the key to understanding language, rather than sticking to the rules of grammar, so maximising the opportunity to communicate with each other is the key to human fulfilment, not the blind adherence to the machinery of ideology. What's wrong with the world is that there are too many machines, too few people looking out beyond their immediate horizons, and not enough Michael Youngs.

The Architect of Social Innovation
Malcolm Dean

Is he an entrepreneur or an inventor? In fact he is both. Like the best entrepreneurs, Michael Young has a gift for identifying a need, focusing on it, and devising imaginative ways of meeting it. Like the best inventors - Thomas Edison for example - his fertile mind produces new idea after new idea. His inventiveness seems to have accelerated as he has got older.

Like most creative people, Michael is a mixture of high intellect and brilliant intuition. If, as psychologists suggest, the creative also have a strong streak of disorder, then that is satisfied too. The archetypal Young enterprise involves an over-crowded office, an over-burdened staff each trying to do four jobs but absolutely committed to the aims and values of the project. He inspires loyalty and exasperation in equal amounts from project staff; loyalty for his creative genius and gentle exterior; exasperation with his iron determination and refusal to let any idea drop.

There remain some puzzling features on the entrepreneurial side. Why is a man who invents such brilliant social enterprises so ready to move on to the next project once the latest idea is safely launched? Why does he not relax and bathe in the success of the creation? After all, from the moment Henry Ford conceived the idea of creating a mass-produced car - one every 90 minutes from his early assembly lines - he remained firmly in the motor car manufacturing groove. Ford's energy went into developing the car, his plant, and the market - 15 million Model T Fords within the first 19 years.

Michael is different. His enterprises, obviously, are designed to produce a public benefit, not a private fortune. But it is more complicated than just that. Undoubtedly he's Britain's most brilliant social entrepreneur of this century. The organisations he has directly launched are numbered in dozens. The people he has helped runs into millions. The Open University alone has 200,000 students on its books. Millions more have been helped by the Consumers' Association, the National (and the International) Extension Colleges, plus the College of Health's campaigns for patients and the briefings for parents pumped out by the Advisory Centre for Education.

So why isn't he satisfied to stick with one - or even two - inventions and use all his energy in developing them? He's too creative for that. He has the same unflagging energy of an Edison, but instead of a succession of physical inventions (the electric lamp, phonograph, cinema projector and several hundred less well-known patents), Michael has produced a string of social inventions. His has been the more difficult field. At least Edison was working with hard science; Michael has been operating with soft, squelchy social science where the principle may be no more precise than the pursuit of social benefit.

A better label for this polymath than either inventor or entrepreneur is social architect. Like a traditional architect, Michael normally moves on once his latest design is up and running. He stays in touch, of course, to ensure the goals and purposes are being achieved. He will suggest new avenues the organisation could explore - or new needs it might be able to meet. But usually he remains at a distance, satisfied the people he has picked are fully competent to run the show.

What is the key to such fertile creativity? He would probably shrink from - and reject - the definition, but beneath that benign and sensitive sociologist's exterior, there lies a brilliantly perceptive structural functionalist of the old anthropological school. All social scientists are ready to describe society - and even to take a guess at the function and structure of its different parts - but only tiny numbers are prepared to go beyond that and say how things could be changed, restructured and improved. Michael leads this happy band: a supreme and endearing optimist.

His social science is a mixture of science, engineering and art. It begins with science: listening intently to people and minutely observing the social structure, whether its base is a hospital, school or neighbourhood. He demonstrates the same skills in looking at social structures as skilled mechanics display in examining cars. Only when you know how something works are you in a good position to know what has gone wrong and how to mend it. But Michael also illustrates the difference between a good mechanic and a brilliant car designer. He moves beyond mere engineering ('if we do this and that then "y" should result') to true art - the inspired leap that has created so many social institutions.

No matter how daunting the circumstances, his observations and creativity do not stop. In hospital with cancer, he devised the idea of the College of Health - or, as he was originally going to call it with his typical sense of fun, the Association of Trained Patients. In the middle of organising the funeral of his second wife, Sasha, he conceived the need to improve the training of funeral directors: the National Funerals College was born.

It is difficult to point to a common theme that links most of his inventions but there may be one: self actualisation. It has its origins in his own education. He arrived at Dartington at the age of 13. It was his fifth school. He had been hunted and harried by the rules of the previous four and the savagery with which they had been imposed. Dartington was different. Just 25 boys. He joined a child-centred community where there were equal rights between adults and children. As he has described it himself, he entered a world that might have been designed by 'Rousseau cross-bred with Baden Powell'. Where once schooling had been 'minced together into 45-minute parcels labelled Latin, Scripture, Arithmetic', Dartington did it differently. He was encouraged to be entrepreneurial: beginning in the school orchard, moving on to set up a poultry co-operative selling eggs, and even into a partnership with another pupil buying and selling motorcycles.

No one is better aware of how people can be put off by formal education. He was a victim. Many of his innovations involve making knowledge and understanding available to people who have been rejected or shut out of the system: mature students who went straight from school to work (the Extension Colleges and Open University); patients who face immense difficulties in discovering how the NHS works or the nature of their illness (College of Health); citizens who are unaware of what is happening in major centres of power such as multinationals or public corporations (Social Audit); commuters who want to catch up on foreign languages or art classes (brain trains); consumers unsure of the quality and value of goods and services (Consumers' Association); refugees or immigrants who do not speak English (Language Line, which provides a telephone interpreting service, originally for Bengalis, Somalis, Vietnamese and Chinese people in Tower Hamlets, now offering over a hundred languages); teachers who are required under the national curriculum to provide lessons in subjects (science) they have not studied beyond GCSE (the Open School, which has adopted Open University methods); parents who want to set up small non fee-paying schools (Centre for Educational Choice); retired or near retired people who want to pursue studies they were unable to follow while in work (University of the Third Age).

This list still misses out various projects started for school children, the unemployed, and communities: self-help garages which provide hands on training for children and adults; recycling workshops for the unemployed; the new Foundation to provide after-school and holiday facilities for children; and a series of neighbourhood development schemes such as LinkAge, designed to bring together people of grandparent age without grandchildren, and people of grandchild age without grandparents.

Not all his inventions promote self development. Clearly the Institute of Community Studies (ICS) is research-based rather than service-based. The Association for the Social Study of Time (Asset) concentrates more on analysis and argument than on service. Then there was the Argo Venture, set up to promote interest in human settlements in space. Back on earth, there are his political innovations: the Tawney Society, set up to examine philosophical principles as well as policies when the Social Democratic Party was launched in the 1980s and *Samizdat*, launched in 1988 as a publication for policy ideas.

The initial source for many of his ideas has been the ICS, the first Young project, set up formally in 1954. It was from this Bethnal Green base that Michael observed the problems facing East End Londoners. His method was simple enough: to listen to ordinary people, set down in lucid prose the problems they had set out, and then to produce some practical solution.

The roots of ICS go back to his discovering how out of touch with the community Labour Party councillors had become. His initial move was to start an association of neighbourhood councils to reduce the scale of government and add a lower tier so that tenants and NHS patients would have more rights. This in turn led to the ICS. It was an ideal base from which to carry out his sociological research, unweighed down by a large bureaucracy even though it did require an endless search for funds.

He was invited by Cambridge to set up the University's first department of sociology, but was appalled by its complacency. He had wanted to double student numbers - to meet the Robbins's goal for higher education - but the dons were appalled by his idea of opening up the colleges in vacation periods to achieve this end.

Some of Michael's ideas came from overseas. And sometimes the idea had to be stored because the time was not ripe. He first thought of the Consumers' Association just before the war when he was working at Political and Economic Planning (PEP), the policy research group. It produced a report on American consumers' unions. He learned then in unsuccessful negotiations with the Board of Trade that a consumer monitoring service would not need statutory protection against libel suits. Even so, the risk of libel remained high when he launched *Which?* magazine nearly 20 years later in 1957. So risky, in fact, that the media which had turned out in large numbers failed to report a line on the new project.

The Consumers' Association is an early example of his skill in attracting key people to his projects. The most urgent need for this pioneering consumer organisation was to deter libel suits. What better move then than to persuade Gerald Gardiner, the future Labour Lord Chancellor but then the country's leading libel lawyer, to let his name appear on the project's masthead. For those of us sucked into later Young projects, one can only admire the width of his personal network, the skill with which he handles the various *prima donna* he brings together, and the boyish charm which makes it impossible for even the busiest of people to turn down his appeals for help.

So how does he compare to earlier pioneers: not the early social 'surveyors' like Mayhew, Booth, Rowntree, but earlier social innovators? The man who is more frequently mentioned in reference to Michael is Robert Owen, the utopian nineteenth century socialist factory owner, who set up a 'model community' in New Lanark. Owen opened the first infant school in Britain and attracted reformers from across Europe to look at the way he had improved housing and living conditions in New Lanark. His proposal for villages of 'unity and co-operation' attracted large numbers of younger workers. Between 1820 and 1830 numerous societies and journals advocating his views emerged.

Yet none of Owen's institutions survived. He withdrew from his New Harmony project in Indiana within three years. Another initiative in Hampshire lasted no longer. Other experiments based on his ideas near Glasgow and in County Cork failed. His campaign for factory reform had little effect, yet his ideas and ideals lived on, clearly influencing the development of the co-operative movement and socialism. Two quotes stand out. Engels described Owen as follows: 'A man of almost sublime and childlike simplicity of character, and at the same time one of the few born leaders of men.' The first part of that sentence applies equally as well to Michael. The other is a reported conversation between Ralph Waldo Emerson in which Owen is asked: 'Who is your disciple? How many men possessed of your views, who will remain after you, are going to put them in practice?' Owen is said to have replied: 'Not one.' That does not apply to Michael. His institutions - as well as his ideals - will live on.

Our Little Systems
Roger Warren Evans

Michael is a sculptor of institutional form. He has surrounded himself with institutional forms of his own creation, projections of himself. They have become part of his personality, interpenetrating his intellect, stimulating, informing, inspiring, constraining. They constitute the framework within which he has structured and commanded a multitude of personal relationships. He has had the strength and wisdom to let many go, to become the structuring principles of other lives; others he has kept to himself.

It is this particular creative ability which sets Michael apart from other sociologists, academics, writers, lecturers, teachers. They have for the most part been content to to adopt the institutional forms of others, rising through an academic hierarchy, publishing successfully, treating the income they generate as conventional personal remuneration. Not so Michael. At every stage he has considered income to be seedcorn capital, generated for onward investment in new institutional forms - selling sculptures to buy new stone, new clay.

His most precious creations, the closest to his heart, are the Institute of Community Studies itself, and latterly the Mutual Aid Centre Limited: they remain firmly with him, providing a framework and stimulus for new creations. Even the differentiation between them of institutional form is significant. In 1954, when the ICS was created as a research and educational trust, little use was made for these purposes of the form of a 'company limited by guarantee,' under the Companies Acts. Michael adopted a trust structure, casting himself as Director of the Trust, and attracting others to act as Trustees of the capital fund that he was generating. His later creations were to abandon trust forms, for artificial persons under the Companies Acts, whether limited by shares or guarantee. He is adept at choosing the appropriate organisational form, to suit the purpose in hand.

In moving to the use of artificial personality, Michael is meticulous. He pays the most careful attention to the control mechanisms in each system he creates, the interlocking powers of Boards and general meetings, voting procedures, casting votes, the consequences of non-participation, and the outcome of dissolution. For example, in moving to the use of limited companies, he realised that there might be disadvantages in having to attach the word 'Limited' to

every use of a company name, as with the Mutual Aid Centre. The
very presence of the word seemed to raise the imputation that the
organisation was a commercial enterprise, even though it was not. After
all, most people are not aware of the differences between such
companies and 'companies limited by shares.' So Michael obtained
from Companies House the appropriate special dispensation to drop the
use of the word 'Limited': even the seal of the Mutual Aid Centre is
permitted to omit the word 'Limited'. In a later creation, the Argo
Venture, formed to promote the cause of space education in 1987, he
did the same; as an artist of institutional form, he has a keen eye for
detail. And in the intervening years, others have followed Michael's
lead; the use of such artificial personalities for charitable purposes has
become widespread.

Michael must have realised, at an early stage in his career, his
potential for institutional innovation; he sometimes refers to his running
a motor repair business when at school at Dartington, in his early teens.
He developed the ability to build, first in the mind and then in the form
of hard legal documentation, the foundations needed for successful new
systems, new relationships. The distinctive evolutionary characteristic
of humankind is the ability to design new social and political forms, to
advance the species and to solve the problems caused both by its
failures and its successes.

For Michael these perceptions were refined, as they were for
Weber, by legal training: in Western society the legal profession is,
after all, the priesthood of institutional form, and institutions are most
commonly created by legislation. Both men had a legal training, before
turning to sociology; Michael qualified initially as a barrister, a
member of Gray's Inn. There are many creative people who imagine
new organisations, new associations or nodal structures, without the
skills to realise them; Michael combines that power of imagination with
the practical ability to give each idea an effective legal form.

Politics has always exercised a strong pull on Michael's mind. In
Western societies, the legislature is the ultimate creator of new
institutions, bringing to each new creation the coercive force of law
and the resources of collective taxation. It must be dream of every
institutional sculptor, to command the Legislature. But his distinctive
personal creativity, and his strong sense of himself as a pivot of
institutional change in his own right, has clearly made him
uncomfortable with the constraints of mainstream Party life. He did
attempt to create a Party himself, in *The Chipped White Cups of Dover*
(1960a), seeking to shape a political base from new perceptions of the
consumer society. But that project was not successful; those
perceptions found expression in institutional form in the Consumers'
Association (1957), rather than a political party. Later, he saw the

Social Democratic Party as a possible vehicle for his creativity, leaving Labour to join its ranks in the House of Lords, and returning when the quest proved fruitless. The proceedings of the House of Lords still exercise for him a strong pull towards the fount of legislation, of institutional formation.

Michael is pictured as the founder of the 'private sector' Consumers' Association. But the public sector National Consumer Council is also a remarkable tribute to Michael's creativity. In the early months of the 1974 Labour Government it seemed that Labour might be unable to retain power: Wilson led a minority Government between April and November 1974, before winning a small working majority in the second General Election of that year. Even then, it seemed doubtful whether the Labour Government would survive to enact major reforming legislation. Michael conceived the idea of forming a company-limited-by-guarantee called the 'National Consumer Council' (dispensing, as was his wont, with the suffix 'limited'), and applying to the Government for grant funding. Michael and a colleague were the first two Directors of that company, and its only guarantor members.

The device was successful: the Labour Government required extensive changes to the company's Memorandum and Articles giving the Secretary of State power to nominate the Board; it will have taken Michael only a few moments to incorporate those changes, at his upper-room table at 18 Victoria Park Square. By mid-1975, long before the new Government could have pushed any legislation through a hostile Parliament, the National Consumer Council was up-and-running, using an institutional form devised by Michael in his back-street workshop. And it has continued in the same form: to this day, there is no legislation underpinning the work of the National Consumer Council, merely an annual grant-in-aid made to a product of Michael Young. His design has stood the test of time, and of extreme political stress.

Nothing is more difficult than to design a successful institution from scratch: most institutions develop over time and reflect an amalgam of personal convention, legal rules, courtesies, custom and practice. Like an English village or country town, its distinctive oddities are all but impossible to create from the drawing-board. Yet with all those constraints, Michael has succeeded in creating systems which have about them the aura of permanence, of self-sustaining independence, and the capacity to grow and change independently of their creator. That is true of the consumers' organisations, those concerned with distance learning, health education, even of newer creations like the National Funerals College.

Yet there have been failures too. In spite of continued commitment, Michael has been unable to broaden the scope of co-operatives in English society: as an institutional form, they have never realised their full potential. The ideals of 'mutual aid' have always lived with Michael, in the almost old-fashioned form in which they were perceived in the inter-war period, as a viable alternative to the institutional structure of capitalism, with its reliance upon systems of private property; they were integral to the concepts of 'common ownership' featured in the former Clause IV of the Labour Party Constitution. The Mutual Aid Centre itself bears, in its memorandum and articles, the mark of those dreams.

At one stage, in the late-1970s, in a further attempt to influence the UK scene, he sought to imitate the success of the OK co-operatives of Sweden. He drew upon his enthusiasm for cars to plan a national chain of DIY user-co-operatives, based on the Swedish model and even using the trade-name 'OK' by agreement with the Swedish progenitor. He established working links with the great OK Co-operative of Sweden and arranged for his followers to visit Sweden. But the movement failed. One co-operative was launched in Milton Keynes, and a second essayed in South London: Michael used again the format of the company-limited-by-guarantee, but this time with a combination of charitable and commercial objectives, adapted to co-operative ideals. But it quickly became clear that the plan was not capable of realisation, in the UK context; in seeking to compete with conventional garages, the co-operatives suffered the disadvantage of being able to charge very limited fees for their DIY bays and other facilities, and the professional managers were forced to develop a wide range of other business activities, simply to cross-subsidise the charitable co-operative and educational objectives. That is how the Milton Keynes OK Service Station functions to this very day: it is still trading successfully, and pursuing its educational and co-operative objectives, sixteen years after its launch, having adapted its operations to changing commercial circumstances. But it stands as the only testament to one of Michael's failures.

Great ingenuity lies in the *modus operandi* of the Mutual Aid Centre itself. In reviewing the range of its products, it is easy to overlook its distinctive features as an institution in its own right. MAC was conceived by Michael, and has operated, as a generator of new institutions. Through its link with the Institute, and its access to the 18 Victoria Park Square premises, MAC commands office facilities and limited 'investment funding'. As new organisational ideas arise, these resources are used to give them initial institutional form until their features are sufficiently well-defined to be able to attract charitable funding or commercial income in their own right. The most recent examples are Education Extra, the National Funerals College, the National Association for the Education of Sick Children, and the

Family Covenant Association. As part of that process, it is understood that the new creations find ways of making reverse contributions to MAC, to replenish its funds and to keep the procreative process going. In each case, an appropriate reverse-payment contribution is identified, whether by way of rent, fees-for-services, copyright fees, goodwill payments, or even dividends, depending on the institutional form and requirements of the creation. Each relationship is given its appropriate, and legally satisfactory, institutional form. MAC is thus itself a distinctive charitable institution, giving birth to other enterprises which are themselves charitable, and replenishing its funds in part from their success.

The character of MAC, as an institution, is quite different from the more static trust, the Institute of Community Studies: ICS remains a conventional academic institution, concerned with appropriate educational and research objectives. When the task has been to create a garage in Milton Keynes, or organise youth training under the Government's Community Programme, or create a new phone-based interpreting service, or give advice on AIDS, that has all been left to the Mutual Aid Centre: it has proved a powerful vehicle for Michael's creativity. And Michael, sensitive to its distinctive institutional function, has always resisted attempts to combine the two organisations. The two paintings hang on different walls.

The ability to generate new institutional systems has an important personal dimension. Michael, like many of the great entrepreneurs of the commercial world, has used his system-building skills to manage a vast network of personal relationships. With few exceptions, each individual is assigned a place within the institutional network which Michael has woven about himself; and Michael clearly prefers people to stay within their assigned position. He manages his own diary, his own address-book and list of telephone numbers: this has enabled him to manage his network of personal contacts with a remarkable and sometimes ruthless facility, within a framework that is itself the product of his own imagination.

No 18 Victoria Park Square has itself played a key role in all this system-building. As every sculptor of the abstract knows, reification of an abstraction requires above all 'an address.' In real life, the mind rebels against the abstractions of virtual reality: Direct Line Insurance and First Direct are genuinely breaking new ground, as a matter of human perception. Even today's great corporations have a 'place' at which they are considered to reside - Marks & Spencer at Baker Street, Sainsbury's at Stamford Street. The human mind has not yet confronted the phenomenon of corporations as true abstractions, existing only at an ethereal number, contactable only by transponder.

And so it is with new institutions: they lose credibility if their first address is a suburban front-room, or a Postbox Number, or an answering service. Michael understands this. Hundreds of his creations have existed first 'at' No 18 Victoria Park Square - some to die there, some to take spontaneous flight, some to be pushed out to make room for others. It is a building which carries with it, for many, an abiding sense of all those births.

Michael's system-building is of a piece with his sociology and his politics: the Mutual Aid Centre is the third leg of the tripod. The study of social systems casts light upon the true character of man as a social animal; their study generates new insights, deeper understanding. Yet those systems are in their turn open to conscious modification by man himself; if they are benign they can be deliberately cultivated - if malign, countered. Humankind must take full responsibility for its own social systems: man is not driven by overpowering instinctual forces which determine human conduct and justify its enormities - all social systems are open to modification, provided that we first understand their true import. Everything is capable of understanding, amenable to change. Hence the drive to investigate, the rigorous intellectual pursuit of greater understanding. Hence the politics, the drive to command the most influential creative systems of society. Hence the Mutual Aid Centre, and the continuing preoccupation with finding new institutional solutions to the wrongs of this world.

Hence Michael.

Making Money for Other People
Robert Gavron

There are very few people in the world of business who can equal Michael Young in business ability and even fewer who can hold a candle to him as an entrepreneur.

I will always retain the memory of him sitting in the plush conference room of an august City institution, explaining to a group of seasoned bankers why one of his smallest and newest ventures with sales of a few hundred thousand pounds and, as yet, no profits, would be worth many millions to an international giant in the same field. They were convinced by Michael, and rightly so. The company is now moving towards profits and, in due course, if Michael so decides, may be realisable for a considerable sum. He doesn't, of course, want the money for himself. He wants it for some more of his charitable undertakings.

Some time ago I was invited to address a university Entrepreneurs' club. The president, a student, wrote that their research had revealed that I had been involved in two ventures which had grown from very small initial stakes, £5,000 in one case and £40,000 in the other, to public companies with substantial capitalisations.

While they commended my efforts they were worried that the outcome had taken some twenty-five years. With the benefit of an MBA, a qualification they would have but, they noted, I lacked, the whole thing would perhaps have been much faster. Nonetheless they would like to listen to, if not follow, my advice. I countered, in my talk, by pointing out that many people believed that successful entrepreneurs are born and not made, that the UK might produce no more than fifty in each generation, and that, typically, they did not pass through tertiary education. There is, actually, no such thing as a typical entrepreneur, although there is evidence that early environment is at least as important as genes. I defined, for the students, certain qualities I believe are helpful if not essential for success.

He (or she) must be prepared to take risks but only when strictly necessary and always carefully calculated risks. He must be more interested in building than in spending. He must be full of self-belief but keen to take advice; intelligent but not arrogant. He must see obstacles clearly but regard them as challenges to be overcome. An entrepreneur must above all things be honest. One cannot build without

117

relying on other people and, in turn, being relied on. He must trust and be trusted. He must understand cashflow. Businesses sometimes fail for lack of sales or profits. But much more often they fail through inadequate cashflow. There must be a core of idealism in a successful venture. People who simply want to make money rarely do. There must be a good product, and genuine concern to do the right thing by employees, customers, suppliers, backers, etc.

There must be hunger: for success, perhaps for recognition or material gain but above all for progress. Today must be better than yesterday, and tomorrow better than today. Planning for the future is paramount, and so is dissatisfaction. There must be grit in the oyster, a constant niggling desire to improve things. A wish to build something solid and then to make it bigger and better. Entrepreneurs are more likely to concentrate on correcting what is wrong with their businesses than being proud of what is right.

Apart from the 'dos' there are the 'don'ts': there must be no self indulgence: many ventures are lost after their first success, and one year with decent results is equivalent to one swallow. Avoid Rolls Royces, premises in Mayfair, luxurious office furniture, hired potted plants, accounts at expensive restaurants, at least until real financial stability has been reached. Never do anything that increases costs without increasing revenue more. Avoid the lethal combination of overdrafts, discounting bills, hire purchase and leasing agreements. If they are unavoidable, clear as much of them as possible at the first opportunity.

This catalogue is far from complete, but it will do as a broad guide. I have matched it to a few successful case histories and it usually works. Michael is the best case history of all; a near perfect model for any budding entrepreneur. He is scrupulously, almost uncomfortably, honest, not only with others but, equally important, with himself. He is the ultimate idealist. He believes the world to be a good place with faults that he can, given time and support, put right. He is highly ambitious for progress and never satisfied. Anyone who has ever worked with him knows that achievement brings demands for more achievement. To please Michael is possible, to satisfy him impossible. Self indulgence is not one of Michael's weaknesses. A business lunch with Michael is a shared (literally) sandwich on a backless stool in the tiny kitchen above his office in Bethnal Green. He is thin and fit not only because he is hyperactive but also because he doesn't eat much.

Michael is an outstandingly able entrepreneur and the evidence is there for all to see. He has made more than one substantial fortune, but never for himself. He registers every venture as a charity. So the profits, often very substantial indeed, are always reinvested, never distributed. The Consumers' Association has a profitable turnover of around £50 million a year. It is only one example of a substantial business thought up and set up by Michael. If he had taken ownership of any of them he would be a very rich man.

He is an excellent businessman. Apart from his entrepreneurial qualities, he is a master of the technical aspects of business. If you set him down with leading captains of industry for an examination in all the qualities required by top industrialists he would rank high in the results. But he has other qualities in addition to those. He is creative; fizzing, almost literally, with ideas. Of course they are not all winners. But there are many more winners than he could possibly pursue. And they are still coming in his eightieth year. He needs two or three lives, and there should always be bright people around him, catching the sparkling stream before it hits the ground and is extinguished, and helping him to put the ideas into practice at a faster rate than any one man, even Michael, can accomplish.

After I had succeeded him as Chairman of the Open College of the Arts, Michael became convinced that we should add cooking to our curriculum. It is an art, he insisted, and one which affects more people's daily lives than most. We should start designing our course immediately; indeed Michael knew the ideal person to design it for us. Michael, it should be said, is a not inconsiderable cook himself, and although austere in his daily life he can, on occasion, appreciate good food and good wine with discrimination and knowledge. The staff and other trustees of the OCA were unanimously opposed to a cookery course. We felt we were a serious art college with an increasingly academic reputation. We wanted popular and accessible courses but cookery was going too far. Besides, the face-to-face element in our courses took place largely in art colleges and institutes of further education. The problems of providing large kitchens and fresh materials were insuperable. Michael was undaunted. He brought the subject up at every meeting, in every letter and in every telephone call.

Eventually, at a trustees' meeting Michael indicated his desire to speak. 'You can say anything you like, Michael,' I said, 'as long as it's not about cookery'. A wry smile indicated that he had been about to raise the dreaded subject again. But without a second's hesitation he launched into a dazzling monologue on how we should internationalise OCA. How we could give pleasure and satisfaction to tens of thousands of students around the world, and garner royalties on a grand scale in the process. We are beginning to move in that direction, and have just received our first royalty payment from Australia. But this was another demonstration that lying just below the surface of Michael's mind, needing only the smallest provocation to emerge, is an inexhaustible fund of ideas, complete with all the necessary background information, answers to objections and, if required, financial justification. I still sometimes wake up in the night and wonder whether we were all wrong and Michael right about cookery.

Michael, again the classical entrepreneur, will not take 'no' for an answer. He is not interested in the words 'practical, reasonable, viable' and so on. He knows that to get things done you have to be unreasonable. He is persistent. He will worry away at a project till he gets a result, approaching it from every angle. He never admits defeat. He hates negativity. He is not a convert to Rab Butler's art of the possible. Everything is possible. The only limitations are the limitations of other people's imagination and vision.

A Funder's Perspective
Patricia Thomas

The world of charitable Trusts is seldom dull but even the most
creative of us are mainly enablers rather than doers. We rely on people
other than ourselves to provide us with a spark, however practised we
are at fanning it into a flame. There are times, even at Trustees'
meetings, when the spark is sadly absent.

It was after one such meeting of the Nuffield Foundation that a
Trustee, Robin Matthews, who shared with Michael Young the
distinction of having been a Chairman of the Social Science Research
Council in its early days, told me that in his view the meeting would
have been more lively if there had been an application from Michael
on the agenda. That was certainly true, so I asked Michael if he would
like to come and talk about his latest list of projects. Shyly he said that
no one had asked him to do this before but that he would be glad to
talk. ·

We talked and Michael outlined his immediate plans. In quite
rapid succession the Foundation received two applications for the
support of work on the education of sick children, one for a book on
death and dying, another for the National Funerals College, and yet
another for research and action in Tower Hamlets. Not all the
applications were late, some of them came in on the prescribed form,
and only one required a decision in two days. (We are quite proud of
our normal decision time of five to seven weeks.) Proposals on such
diverse subjects took different routes: two small research projects were
awarded grants through the Small Grants Scheme for the Social
Sciences; the National Funerals College won support through the
annual Phoenix Fund competition for projects that help old people.
Two projects were funded by the Trustees at their quarterly meetings.
The different proposals were scrutinised in distinct ways, most were
sent to independent referees for advice, while one was considered by
an expert Committee. All of them succeeded, though there were tense
moments when it was uncertain whether Michael's laconic prose style
and lack of detail would prejudice the soundness of the idea he was
putting forward. Not only did all the applications succeed, but Michael
managed to bring off the enterprises he was planning. The Trustees can
be pleased with the results of their investment, because Michael is not
one to take the money and default on the project. If his proposals seem

casual in their terseness, the work is pursued with an energy unusual in someone a quarter of the age that Michael is about to become. There seem to be no false starts, no petering out, only a solid record of social invention.

I began by saying that grant-givers rely on the world outside to inspire them. As I have known Michael since he was Chairman of the Social Science Research Council twenty-five years ago, it has been particularly pleasant for me to have played a part in securing Nuffield funding for his initiatives. It is fair to say that I may occasionally have felt a little smug.

And there the story might have rested had it not been for the fact that charitable Trusts have their own club, the Association of Charitable Foundations, which brings together Trusts in special interest groups to hear outside speakers and to compare notes with one another. There is an unwritten rule that grantseekers are barred from these meetings, but Michael found himself invited to talk to us about yet another of his ideas that was looking for patronage. I have no idea whether or not he was successful in this venture and this was not an initiative that I thought would take the fancy of my Trustees. When the sandwiches arrived and the Trust representatives began talking amongst themselves I realised that most of us had supported Michael's enterprises in a major way, that those of us who had done so were pretty pleased with ourselves - and here is the mark of genius - we all thought ourselves to be Michael's exclusive supporter, though I suppose we knew that he must have got the odd grant elsewhere. It was not that Michael had misled anyone. Trust administrators may be more prone to self-congratulation than most, but it says much for Michael's quiet intensity that we all thought that only our own Trust had the vision to break all the rules by giving Michael's initiatives serial funding. When we discovered that Michael had an average of five grants from each of us, we simply marvelled that one person could be so persistently inventive. And I believe that we all continue to make grants to Bethnal Green, though perhaps some of our smugness has worn off.

The Sociologist as Man of Action
Daniel Bell

What is striking about Michael Young is how he brings to sociology a combination of practical concerns and passions which is so unlike anything to be found among my fellow American observers. He is a modern blend of Charles Booth, Charles Babbage, Edwin Chadwick, and Isambard Kingdom Brunel, with a sprinkling of William Morris or H G Wells thrown in for spice. And these names are not invoked emptily. Quite simply, Michael Young is one of the most imaginative, innovative and unique sociologists in the world today.

Perhaps the best way of substantiating this claim is to look at the Victorian forebears I have named, not because he repeats their work, but because he embodies the inquisitive spirit which animated them, and the realistic utopianism which marked their achievements. Charles Booth wrote the great *Life and Labour of the People in London* (1902), an eighteen-year investigation of the London neighbourhoods, which is the prototype of the modern social survey. Charles Babbage built the first calculating machine, the first practical application of the mathematics he taught at Cambridge. Edwin Chadwick, the leading social reformer of his day, wrote the famous report on sanitation which led to the modern system of public health inspection of housing conditions and sewage. And Isambard Kingdom Brunel was the pioneering English engineer largely responsible for the railway tunnel, bridge, and viaduct construction and the great iron train sheds of Victorian England.

Michael is not a technologist or a planner, as these terms are commonly understood, but a social designer; an architect, in the metaphorical sense of the term, whose passions lie in the social use of social knowledge, a devotion to empirical research and the application of that research to social practice, and a sophisticated awareness of the political process through which social policy and new social institutions have to be guided. John Stuart Mill once observed that the critic was the lowest order among the potentates of the human mind. To be critical is always necessary. But if one is only critical, who is to take the responsibility to create and implement what we need or want to do? Too often the sociologist has remained only the critic, and evaded the larger responsibility.

There is a second kind of sociologist, who often has ideas for social reform, but who rarely does the necessary research to find out if the reforms are viable. And there are the sociologists who, to their credit, will do both. Yet as Adam Yarmolinsky noted twenty years ago - drawing upon his experiences as one of the designers of the war on poverty in the Kennedy/Johnson administrations - if one is to effectuate ideas, there is a series of many further steps which few persons understand, and even fewer take. It is relatively easy to spout ideas, but it is much more difficult to translate these ideas into specific policy, and even more difficult to translate that policy into legislation. The next step involves mastering the political process to get that legislation passed and then, the most difficult of all, the tasks of creating the necessary institutions and agencies within the bureaucracy to carry out those initial ideas and policies.

Michael is that rare sociologist, a man who has done pathbreaking empirical and survey research, who has applied that research to practical social policy, and who has moved on to the more demanding challenge of building institutions - and successful ones at that - to carry out social practice. In Britain he has made distinctive and enduring contributions in the areas of family, education, the consumers' movement, social forecasting - and even in the building of the new political party.

Michael came to international recognition with the publication of the book (co-authored with Peter Willmott) *Family and Kinship in East London* (1957), which has sold a staggering number of copies. The book dealt largely with the consequences of the new social planning of the Labour local governments in London, which had resulted in the creation of the great blocks of tower flats in East London, one of the oldest and most dilapidated areas of the metropolis. The immediate problem was the residents' dissatisfaction with this housing, even though there were some amenities such as green space, open vistas and fresh air, none of which had been present in the crowded London described by Charles Dickens and sketched by Gustave Doré. The reason for the dissatisfaction was that the planners who built these flats had never actually considered the nature of English working-class life, in particular the continuing closeness of the family, and the desire of many English workers to have their parents living near them. In effect, the new housing was breaking up both kinship ties and community. But it was more than the short-sightedness of planners that was the thrust of the Young-Willmott book. They were also destroying one of the most cherished - and invidious - and unfortunately still persistent myths in contemporary sociology; the ideas embodied in the terms *Gemeinschaft* and *Gesellschaft*.

Much of sociology, in moving away from history, created a set of ideal types which, unfortunately, most people have accepted as a historical or literal reality. This was the idea that 'the past' was orderly, settled, traditional, intimate and personal, the notions summed up in the word *Gemeinschaft* (or community), and that the present is anomic, impersonal, bureaucratic, a world in which individuals are rootless or depersonalised. This is a myth derived from romanticism, and often shared by left and right alike. But it is a dubious myth in two ways. One is that no 'past' has ever been settled, its inhabitants' lives unravaged by plagues, epidemics, migrations, conquests, war, or even simply the monotonous brutalities of farming life, a picture depicted so vividly in Ronald Blythe's book *Akenfield*. Nor is the present as fragmented and impersonal as the reverse side of that myth suggests. In a cosmopolitan world, individuals can escape from the conformity of small-town life, while in the large metropolises there are also strong and enduring family-kinship and communal ties. These are some of the truths which Michael, along with others like Richard Hoggart, have been able to demonstrate. It was the neglect of this 'practical' social knowledge which had led the planners astray.

Michael has also been very influential in the field of education, where he was one of those responsible for the creation of the comprehensive schools - one of the most sweeping and controversial reforms in English society in the last generation - and the Open University, which has become one of the largest educational projects in the world. Similarly he played a crucial role in the creation of the Social Science Research Council as an official government body. Until the creation of that SSRC there had been no central public source in the U.K. to fund social research and to initiate social investigations. One of the first such groups was the Committee on the Next Thirty Years, which Young founded with Mark Abrams in 1969 to develop social forecasting. Given the extraordinary number of such initiatives, it is not far-fetched to say that Michael Young is probably the most successful 'entrepreneur' of social enterprises in the world.

What is most characteristic of the man, however, and which in his eightieth year is still as evident as ever, is his intellectual restlessness and extraordinary energy. Most people might be content to set up a successful institution, remain at its head, and reap the kudos and benefits from that position. It has been Michael's practice, once an institution has been launched, to make sure that it can keep going, and then to move on to other fields through the unique combination of new social research to be translated into new social policies and into new social institutions. It was in recognition of these distinctive achievements that he was put forward by the Labour government of James Callaghan, in 1977, for a life peerage.

Perhaps the roots of this vigour, and certainly of the form it has taken, can be found in his own education and upbringing. Michael was born in August, 1915, in Manchester, of an Australian father and an Irish mother. His early years were divided between England and Australia, before attending Dartington Hall School, a unique progressive school which had been founded by Leonard Elmhirst and his American wife, Dorothy Whitney Straight Elmhirst. Some people have seen Dartington as a kind of forerunner of the counter-culture alternative-schools movement which flourished in the late 1960s and early 1970s in the United States, but the resemblances are superficial. The animating impulse of Dartington was aesthetic and naturalist, and bore close resemblance to the German youth movement before World War One, the *Wandervogel*; to the spiritualism of Hermann Hesse; and to the anarchist Ferrer Schools which took occasional root in Europe and the United States. (Interestingly, Bertrand Russell and his then wife, Dora, started such a school in England, its great notoriety arising from the fact that all the children were allowed to romp naked. In a different vein, Dartington was a parallel to schools such as A S Neill's Summerhill.) But Leonard Elmhirst was more interested in stressing a union of agricultural and aesthetic pursuits, and the students were taught rustic skills, as well as encouraged to develop imaginative and artistic talents. It may well be that Michael's intellectual restlessness as well as his practicality have reflected that environment. In any event, Dartington left its imprint on him in many ways; and his own activities have continued and enriched that tradition. He became a trustee of Dartington Hall in 1942, a position which he has only recently relinquished, and also published a book about the Elmhirsts and Dartington Hall (1982a), and in homage to that place designated his title as Young of Dartington.

His further education was at Gray's Inn, and at London University, where he took his PhD in social administration under Richard Titmuss. Social administration in Britain embraces both sociology and social work, and Michael's contemporaries include some of the best-known names in this discipline in the UK. His own contributions have helped to keep these evolving academic areas in touch with older English strains of pragmatism and moderation.

During the war, Michael was director of PEP (Political and Economic Planning), the leading such body of the time, and in 1945 he became the secretary and key figure in the research department of the British Labour Party. He was influential in drafting the postwar election programme of the Labour Party, and was one of the principal aides to Clement Attlee in helping shape the major welfare-state programme which undergirds Britain today.

While he retained an interest in politics and served as an adviser to several Labour governments, particularly to Anthony Crosland - some of that close association is recounted in the extraordinary and moving memoir of Crosland written by his widow, Susan Crosland - Michael was also tempted by the academic life. In 1961, when Cambridge established, for the first time, a degree programme in sociology, he was named as the first lecturer. But living in the closed world of Cambridge University soon palled, and Michael resigned to return to active research and policy activities through the Institute of Community Studies, which has remained his true base throughout.

Michael's unique strength lies not only in research and social practice, but in his intimacy with the political process, an intimacy gained by close association with the Labour Party and its several governments and, more recently, given new lease by his accession to the House of Lords. In 1960, Young had begun to feel that the Labour Party was becoming more and more ineffectual, and would continue to be so, in large measure because of its increasing dependence on the trade-union bureaucracy. He believed that the interest groups and the corporatist character of the unions were inhibiting innovation in British society. In that year he drafted a proposal for a new 'consumer party' which would speak for the broader interests of British society, rather than the enclaved industrialist-and-trade-unionist combination which emphasised the syndicalist features of British society. It was a prescient document, for what he proposed then did in fact come into being with the formation of the new Social Democratic Party in Great Britain. Young was one of the leaders of this new party, and in 1982, to help give it a strong intellectual direction, he created the Tawney Society, with Tony Flower as its General Secretary, as a competitor to the old Fabian Society, which had been the intellectual ginger-group of the Labour Party. The symbolism of that organisation is obvious. It is named for the great intellectual figure of British socialism, R H Tawney, and derives its purposes from the two books which defined Tawney's attitude toward the negative and positive features of contemporary life; namely, *The Acquisitive Society* and *Equality*.

I said at the start that Michael Young embodied and carried on the spirit of a number of Victorian forebears. It is now time, perhaps, to vindicate my references to William Morris and H G Wells. For Michael is also a novelist, and the author of one of the most imaginative social-science fictions of the 20th century, *The Rise of the Meritocracy* (1958) - a utopian fable which pictures a society in which everyone has achieved his place on the basis of merit, rather than by inheritance. My references to William Morris and to H G Wells are not intended to indicate distinct lineages. (If anything, Michael Young's idea of meritocracy is more a realisation of Tawney's idea of 'function' as the just principle to replace the acquisitive society.) However, the mood of Morris is there in the novel's idealisation of a just society and the hoped-for gentle temper which the abolition of privilege would bring.

(In fact, Morris's *News from Nowhere*, published in 1890, actually seems to anticipate the intentions of Dartington Hall.) The echo of H G Wells is more distinct, in that Wells believed in an aristocracy of talent, which he quaintly called the samurai, and who by their superior talents, scientific knowledge and organisation would overcome the social divisions of a brawling society, and create a new harmony - a scenario sketched most elaborately in Wells' *The Shape of Things to Come* (1933).

Young's meritocracy had its own delicious denouement. Since all men of talent had been given recognition, those below had no excuses for failure, and had only the stigma of rejection. And so, in the end, the Populists revolted. Yet they could only succeed because of their alliance with 'a new class', the high-status women who were the wives of the leading scientists. Relegated to the household because of the need to nurture high IQ children, the activist women demanded equality between the sexes and a view of life which would not be determined by 'a mathematical measure'. The good life that is demanded - but would it emerge? - is one which would emphasise each person's diverse capacity for diversity.

It is the promotion of this vision of the good life which has continued to drive Michael, and which underlies his ability to relate social research to social practice, and ideas to policy, and policy to planning - planning not dictated by social technologists, but planning responsive to the diverse natures of human society and the efforts to achieve a more rational co-ordination of the interconnections and interdependencies of these communities. Max Weber noted on a number of occasions that the sociologists who understood the world best were those who did not stay detached from real life, but threw themselves into its problems and attempted to grapple with them. Surely there is no one who exemplifies this observation more convincingly than Michael Young.

Education and Ethical Socialism
A H Halsey

I have known and admired Michael Young since the early 1950s. We never served the same institution, though we were both children of the London School of Economics, and both indebted to the teaching of Edward Shils. I tried to teach Michael to lecture without notes when he went to Cambridge and to abandon the temptation to join the 'gang of four' who started the Social Democratic Party. But I failed in both efforts.

Now that he is aged 80 it has become more clear than ever that Michael looks for redemption in childhood. He seeks, that is, the foundations of high civility, creativity and fellow feeling in the way in which human beings are reared. Properly understood this is a significant theme if not the central theme of his life. Also properly understood, it means that he was always seeking to weigh the forces that contribute to the stature of a person. The final outcome, if it is ever final, is the product not only of formal schooling but of the ensemble of social institutions and encounters which are engaged in turning a biological entity into a social personality. So Michael has always sought the educational dimension of living in the family, the neighbourhood, the school and the college. He sees the process of learning, moral as well as cognitive, as taking place in work and leisure and retirement - literally from the cradle to the grave, and literally as the totality of experience. Thus pubs, street corners, theatres and holidays are always schools. Even Robben Island has to be counted, and it is entirely characteristic that he focused on it as a potential site for the Open University of Southern Africa when he visited Cape Town in 1994. And mothers, mates, companions and social workers are all part of the network of potential educators as well as formal lecturers and teachers.

Hence his outlook is as broad as it is possible to be. Perhaps in his early days he neglected the educative possibilities of church, chapel and voluntary associations (scouts, trades unions, co-ops, cycling clubs etc). But he neglected little else. He thought of a manifold ensemble and he had immense faith in it as the origin of human achievement and therefore of the virtually unlimited power of people to invent, to create, and to co-operate everywhere. His ingenuity as a social engineer is fabulous, and the fable is illustrated throughout this collection. But he has been no philosopher and no mathematician - which makes his story more interesting in that had he been a philosopher he would have seen himself as dedicated to optimising the balance between liberty, equality and fraternity (which today for obvious reasons we call community). He was a Rawlsian before Rawls. This was, after all, the project of the post-war Labour Party. Instead he guided policy by instinct, avoiding too complete a victory for liberty, or for equality, or for fraternity. And if he had been a mathematician, he might have followed up his invention of the idea of meritocracy to produce a sophisticated genetic/psychological/social theory of selection in human society. There has been a debate since Cyril Burt and the eugenics movement about the multiple determinants of intelligence, the role of intelligence in shaping patterns and pathways of mobility, and the significance of work as well as education in approximating modern countries to a meritocracy rather than to the caste or estate rigidities of medieval societies.

Michael was content to leave his readers with a now famous formula: $IQ + E = M$, where IQ is measured intelligence, E is effort and M is merit. Sociologically this is a good frame. But unfortunately none of these variables could be measured in ways from which policy could be unequivocally inferred: but that only deepened and widened the discussion. Part of the thesis, after all, was that the revolution as well as the counter-revolution was dependent on advances in psychometrics and the application of the findings beyond the education system to the entry of recruits to industry and their subsequent career progress. The development of Regional Adult Education Centres was envisaged, where records of re-testing were kept and the lazy genius eliminated while the second or third chance was perennially on offer to the diligent student. A simple formula was sufficient to start a complex debate over policy - a debate which still goes on.

But these academic games did not in themselves interest him. He wanted to change the world, to create a new society free from the trammels of class and medieval restraint, a world of happy, inventive, convivial learners. Like all gut liberals he hated the constraint of inheritance and was ready at all times to engineer improvements of environmental circumstance. So he attacked with passion the single-minded idea that the country is best governed by those with brains. He was for ever on the lookout for innovations and reforms that would enable any child to be more inventive and clever than before. In that sense he was always a liberal. But he was equally suspicious of any hardening of the bureaucratic arteries that might foster ascription between the generations. Those who had the freedom to bless their offspring with the resources that issue as achievement should be prevented from turning their freedom into justified inequality of learning provision. His intention in that context was to strike a blow for socialist equality against liberal equality of educational opportunity. He knew, perhaps more than anyone else, that the British class and status system was especially apt to resist the equalisation of the comprehensive school and the devaluation of mass higher education. He was therefore a steady supporter of both the comprehensive school movement and of the Open University, a concept which he is still selling all over the world. In that sense he is and was, as usual, holding the ring between the claims of equality and liberty. One hardly needs to point out in the mid-nineties that his instincts were politically and socially sound. The sad story of polarisation since 1979 in health, education and welfare, as well as income and capital, could have been written by Michael and certainly has been a pattern which his inventions have been designed to oppose.

Why is this? It is because in the end Michael's social ideal is that of community. He loves fellow feeling. He admires the views of Hume on this subject. Though his liberalism has frequently led him to doubt the perfection of a Bethnal Green life, especially an analphabetic one, his nostalgic sense of a 'conscience collective', his fundamental belief, following Hume, that human beings may be relied upon to care for each other and to invent new pathways to that utopia, have always made him a communitarian socialist. It was that side of the movement, the belief in the essential and enduring goodness of people that led him into the Labour Party in the first place. And it was the other two sides - centralism which set out to conquer Westminster and Whitehall, and Marxism which offered a theory of automatic historical victory for the working class - which made him forever vigilant on behalf of a much more humanistic socialism. These forces even made him foolish enough to defect from the Labour Party in the early eighties and to lend his vigorous support to the Social Democratic Party. However, his instinctive balancing of the three great aspirations of the Left - liberty, equality and community - brought him back to the Labour Party where, despite the immense damage done by defection, there is high scope for his inventive wisdom.

The Rise of the Meritocracy (1958) is the nearest Michael has ever come to a general theoretical treatise on the structure of society, and I am not forgetting either *The Symmetrical Family* (1973a) or *The Metronomic Society* (1988b). It was an amazing venture in prophetic insight. It even anticipated the rise and the possible fall of the feminist movement.

But its satirical purpose was again to argue for the open society of maximum opportunity through equal spread of learning resources as against the restricted application of quasi-liberal principles in the restricted conditions of Britain in the nineteen fifties. It could be published today without changing a word, and without losing an iota of its relevance.

The importance of community as the necessary underpinning of a decent society has never been greater than it is now when we have been through sixteen years of the pursuit of liberty in the guise of licenced individualism. *Meritocracy* insisted on the claims of equality and thought of the comprehensive school as the nursery of community feeling. And much the same can be said about his contribution to the Plowden Committee and to my studies of the Educational Priority Areas which followed. For the movement towards the community school and the development of multiple, co-operative links between schools and their families has its origins in these pioneering efforts. We could not know at that time that both ends of the link would weaken catastrophically: the family because of break-up, unemployment, mobility and decline in the public services of support; the school because of funding failures. In the case of the schools we must incidentally be clear that the proportion of national income devoted to education as a whole has risen year by year since the 1960s; but the educational expenditure as a proportion of GNP, and as a proportion of all governmental spending, has declined since 1979, despite the expansion of both pre-schooling and the tertiary system of education beyond school. There is still a long road to be travelled in order to reach the society of life-long learning that many of us, including Michael, long to see. What *Meritocracy* did was to map that journey onto a clearer conception of the country in which we wanted to live and onto the traditional values we had sought in giving a shape and direction to family and educational policy.

The EPA studies are also a characteristic illustration of Michael's knack of innovating between the interstices of bureaucracy. He was the Chairman of the SSRC, his life-long friend Anthony Crosland was the Secretary of State for Education, and I was Crosland's advisor. Crosland had persuaded the Cabinet to provide sixteen million pounds for improving the educational standards of those living in the slums, Young had identified best practice from the Plowden enquiry, I had some ideas from the American war on poverty and the three of us devised a plan which sent Michael and me off round the country to seek and appoint teams of innovators and researchers in London, Birmingham, the West Riding and Dundee. The SSRC was to give the research money, I was to co-ordinate operations from Oxford, Crosland and the LEA's were to provide the 'action' money, and out of it all we were to demonstrate how multiplier effects could emerge from enthusiastic intervention.

Michael himself, we should note, was just as interested, indeed more interested, in the processes of invention and their prosecution in the real worlds of the school, the Local Education Authority and the Ministry as in the interests of the SSRC to fund research. He was fascinated by the whole process of thought and funding from the classroom back to the town hall and even back to Whitehall. His mission has always been both to think and to fix. Notice too, another typical Michael behaviour, that he was perfectly content to leave me to it when he felt that the scheme had been effectively launched. It all ended up, such is the rhythm of politics, research and administration, in my reporting to Mrs Thatcher: but that is another story.

For a while in more recent years Michael transferred his focus onto the later stages of the life cycle. He interested himself in the passage of time, in the Third Age and in retirement, disease, bereavement and death. These are all necessary features of a rounded view of life. But in the end he returned to his permanent preoccupation. He wanted to help the Commission on Social Justice to formulate a strategy for achieving a new socialism - not a *Marxisante* march to national affluence, not a better programme of centralisation and nationalisation, but a child-centred or family socialism, a new amalgam of community, caring for neighbours, and freedom for individuals, which would be fully sensitive to the realities of a global economy. At the same time, which in practice delayed our efforts, he wanted to start the new Family Covenant Association as a voluntary movement towards strengthening kinship bonds by naming ceremonies for children born outside formal marriage, convivial connections of grandparents with the cohabitant partners of their offspring, and clarification of the laws governing inheritance and property of those who live together. We did this, with Rosie Styles as the first director. Then we completed a pamphlet for IPPR (Young, 1995c) to push forward a national discussion of necessary steps towards a more just, more integrated, more equal and more free society.

So what is the message? First, it is clear that the underlying motif of Michael's life has been to conduct a peaceful but permanent revolution towards a more just society of individuals rejoicing in their common interdependence. In that sense he is finally a communitarian. Most recently I have sensed that he is emerging as a fully fledged ethical socialist. He is not formally a Christian, but he appreciates the connection of socialism to individualism through altruistic feeling allied to rational action. That is why he cares so passionately for the fostering of strong families, both nuclear and extended. That is why he is willing to think of a child-centred socialism with splendid schools, architect-designed child-friendly neighbourhoods, and strong state support for citizen incomes linked to parenting. I have never explicitly put it to him but I would wager fairly heavily that he subscribes faithfully to the six conditions for entry to the ethical socialist camp.

The first three are Liberty, Equality and Community in harmonious balance; and he loves them all. The others are a bureaucratic state, a moral conviction that the duty of the state is to make individual excellence as easy as possible and that the duty of the individual is to do as well as possible on as little as possible.

He is, I think, the outstanding practical British sociologist of the twentieth century. If the House of Lords were compatible with democracy, he would deserve an honoured place in it.

Politics and Michael Young*
Trevor Smith and Alison Young

Michael Young has pursued three main, but complementary careers:
those of social reformer, social theorist and political activist. We will
focus on the last of these. The character of his political interventions
are all-of-a-piece with his personality and general *modus operandi*, so
that in terms of his own admittedly complex make-up there is nothing
eccentric about them. What makes them unusual is the range of roles
he has taken on - together with their somewhat febrile or intermittent
nature - for, after all, most activists show a greater consistency and
dedication of purpose and restrict themselves to one or two roles. Thus
in politics, as in his other endeavours, he is something of a gadfly,
finding it difficult always to integrate his own ideas with those of a
single political party. It is not that his partisanship is particularly
promiscuous so much as that he gets quickly frustrated by the
inevitable 'patience' demanded of ideas: it is as though the urgency of
the social reformer gets the better of the successful politician's timely
opportunism. And yet party politics have had a fascination for him
from an early age.

His first introduction came at the age of fourteen when his father
was acting as Liberal agent for the Cirencester constituency in the 1929
general election. In emulation he stood as a Liberal in his school's
mock election and, while he gained only two votes, vividly remembers
the excitement of receiving a letter from his father in an envelope
bearing the stamp 'Election Communication': it was a paternal
certification of his formal engagement with politics which would have
been important to him because although he was something of a loner,
paradoxically he has also a very dependent personality. The Elmhirsts
were later to give him endorsement of a parental kind. As a student at
LSE in the late 1930s he briefly joined the Communist Party, was
rejected for the International Brigade fighting in Spain, left the party
over the Molotov-Ribbentrop Pact and joined the Labour Party at the
outset of war. His internationalism was reflected in his strong support
for the League of Nations.

---

*   Adapted from: *The Fixers*, Trevor Smith and Alison Young (no relation),
     Chapter Five, Dartmouth Publishing Co. (forthcoming).

As with everything else about him, his interest in politics and the nature of his politics stems very directly from the formative influences of the Elmhirsts of Dartington. In terms of his subsequent political development these were two-fold: experiential and ideological.

The experience they gave him could only have been equalled by a young scion of one of the great ruling dynasties such as the Cecils or the Marlboroughs. When he had nowhere to go in the holidays, they took him in his father's cut-down suit to New York on board *RMS Majestic*. On arrival they were met by a fleet of Cadillacs in which they drove to Dorothy's Park Lane penthouse. The summer house on Long Island had twenty servants and stabling for twenty horses - a stark contrast with life with his father which meant sharing a bed in a one room flat in Notting Hill. Dorothy Elmhirst had been at school with Eleanor Roosevelt (who, interestingly, had attended Allenswood School - an early English progressive school patronised by the Bloomsbury set) and in 1933 Michael Young himself stayed at the White House and dined with most of the United States cabinet. All this must have made a deep impression on a seventeen year old boy, experiencing greater extremes of riches and poverty than most people, and it was one that was not lost on him.

Ideologically, he would have been profoundly affected by the progressive ideas of the New Deal politicians and the excitement of President F D Roosevelt's reforms, but of even greater impact was the example of the Elmhirsts themselves and their motivation behind the Dartington project. They were not intellectual originators, but had been attracted, particularly Leonard, by Rabindranath Tagore's theories of education and rural development. These were to be transmitted directly to Michael, as can be seen in his strong preference for small-scale, bottom-up innovation rather than nation-wide reformist programmes. Born a generation earlier, he might well have subscribed to the syndicalism of G D Cole and his fellow Guild Socialists.

His first political role was that of a think tank staffer. PEP was set up with money from the Elmhirsts in 1931 as a non-party, reasonably progressive applied research agency. While a student, Michael undertook some part-time work for its director Max Nicholson and joined the staff in 1939. PEP's studied political neutrality, its emphasis on well-researched and well-written reports that sought to build bridges between research and policy-making, provided him with a grounding that he would put to good use in later years. During the war PEP acted as a sounding board for Whitehall and Michael was involved in its close interaction with civil servants. While at PEP he was simultaneously contributing to a series of Labour Party pamphlets. It was not surprising that in February 1945 he moved across to Transport House as secretary of the research department where he played a major role in drafting the manifesto for the general election and stayed in post throughout the period of the Attlee government.

While heading the research department at Labour headquarters, the indefatigable Michael Young was simultaneously working for his PhD at LSE under Harold Laski, professor of political science and controversial chairman of the Labour Party during the successful 1945 election campaign. At LSE he met Edward Shils, a young and persuasive American sociologist. In his obituary, Michael was to write:

> 'Edward Shils changed my life when he was on the sociology staff of LSE in the 1940s. I was then the research secretary of the Labour Party and still thinking I might try for a parliamentary seat, when he invited me to join his post-graduate seminar over which he presided with irrepressible intellectual brio. By some magic and to my surprise he made me feel I was already more of a sociologist than a politician and should make his strange trade mine.' (1995a)

Thus Shils temporarily resolved the tug Michael would always feel between the political and the social and thereupon he swopped Laski for Richard Titmuss as his doctoral supervisor, one of the founding fathers of social administration as a university discipline. If the Elmhirsts had been surrogate parents, both Shils and Titmuss were to stand proxy as elder brothers and both were to assist him in establishing the Institute of Community Studies (ICS) in 1954 at Bethnal Green. Their intellectual influence reinforced that of the Tavistock Institute (where he spent a year after Transport House) so that his focus shifted away from politics towards thinking about non-state action, that is to say, away from government to concentrate rather more on an understanding of society and more particularly local communities. Dormant Tagorian impulses were being reawakened and it would be some time before a period of political activism would break out in him again. Nevertheless, the value of his experience as a think-tanker at PEP (and as an *apparatchik* in Transport House) was imprinted on him so that later, with the advent of the Social Democratic Party (SDP), he would launch the Tawney Society as an intellectual resource for its policy deliberations.

He was relatively inactive politically for most of the 1950s, reflecting perhaps the 'end of ideology' that characterised the decade, Suez and Hungary apart. Labour's third election defeat, however, stirred the activist in him once more and he became a major influence in the modernising, revisionist movement that engaged a large section of the party and extended more widely into a national soul-searching that manifested itself in a series of *Penguin Specials* such as *The*

Stagnant Society by Michael Shanks. The ICS study of the suburb of Woodford appeared to validate the revisionist thesis that consumption not class was becoming the main determinant in voter preferences. To support further this contention Michael, together with Rita Hinden, the editor of *Socialist Commentary*, commissioned Mark Abrams to undertake an opinion poll, the results of which were published by Penguin in *Must Labour Lose?* All of this provided ammunition for Gaitskell's unsuccessful attempt to amend Clause Four of Labour's constitution which committed it to nationalisation policies that were seen to over-emphasise the class basis of the party's programme.

Michael was clearly identified with revisionism, which provoked a fierce reaction from Labour's left-wing, but he wanted to push the case further than most of its supporters. In developing new ideas to bring Labour back from the political wilderness, he wrote a pamphlet which the Fabian Society refused to publish; the general secretary at that time was Shirley Williams, later a founder member with Michael of the short-lived SDP, but in 1960 unwilling to make the leap which he was ready for - a new progressive party. Not that he thought the Labour party was necessarily beyond redemption. In the pamphlet *The Chipped White Cups of Dover* (1960a), he argued that if Labour was successfully to fight off the challenges of the Liberals, it must return to being a party of reform and adopt an internationalist approach. He also focused on consumption: 'class based on production is giving way to status based on consumption as the centre for social gravity'. A reforming party would attack monopolies and restrictive practices and would immediately apply for entry to the Common Market. Education expenditure would rise substantially, more motorways would be built. Labour, if it was to regain its credibility, would have to dispel the impression that it opposed consumer prosperity. He also saw the trade unions as a great liability to the party, 'with smaller and smaller votes behind them in the country to set against their large blocks of votes at the conference'. Internal union democracy must be introduced and the links between constituencies and local union branches should be improved. If all this was too radical even for his fellow revisionists, it was nevertheless a remarkably farsighted piece of analysis. While *The Chipped White Cups of Dover* articulated the importance of the citizen as consumer to a degree not previously stated so forcefully, as a political manifesto it was at one with his research findings and his work as a social reformer which was beginning to reach its climax.

In 1957 he created the Consumers' Association with the launch of the magazine *Which?* This was an immediate, overnight success and developed into a publishing empire which included books and magazines ranging from *The Good Food Guide* to *Which Way to Health?* - catering for all the middle class preoccupations in between by means of *Money Which? Motoring Which? Gardening Which?* and *Holiday Which?* among others, and by 1990 the Consumers' Association had a turnover of £38m. He had assumed yet another political role, that of a serial pressure group propagator. He was later to inspire the creation of a variety of other lobbying organisations including the Advisory Centre for Education and its magazine *Where?* the Centre for Educational Choice, Education Extra, the College of Health, the Mutual Aid Centre and Social Audit. All of these initiatives chimed well with his vocation as a social reformer.

There were three occasions when he accepted official missions from government: sitting on an advisory committee and being the founder chairman of two quangos.

In 1963, Sir Edward Boyle, Conservative Minister for Education, appointed him to the Central Advisory Council for Education which, under Lady Plowden's chairmanship, was about to inquire into primary school provision. A J Ayer and David Donnison were also members. Donnison and Young became the kernel of Working Party No. 2 which looked at social influences on educational achievement. Clearly there was some official sympathy with new educational thinking. It was from this group and especially from Michael that the idea of the Educational Priority Area (EPA) sprang. As an idea it had more impact than any other aspect of the Council's recommendations. The inspiration lay in experience from the United States - where in turn the Plowden Report was enthusiastically received.

After the report had been published Lady Plowden continued campaigning for EPAs. Donnison and Michael and a few others also pushed the idea in private, including an evening seminar at the Minister for Education, Anthony Crosland's London home. In a sense, all this pressure was successful; £16m was allocated to put the EPA idea into practice with some pilot studies, as Professor Halsey's contribution in this collection records. But because of budgetary horsetrading between the Treasury and the Department of Education and Science, almost all of it was allocated to buildings and it was in vain that Michael tried to impress upon Crosland - who was pre-occupied with introducing comprehensive schools - that other things were often more important and that allocation of most of the sum to buildings meant sacrificing other more vital aspects of the idea.

From 1965 to 1968 he served as the first chairman of the Social Science Research Council (SSRC), one of the more enduring monuments to Harold Wilson's 'technological revolution', that later narrowly survived Sir Keith Joseph's critical scrutiny by changing its name to the Economic and Social Research Council. Although he had long advocated the creation of such a body, the post was essentially a consolation prize for not getting his first preference - the chairmanship of the Public Schools Commission which went to Sir John Newsom, a mildly progressive Establishment educationalist. He applied himself to the task of building up the SSRC with considerable assiduity: 'I was paid half-time but worked full-time' he claims. The Minister, his friend Anthony Crosland, gave him a free hand and a list of one hundred possible members concocted by civil servants. 'I chose very carefully', he says, conducting a poll among thirty or more leading social scientists and constructing an elaborate grid that indicated who had recommended whom. The civil servants, he claims, were dazzled by this example of applied social science and by the names that emerged. All his nominees were accepted, and included, in addition to respected academics, two 'consumer' representatives in the form of Campbell Adamson, Director-General of the CBI, and Len Murray, General Secretary of the TUC. Crosland warned the Council members that while their chairman 'looked meek and mild it was not so: he will run away with it if he can!'. In retrospect Michael thought that his appointees came too much from the 'great and the good' of the academic Establishment and he made the 'fatal mistake' of entrenching the sovereignty of university disciplines by getting them to preside over committees that too closely adhered to their own well established specialisms. All of this was very uncharacteristic of his usual method, which would have been to contrive a creative cocktail from different sources that would have included some more humble but vitalised ingredients.

A decade later he was asked to be chairman of the newly formed National Consumer Council set up by Shirley Williams when Minister for Consumer Affairs. He had just returned from a period in Africa and was not fully attuned to the role of the new agency, allowing the civil service to recommend its members. But he did strive to guide it to look at the provision of goods and services from the perspective of the poorer sections of the community who did not avail themselves of the findings in *Which?*.

These three official forays into government were clearly not among his happiest experiences. He is by nature neither a civil servant nor a politician, finding difficulty in settling down to the routine hard slog which in their different ways both roles require for successful outcomes. He prefers to expend his considerable energies over a wide range of activities.

Among these has been a consistent, if periodic, interest in putting more life into local politics, particularly in inner-urban areas. As a promoter of community politics, in 1971 he helped form the Association of Neighbourhood Councils that aspired to introduce into urban areas the concept of the parish council. Parish councils were the smallest unit of local government, introduced in 1888 to give a sense of communal and political identity to villages and hamlets. Megalopolis, argued Michael, needed to be broken down into units more manageable than the large boroughs of the conurbations. Two informal experiments were undertaken: one in the Golborne ward of Kensington from 1970 to 1973, and another in Birmingham. While the latter was the more successful in mobilising local opinion they were not immediately successful, largely, in Michael's view, because the local government boundary commissioners fought shy of such radical reforms. Nevertheless, during the period of Liberal Democrat control of the London Borough of Tower Hamlets that ended in 1994, a highly disaggregated system of Neighbourhoods was constructed which, despite a somewhat chequered existence, remains one of the few bold experiments in decentralised politics, taking subsidiarity to the ultimate degree and bringing government very close to the people. It was a practical manifestation of Michael's earlier experiment and occurred on his own doorstep in Bethnal Green.

During the 1980s he responded and contributed to the highly volatile electoral mood of the nation. His over-riding concern for the potentialities and values of community life were at total variance with the prevailing Thatcherite emphasis on the individual and its corollary that 'there was no such thing as society'. He must have felt that Margaret Thatcher had thrown down the gauntlet personally to him. His reaction was to participate in attempts to maximise the anti-Conservative vote by means of tactical voting and, once again, he took up the cause of political realignment. *Tactical Voting '87* was formed to mobilise Lib-Lab collaboration, which later successively became *Common Voice* in 1988, and *Voting Reform Information Services* in 1993. Michael was only directly involved in the first of these, though in parallel with the formation of *Tactical Voting*, he helped launch the magazine *Samizdat*, to provide theoretical discussion and support, which in its first issue proclaimed itself as fostering 'the popular front of the mind'. But the ebbing electoral fortunes of the SDP, the failure of the Alliance, when the SDP and Liberals fought on a joint manifesto in the general election of 1987, followed subsequently by the failure of David Owen as leader to join the majority of his followers in a merger with the Liberals to form the Liberal Democratic Party, drove Michael back into the Labour Party. Perhaps he had never wholeheartedly joined it, nor wholeheartedly left it. Instead, he had personified and validated Raymond Aron's critique that the trouble with British sociology was that it was 'an attempt to make intellectual sense of the political problems of the Labour party'.

His outbreaks of rather frenetic and short-lived political activism - more recently, as referred to in Kate Gavron's piece in this collection, he was involved in a successful tactical voting campaign to rid the

Millwall ward of Tower Hamlets of its new BNP councillor -illustrate
that his real centre of gravity is as a social theorist and reformer. He
has, as a life peer, the formal status of a legislator but it is a role he
largely eschews. He attends and/or participates in the work of the
House of Lords only when there is a topic on the agenda that is of
direct concern to one or other of his interests or rather, since they are
so extensive, those that currently or consistently engage him. Andrew
McIntosh's discussion below shows that education, consumer affairs,
the health service and community care, will see him contributing or in
attendance. But, for the most part, he is rarely there. The House of
Lords is too elitist, too centralist, too remote and too irrelevant to
engage him. Even if its composition were to be radically altered, it is
doubtful if it would appeal much more to him. By temperament he is
not naturally part of the political infantry: he belongs more to the
political equivalent of the Special Air Service.

The significance of Michael Young's incursions into politics is
two-fold. Firstly, and probably to his intense frustration, his main
successes have only emerged in the medium to long term. Many of the
centrist policies, currently propounded so assiduously by John Major
and Tony Blair, owe their intellectual antecedents to Michael's
prescience in recognising that British politics would revolve in future
around the preferences of the citizen *qua* consumer, rather than the
citizen *qua* producer. He clearly foresaw before others the reorientation
this would involve, even if his chosen vehicle - the realignment of the
parties - has so far not come about; though tactical voting is coming to
the fore again and may yet achieve his goal. But it has taken more than
thirty years, with any number of false dawns, of which the SDP was
the most spectacular.

Secondly, he has been a harbinger of the shape of things to come
in one other respect. The multiplicity of political roles he has played
exemplify the main features of the emerging *nomenklatura* in Britain,
whereby those from a variety of backgrounds, be it as a pressure group
activist, professional lobbyist, legislator, party *apparatchik*, think
tanker, management consultant, quango placeman, or civil servant, take
on roles that become increasingly interchangeable. He has played most
of them. Some of these newcomers may display his agility, but it is
likely that few will possess either his ingenuity or his integrity.

Michael in his Peer Group
Andrew McIntosh

Michael Young, ennobled as Lord Young of Dartington, made his maiden speech in the House of Lords on 5th April 1978, in a debate on consumers and the nationalised industries. Conventions dictate that maiden speeches should be short - usually taken to mean 10 minutes or less - and unprovocative. Michael flouted the first convention, speaking for 18 minutes. He attempted to meet the second by proposing to speak about *'mundane matters - although because something is mundane does not by any means mean it is uncontroversial'*.

Mundane or not, the speech brought together themes which had been prominent in his thinking over many years, and were to be brought out in his rather infrequent interventions in the Lords in subsequent years.

Lords' Hansard is not an obvious primary source in the history of social thought and social policy; and Michael has not used the House of Lords as a platform to announce major advances in his thinking. However, his speeches there, on issues which have been important to him and to us - including the consumer movement, public services and local democracy, education and training - have brought to the parliamentary arena his abiding concerns for the individual, and the need to tame corporate and state power when they infringe upon individual rights. This chapter is written in the belief that these speeches illuminate Michael's thinking on social and political issues, and deserve a wider audience than historians of a second chamber whose legitimacy Michael always questioned.

Consumers

Michael's maiden speech was part of a debate opened by Baroness (Elaine) Burton, drawing attention to the government response to a NEDO report of 1976 on nationalised industries, and a report from the National Consumer Council of which he had been the Chairman, on the same subject. Both reports demanded more teeth for consumer bodies; the response (by the Labour government which had appointed Michael to the Lords) was more equivocal, and Michael had no hesitation in saying so:

> *'These are State monopolies, protected by the State and by
> law, and, just because they are in this highly privileged
> position, these monopolies can set more or less what levels
> of price they choose, and can provide what standards of
> service, and what services, they choose'.*

The government response, though there were welcome increases in
consumer representation, lacked a *'general position ... in relation to the
problems of the nationalised industries'* and

> *'if there is no general position, one cannot very well expect
> that the recommendations that ensue will be very
> convincing'.*

Michael's solutions include - and go beyond - many of the sanctions
now part of the Citizen's Charter. For British Rail,

> *'if high speed intercity trains are late beyond a certain point,
> I see no reason why there should not be a partial refund to
> passengers'*

For telephones, gas and electricity, *'if supplies are disrupted by strikes
or by a failure to carry out repairs...could not the standing charges
also be suspended during the period when service is no longer
available?'*.

Four years later, in May 1982, Michael Young, by now a Social
Democrat, returned to the theme in debate on Fred Willey's Supply of
Goods and Services Bill, which extended consumer protection already
available for physical goods, to contracts for services. The bill was
necessary, Michael said, because of the continuing increase in the size
of the service sector; because *'consumers can so much more readily be
'done down' over services than they can over goods'*; and because the
law has provided inadequate protection against unscrupulous tradesmen.

Another strand in Michael's thinking about consumers came to the
fore in 1983, when he initiated a debate on the reform of building
societies, following an earlier Mutual Aid Centre report. He contrasted
the formal mutual status of building societies with the reality of

> *'self-perpetuating oligarchies (which) are ready to go to
> almost any length to keep power in their own hands'*

and described the (successful) devices of the Nationwide Building
Society to keep a reformer off their board as the principles of the
Militant Tendency rather than of mutuality. He then recommended -

many years before it took place - the appointment of a building society ombudsman.

Debates and legislation on Sunday trading provided Michael with further opportunities to champion the needs of consumers - in this case customers like working women who *'could not shop at the ordinary hours, so they needed to be able to shop on Sundays'*. To the Bishop who spoke with distaste of the 'bustle' in Edinburgh on Sundays, in the absence of restrictions on Sunday trading in Scotland, Michael's response was *'what is wrong with a little bustle, even in Edinburgh ... on a Sunday?' What should be done to people who create that bustle and who shop? The answer we have had all the time is to stop them. Is the traditional Sunday really in such disrepair that it has to be enforced by the police?'*

A continuing theme in his thinking about consumers is the need for 'action kits' to help consumers to take action on their own behalf. This emerged in a debate in 1984 on the distribution, servicing and pricing of motor vehicles, when he recommended an action kit to help people to handle personal imports of cars, and described his DIY garage in Milton Keynes. As ever, his concerns were practical, helping consumers to act on their own behalf, rather than merely idealistic or theoretical.

Public Services and Local Democracy

The link between concerns for consumers with concerns for the quality and efficiency of public services has been clear from the speeches already cited. It was even more explicit in a speech in 1985 on new technologies, in which Michael drew attention to the under-used power of the Government as consumer:

> *'The Government are an enormous consumer. The question ... is whether the Government are a good consumer. My answer is that they are not, and ... not nearly as helpful to industry as they could be ... if the purchasing power of public authorities (were) used quite deliberately to improve the efficiency of British industry, so much could be achieved. If such powers were properly deployed, perhaps we would see fewer reports from the Consumers' Association ... about the technical inferiority of British products ...'*

Other than the issues of quality and efficiency, Michael's main concern about public services has always been that of accountability - not so much in the party political sense, but to local communities.

This was the theme of a speech on expenditure cuts and the public services, in April 1981. In this speech he sought to define his new-found allegiance to the Social Democratic Party in terms of *'municipal socialism'* which he said the *'modern Labour Party'* had rejected in favour of nationalisation of *'all manner of services including gas, electricity, buses and health'*. He criticised successive Labour governments as having been

> *'great centralisers - for good reasons (for the fairer distribution of resources) and for bad reasons (that there seemed to be economies of scale to be had from larger organisations)'*

and he associated himself, in his previous Labour allegiance, with this criticism:

> *'I am as much at fault as many others in having believed that economies of scale were so important that it was worth sacrificing a lot else to get them'*.

His alternative, then and on many occasions before and since, is decentralisation, and increased local democracy; the view

> *'that local councillors tend to be, by and large, nearer the ground and more aware of the intimate needs and the important personal needs of the people whom they serve in their own locality...they know better than the people in Whitehall that if a housebound old lady in, say, the back streets of Gateshead is deprived of the services of a home help she badly needs, that could, and often does, lead to grievous suffering for that old lady'*.

But his passion for local democracy has never stopped at the Town Hall. As early as 1970, he organised a survey of residents in Hornsey, where he then lived, in which he showed convincingly that people who live formally in the Hornsey borough and constituency, and within that in electoral wards with boundaries drawn to produce numerical equality, actually *think* that they live in communities, in neighbourhoods, of perhaps 3,000 - 5,000 people, which they can name, and which are usually smaller than, and not coterminous with, electoral wards.

This led him to the view that neighbourhoods were a reality to people living in cities, who were deprived by law of the right to form statutory local or parish councils comparable to those existing for many years in rural areas. With the support of the usual stage army of the great and the good, he formed the Association for Neighbourhood Councils, to lobby government for local democracy, and provided funding through his influence on the Elmgrant Trust.

I was at the time the chairman of the Hornsey constituency Labour Party; and at Michael's urging I succeeded in getting a commitment to neighbourhood councils included in our manifesto for the 1971 Haringey council elections - only to have it rejected by the victorious but conservative Labour group. In 1974, a Sunday evening telephone call and neighbourly visit from Michael made me, next day, the chairman of the Association for Neighbourhood Councils - perhaps one of the less shining examples of his ability to start new movements and find other people to carry them forward.

So when, in April 1984, I introduced an Urban Parishes Bill, which would have given 20 per cent of the electors in any urban community the right to demand a parish council with limited revenue-raising powers, Michael was the first to speak in its favour, arguing that

> *'it is to small-scale areas that popular loyalties attach, and not to larger units, such as have been created - always larger on each occasion - out of the long line of reorganisations which started in the last century'.*

Though the Bill went through all stages in the Lords, with government acquiescence but disapproval, no time was found for it in the Commons, and it died at the end of the session. Perhaps there may yet be an opportunity to advance Michael's long-lasting desire, to *'put back into local government in urban areas some of the spiritual fundament that local government needs if it is to survive and flourish'.*

Education and Training

Michael Young's time in the House of Lords has been an era of incessant government legislation in the field of education - the most active period of reform, for good or ill, since the Butler Act of 1944.

Michael pointed out, in a speech in June 1982, a major problem of education and training policy which government had not tackled then and has not tackled since: the division of responsibility between school and post-school education on the one hand, and vocational training on the other. The first has continued to be the responsibility of the Department for Education, and (despite attempts to diminish their role) of local education authorities; the second has been under the Department of Employment and its agencies, originally the Manpower Services Commission.

The *'strategic division'* which he identified ...

> *'taking a long view, and not a short view on administration,
> is whether responsibility should be with the Manpower
> Services Commission, using allowances and subsidies for
> training and sometimes to cover young people's wages (or)
> local education authorities having the prime responsibility
> and using not training allowances but education and
> maintenance allowances in one form or another'.*

He came down firmly on the side of *'the responsibility being given to
local education authorities and not to the Manpower Services
Commission'*, in part because *'most...young people in colleges of
further education, and many in schools, are already taking courses of
direct vocational relevance'* and *'there is a need for something much
more than narrow vocational education for the trainees'*,

and concluded with the hope ...

> *'that one day we may even have a Government who are
> prepared to see the Department of Education and Science
> become the Department of Education and Training'.*

But, as with local government, Michael's concern for individuals in
education did not stop at the Town Hall. In the second reading debate
on the Education Reform Bill in April 1988, he poured scorn on the
government claim that the Bill removed the balance of power from the
producers and gave it to the consumers of education.

> *'The guts of the matter ... is that there can be no genuine
> choice without diversity....we need diversity not only to
> enhance freedom but also to stimulate and nourish the
> mainstream schools. The history of education in this and
> other countries is the story of experiments and diversity
> which become adopted as orthodoxy later on.'*

The only new kind of school proposed by the Bill was the City
Technology College. Michael's question was:

> *'why only that? Why should the Bill not also allow parents
> and teachers in rural areas as well as cities to have a go
> and set up new, non-fee-paying schools with emphasis not
> just on science and technology but also on the visual arts
> and the performing arts, outdoor pursuits, a particular faith*

*or philosophy that may be held by a group of parents, or
new methods of learning?'*

Rejecting the orthodoxies of both left and right, he praised the 'free
choice schools' attended by 10 per cent of children in Denmark, and
concluded:

*'My hope is that one day we in Britain will also have
mainstream schools with a ring of small maintained schools
around them, all benefitting from the variety that they
represent and from the exchange of ideas and experience
between different types of school, between teachers with
different experiences and between parents who have had
different experiences of their children's education. I fear
that, unless that is done, real choice in education in this
country will remain the privilege of a privileged class. If you
are well off, you will have the choice of all manner of
schools. If you are poor, you will have none or very little.
Britain is divided and the social classes are, to quite a large
extent, divided between those with money who can afford
fee-paying schools and the great majority who cannot.'*

In subsequent years, Michael was to continue to advocate choice and
diversity in education, often in opposition to the policies of the Labour
party to which he had now returned.

As an example, in March 1991, he supported a private member's
Bill introduced by Baroness (Caroline) Cox, which would have
extended public support for non-fee-paying independent schools, and
in particular for religious schools other than Christian or Jewish
schools. He did so partly because of the need to *'recognise that we
must shape our education system better to fit the new social and
religious composition that has been brought about by the great
immigration of the past decades'* and partly because of his abiding
interest in *'small schools...in experimental schools, in progressive
schools'* including, of course, Dartington, and small schools in rural
areas. He drew attention to the foundation of the European Forum for
Freedom in Education, which was assisting in the creation of
independent but state-supported schools in eastern Europe.

In the following year, in February 1992, he saw some merit in the
objectives of the government's Education (Schools) Bill, which set out
to improve the information available to parents about their children's
schools, and to extend the role of trained lay people in school
inspection.

However, he was very critical of the means proposed in the Bill to achieve these objectives. The new inspection teams would replace, not augment, Her Majesty's Inspectors of schools, and would not provide reliable information. *'Information for consumers,'* he said, *'is not of much value if it is low grade information'*.

In Michael's view, the Bill broke *'three of the fundamental rules...for the provision of good quality information for consumers'*. First, because the inspectors would have very little expertise in education, the information would not be reliable. Second, *'because the standards used to judge different schools will be different according to the inspection teams that are applying them,'* the information would not make comparisons possible. And third, because the Bill did not provide for *'decent follow-up to the inspections;'* the requirement that *'something should happen when weaknesses are revealed'* was not met.

A further issue which brought him into potential conflict with his Labour colleagues was his attempt to add to the Education Bill of 1993 a provision that education for children in hospital, and home tuition, should be grant-maintained, responsible directly to the Funding Agency for Schools and the central government, rather than provided by local education authorities. Driven at least in part by the pressures on local education authority funding, his amendments were designed to remedy the differences between LEAs in adequacy and quality of hospital education provision.

In the end, a compromise was reached which enabled Labour colleagues to support an amendment to protect hospital schools without detracting from local control of education; and his amendment was, of course, defeated. But the episode illustrated Michael's independence, stubbornness, and passionate concern, if necessary in defiance of party loyalties, for individuals in a complex and often overbearing society.

Conclusion

Michael Young will not be, and will not wish to be, remembered as Lord Young of Dartington: even his chequebook still says 'M D Young'. But he has, in his time in the Lords, made an idiosyncratic and effective contribution to that curious and indefensible institution. As recently as April 1995, together with Frank Field MP, he has campaigned to give official recognition to non-religious naming ceremonies for children. His colleagues in the Lords are grateful for the way in which he continues to use the House, from time to time, as a platform for the defence and promotion of ideals which we share, and which he embodies for all of us.

IDEAS

The Ups and Downs of the Meritocracy
Paul Barker

The Rise of the Meritocracy has never been easy to categorise. This may be why it is the best and the most influential of Michael's books. In some ways it is an extended pamphlet. But if that were all, it would have faded into the dust of old disputations. The books that last longest are those that can be read more than one way.

From its first publication, in 1958, it created a puzzle for those who wanted to cram it into one category or another. I was given a copy the following year, as a birthday present, perhaps with ironic intent. But then irony is an essential part of the book itself. The magazine I eventually went on to edit, *New Society* (launched in 1962), was described by Robert Hewison, in his cultural history of those years, as 'a forum for the new intelligentsia'. A less friendly interpretation might be 'a forum for guilty meritocrats'.

I first met Michael in 1967, and soon afterwards wrote a profile of him for an American magazine. I described *The Rise of the Meritocracy* as 'his most important and most maverick work'. I hold to that. But what, exactly, was its first impact? What was its practical influence? What is its continuing importance?

To look back at the reviews it got in 1958 is to enter the world of the assumptions that marked the first period which could really be called 'postwar'. The Attlee years, when Michael ran the research (i.e. propaganda) department of the Labour Party, were preoccupied with trying to hold a precarious balance between the disastrous financial implications of the Second World War and the determined enactment of social legislation based on prewar and wartime ideas. R A Butler had brought in the 1944 Education Act as Education Minister in the wartime coalition government. (Michael wrote, in his 1947 book, *Labour's Plan for Plenty*, that 'Of all the social services, education is far and away the most important.') But in 1953, as Chancellor of the Exchequer after Churchill's return to office, Butler brought in the first budget since the war's end which didn't put up taxes. Food rationing, once defended as socialism in action, was abolished. Domestically, the 1950s had a golden glow.

Among the first sociology Michael published was an article on the meanings of the 1953 Coronation. It was sympathetic to national sentimentality about the young Queen. In *Meritocracy*, the 1950s and

1960s are referred to as the 'Elizabethan' era. In fact, this usage barely outlasted the mid-1950s. After the Suez debacle of 1956, the sun quickly began to set on the British Empire and 'Elizabethanism' alike. In the year the book was published, the Campaign for Nuclear Disarmament held its first Aldermaston march. (It started at Trafalgar Square. The order of march was thereafter reversed, for better publicity.) It inaugurated a. new style of middle class, often meritocratic, dissidence.

> *'Dr Young has written an admirable tract on latter-day Platonism. He has shown how social inventions, like technological inventions, can turn and bite the inventor. It is not many years since horticulturalists discovered that DDT was not an unmixed blessing ... Dr Young's fantasy is a discovery that the Education Act [1944], too, was not an unmixed blessing. In saving Britain's intellect, it may destroy Britain's soul.'*

Thus, Sir Eric Ashby, botanist and education grandee, in the books pages of *New Scientist* in December 1958. He took it all with a mandarin calm. Not so, for example, Alan Fox, an Oxford sociologist, writing in *Socialist Commentary* (a magazine of the Labour right). 'Was there ever such a society as ours, one wonders,' he expostulated in the November 1958 issue, 'for projecting nightmare visions of its own future?' He cited Aldous Huxley, George Orwell, Arthur Koestler and, interestingly, James Burnham. In *The Managerial Revolution* (1941), Burnham predicted inexorable dominance by a manager class. His thesis is an acknowledged influence on *Nineteen Eighty-Four*. It is also part of the intellectual undergrowth out of which Michael's book sprang.

'Well, here we are still taking punishment,' Fox went on. Young (he said) had produced 'another spectre to make us gasp with anguish.' Fox's anguish was matched by other reviewers. The *Economist* was vitriolic: 'Should we really exalt the saintly moujiks of Tolstoy above, say, Leonardo da Vinci?' The truth was (it said) that 'A "meritocracy" of one sort or another is on the way. Not even the most rigidly comprehensive schooling, so long as it does not flatten superior ability, will keep that ability in the working class.' Nor was the book in any sense positive: 'Mr Young has retreated behind a smokescreen of entertaining jibes.' (Sir Geoffrey Crowther, not long retired from editing the *Economist*, was preparing a government report on the education of 15 to 18 year olds [15 was then the school leaving age]. It emphasised how much working class talent was going to waste. Was he tempted back as a reviewer? As editor, Crowther's advice to his journalists was: 'Simplify, then exaggerate.')

The educationist, Boris Ford, told the readers of the *Spectator* that 'Michael Young is a sociologist not altogether approved of by his fellow-sociologists.' Not only did he take 'too few statistical samples' - the contemporary, and often-repeated, reproach against the Institute of Community Studies' first book, *Family and Kinship in East London* (1957) - but he had also been 'dilatory in shouldering his pole of the banner of Social Mobility'. Ford didn't mind, because Young was confronting 'outstandingly important issues'. The meritocracy the book feared derived, Ford said, from the 'inheritance of wartime assumptions about efficient selection and promotion, reinforced by an LSE sociology intent on demolishing roadblocks in the way of talent,' and all 'backed up by the proliferating growth of the power and outlook of the Civil Service.'

In Michael's introduction to a new American edition (1994), he says he hawked the book around London publishers for years. It was only by accident that it appeared after *Family and Kinship*. It was also only by accident that it ever appeared at all. He met an old friend, Walter Neurath, on a beach in North Wales. Neurath had just founded the publishers, Thames & Hudson. Their speciality was, and remains, art books. But Neurath published the book anyway. 'Fortunately,' Michael writes, 'his kindness was rewarded this side of the pearly gates.' Penguin followed up with a paperback in their Pelican series. It sold many thousands of copies. The Pelican list had an authority hard to imagine today, when so many paperback series compete.

The re-publication in the United States demonstrates the book's continuing power to provoke. *The Bell Curve: Intelligence and Class Structure in American Life*, by Charles Murray and the late Richard Herrnstein, was also published in 1994. Among Americans, *Meritocracy* has always found itself caught up in the crossfire of the bitter battle between environmental and genetic explanations. (Murray himself is an admirer of the book.)

Reviewing the new edition, the *Atlantic Monthly* attacked it for sneering at the idea of equal opportunities for all. And when it was first published in America, in 1959, the *Wall Street Journal*'s reviewer wrote angrily:

> *'What Mr Young seems to be saying is that society is better off for being a hodge-podge, with some people getting by on ancestry, some on inherited money, some on favouritism or nepotism, and some on brains. From 1946 to 1951 Mr Young, as head of the Labour Party's research department, helped build Britain's welfare state. Since he now evidently holds with Lord Melbourne that it is better to leave things*

*alone, his past hardly explains his present. Or maybe it does
explain it; maybe he has "had enough".'*

In Britain, the book was received more often with puzzlement than
with hostility. In the *New Statesman*, Peter Shore - who held Michael's
old Labour Party post between Hugh Gaitskell's failure in the general
election of 1959 and Harold Wilson's modified success in 1964 -
worried away at its 'harsh and pessimistic' vision, though he judged it
'certainly not implausible.' It was, he reckoned, 'a reasonable
projection of Mr Butler's Opportunity State.' This was an odd use of
'reasonable'. Perhaps the magazine's literary editor was unwise to mail
a satire to a man without much evident sense of humour.

The literary and cultural critics, Richard Hoggart and Raymond
Williams, were especially important reviewers at the time. What they
said showed which way the centre-to-left wind was blowing. The
heyday of their influence was just beginning. Hoggart's *The Uses of
Literacy* was published in 1957; Williams's *Culture and Society* in
1958. Both wrote reviews which walked around *Meritocracy* like
hesitant border terriers, rather than confront it direct. Both had risen
(from working class Hunslet and Abergavenny) through the operation
of the gospel of equal opportunity, though both in their different ways
saw its shortcomings. Williams grew increasingly angry and, over the
years, ended up boxed into a semi-marxist corner. Hoggart portrayed
poignantly the way the rising lad (less often, then, lass) had to cut
himself off from his own family.

Williams told the readers of the *Manchester Guardian*, rightly,
that 'The logic of the future-story is the logic of extending tendencies.'
(Nothing 'reasonable' about it.) For him, the best in the genre was
Swift's *A Modest Proposal*, which suggested that the way to cure, at
a stroke, poverty and over-population in Ireland was to fatten up the
children of the poor as food for the rich. For Williams, as for Hoggart
in his *Observer* review, *Meritocracy*, short though it is, was too long
for its own good. The theme, Hoggart said, was 'sufficient only for a
good short squib.'

Williams used the book as a way to hit contemporary society over
the head. (And why not? All books about the future are really critiques
of the present.) 'I see no evidence,' he wrote, 'in contemporary
England, of *power* being more closely connected with merit, in any
definition. The administrators, professional men and technicians are
increasingly being selected on educational merit, but the power is still
largely elsewhere, "and no damned merit about it".' The meritocrats of
1958, he argued, were no more than a superior servant-class. 'To be an
upper servant may be as high, really, as we can raise our heads.'

He thought that Young was extrapolating from some supposed

'cultural decline' of the working class, due to their 'limited intellectual potential.' This was beating the book with the wrong end of the stick. The stick would have fallen more accurately on many pages of *The Uses of Literacy*, with their sentimental view of urban working class life (another reproach often made, also, against *Family and Kinship*, published the same year). Working class culture, Hoggart thought, was careering downhill under commercial, and especially American, influence. In *Theatres of Memory*, the social historian, Raphael Samuel, recently quoted Hoggart's denunciation of milk bars 'as a caution against a too immediate hostility to what is alien and innovatory':

> '*Girls go to some, but most of the customers are boys aged between fifteen and twenty, with drape-suits, picture ties, and an American slouch ... the "nickelodeon" is allowed to blare out so that the noise would be sufficient to fill a good-sized ballroom, rather than a converted shop in the high street.... Compared even with the pub around the corner, this is a peculiarly thin and pallid form of dissipation, a sort of spiritual dry-rot amid the odour of boiled milk.*'

The first Teddy Boy on record was seen in South London in 1953. The first milk bar reached my West Riding home village about four years later. Anthony Burgess's novel, *A Clockwork Orange*, which opens in a milk bar, was published in 1962.

Appearances barely feature in *Meritocracy*. But the world Hoggart decried was, in fact, an accurate foretaste of the way things would go. For his *Observer* readers he suggested an alternative future to Young's. He imagined 'an unequal society in which "equality", far from being discredited, had *formally* been allowed to rule in fantastically diverse areas of experience; a society so generally prosperous that material differences between people would be exploited only, but intensely, to rouse marginal rivalries.' This sounds very much like the Britain we ended up with (though it supplements meritocracy, rather than supplants it).

When I first read it, the book's science fiction thesis of an IQ-justified hierarchy seemed far-fetched. Re-reading it, the section closest to science fiction - the eventual revolt against that hierarchy - still seems weak. But it was in line with Michael's recurrent, admirable recognition of the right of the poor, the bloody-minded and the unintellectual to be the way they want to be, and to have their lives and their preferences respected.

Many of the reviewers also preferred Part One, where Michael has a lot of fun with his new idea. In Part Two, we are due to find out more about the attempt to counter it. But the 'Chelsea Manifesto' -

supposedly forged in an alliance between revolution-minded 'shaggy young girls from Newnham and Somerville' and 'aged men' who still remember the Labour Party's original ideals - may be radical but is undoubtedly very skimpy.[1] The *Times Literary Supplement*'s anonymous reviewer enjoyed the first two thirds of the book, but found the final revolt 'too sketchily contrived to be convincing.' The sympathetic Boris Ford found that 'positive values are insufficiently explored.' The unsympathetic Alan Fox said that 'Dr Young clearly rests much importance on his concept of "plural values"', but to this reviewer it 'fails to provoke cries of "Eureka".'

It is easy to understand reviewers' puzzlement. Irony is a dangerous freight to carry. Like waggons bearing nuclear materials, it should come with a warning for the unwary. The message of the book could be taken in at least two ways, possibly three.

Because of the title, it was often taken as simply the pre-history of a new phenomenon. As the *Oxford English Dictionary* confirms, Michael had invented a useful neologism. His new word must have appeared in print millions of times from the pen, typewriter or word processor of writers who never read the book. As he says in the new American edition, 'the most influential books are always those that are not read.' (*Das Kapital* is the most famous example, though *The Origin of Species* must run it close.)

Alternatively, it can be read as a simple attack on the rampant meritocrats. In this guise, in the 1960s and 1970s, it had its most far-reaching practical influence.

But, thirdly, it can be read - and, I would argue, best read - as sociological analysis in the form of a satire. Whatever its weaknesses, it still beats most sociology.[2] 'Meritocracy' is the only concept put forward by a British sociologist recently which has attained common

---

1. A folk-memory is invoked of an even earlier set of ideals. One of the 'vivid' young women leading the revolution is Lady Urania O'Connor. She shares a surname with Fergus O'Connor, the best-remembered Chartist leader. Further irony lurks. Urania was the name of a project, launched by Charles Dickens and the bank heiress, Baroness Burdett-Coutts, in the last days of political Chartism, to rescue fallen women. It failed, like other Burdett-Coutts philanthropic projects. One of the few remaining signs of the baroness's well-meant efforts is a luxuriant marble fountain, regularly vandalised, in Victoria Park, a short walk from the Institute of Community Studies.

2. Michael is the sole living British sociologist I can find in the current edition of *Chambers Biographical Dictionary*. It gives most weight to his consumerist campaigns and educational innovations. *The Rise of the Meritocracy* is his only sociological publication mentioned by name.

currency. To match it you might even have to go back as far as Herbert Spencer, who invented the 'survival of the fittest' - a concept Spencer wasn't in the least ironic about.

One reason for the book's continuing power is that its forecasts have worked at more than one level. Historically it is an important intellectual propellant behind the educational attack on the 11-plus, streaming and grammar schools generally. Here, the crucial link is personal. Anthony Crosland is among the varied collection of people listed in the note of acknowledgments. (They range from Margaret Cole and Peter Townsend on the left to Irving Kristol and Edward Shils on the right.) Crosland became Secretary of State for Education in Harold Wilson's 1960s administrations.

Under his regime, comprehensive schooling moved from being an ideal, which appeared to have worked well on a small scale, to a doctrine to be imposed everywhere. Even in 1954, after the London County Council decided to put its own money on comprehensive schools, one friendly early critic pleaded for experimentation, rather than homogenisation.[3] But this was Mr Secretary Crosland, as recorded in his wife's published memoir of his life:

'If it's the last thing I do, I'm going to destroy every fucking grammar school in England,' he said. 'And Wales. And Northern Ireland.'

'Why not Scotland?' I asked out of pure curiosity.

'Because their schools come under the Secretary of State for Scotland.' He began to laugh at his own inability to destroy their grammar schools.

Over the next ten years, under a succession of Education Secretaries and their civil servants, Crosland's anti-meritocratic ambition was almost fulfilled. Yet the flaw in neighbourhood schools had already become clear in the United States, home of the original model. They locked children into their background. This was fine if the background was fine; less fine if it wasn't.

This administrative doctrine was laid down by a minister who was

---

3. Having been at one of the first comprehensive schools, as well as (thanks to the 11-plus) a local grammar school, I always agreed with this. I thought, and tried to convey through the pages of *New Society*, that what happened inside classrooms was far more important than external systems of administration. Teachers and the curriculum are what deliver, or don't deliver, the goods.

educated at public school and who left fee-paying schools untouched. (The Butler Act's most important innovation in secondary education was to abolish fee-paying as a way into grammar schools. This was thepoint, and the effect, of the 11-plus examination, IQ test and all.) The public schools were therefore ready to receive an injection of talent from the children of anxious parents. Oddly, it was also Crosland who promulgated a two-tier system of higher education (now abolished): polytechnics on the one hand, and universities on the other. This exactly corresponded to the divide between secondary modern and grammar schools that he was attacking. But perhaps he saw polytechnics as comprehensives, and universities as public schools.

What was wrong about Crosland's policy, and his reading of *Meritocracy*'s satire, was the rush to ditch something good before you were sure it was being replaced by something better. The supposed groundswell of public support for comprehensives was misleading. One segment consisted of modestly placed parents who were well enough off to pay the pre-Butler grammar school fees, but couldn't afford public schools; their children were now shut out from grace if they failed the 11-plus. Another, larger segment were voting *against* the secondary modern schools, to which most who failed went, rather than *for* comprehensives (as David Donnison pointed out as early as 1967).

Painfully, the bureaucratic homogenisation is being dissolved. As this goes ahead, it becomes clear that the sociology in *Meritocracy* is more enduringly true than any short-term misinterpretation of it. The unstreamed comprehensive schools, with mixed-ability classes, never achieved total dominance. From the mid-1980s, a gradual reversion began, towards a more meritocratic model. It seemed to be what people wanted.

Even higher education has gone the way the book foresaw. In its pages, Eric James, then the High Master of Manchester Grammar School, is regularly cited as the flag-waver of the meritocracy. When James became the first vice-chancellor of the new University of York (founded in 1963), he wanted it to become a grammar school among universities. A generation later, this meritocratic, work-based ideal has lasted better than the 'plural values' of the other new universities of its day. York is one of the best-regarded.

In 1958, reviewers thought Michael was stretching the limits of probability when he suggested that Oxford and Cambridge might end up purely meritocratic. But with Oxford's final acceptance in 1995 that entrance should turn on A-level grades, this is what happened. Unfortunately, for the time being, this locks Oxbridge colleges even more tightly into taking entrants from fee-paying schools. As he also predicted, these have become devoted to churning out good grades, rather than good chaps on the rugger field.

The immediate influence of *Meritocracy* was unfortunate. A politician without ideas is a sad sight, but a politician in the grip of an idea can be dangerous. The Thames & Hudson edition went out of print in 1970, and the Penguin edition in 1979. My interpretation is that, by the end of the 1970s, it was felt that the book's political message had had its day. The task was complete: the meritocracy had been shafted. (Yet this coincided with the apotheosis of our highest-flying postwar meritocrat, Margaret Thatcher.) By contrast, *Family and Kinship* has remained in print. But this is less, I think, because of such sociological concepts as the 'Demeter tie' between working class daughters and mothers than because of its friendly observation of an apparently bygone era of inner city life[4]; as fascinating as similar pages in Henry Mayhew or Charles Booth.

In his new introduction, Michael says that one publisher who rejected his manuscript suggested he re-wrote it as a novel. In principle, this wasn't a bad idea. The most powerful dystopian and utopian books have usually been presented as stories about more or less plausible people. The utopias have always been thinner on the ground; but both Edward Bellamy in his utopian *Looking Backward*, and William Morris in his *News from Nowhere* (written to counter Bellamy's all too accurate prediction of the bureaucratic, even Stalinist, course of much socialism) used the form of a novel. So, among dystopians, did Samuel Butler in *Erewhon*, Aldous Huxley in *Brave New World*, George Orwell in *Nineteen Eighty-Four*. They all crop up in the pages of the *Oxford Companion to English Literature*. But *Meritocracy* does not (or doesn't yet), even though the fact that it is *almost* a story has probably done it no good among academic sociologists.

In its review, the *Financial Times* regretted that the reader 'waits in vain for the sound of a human voice or a glimpse of earthy people.' The attractive hubbub of such voices is one reason why *Family and*

---

4.   A study should be written of the remarkable group of middle class Englishmen who, in the mid-1950s, found in the working class an appealing sense of fraternity, an alternative family, that they themselves hadn't known as young children.   They are Colin MacInnes (key work, *Absolute Beginners*, 1959), Peter Opie (key work, with Iona Opie, *The Lore and Language of Schoolchildren*, 1959), Michael Young (key work, with Peter Willmott, *Family and Kinship*, 1957), and the photographer Roger Mayne, with his extraordinary portrayal of a cluster of mid-1950s streets in Kensal Town and Notting Dale. Photographs by Mayne appeared on the dust jackets of the first editions of MacInnes's novel and the Opies' book, and on the 1961 Penguin edition of Young and Willmott.

Kinship is still so widely read. But *Meritocracy* embodies an all-embracing view of the way society might go; and, as it turned out, is going. Even its own influence in causing politicians and administrators to attempt to stem that tide did not, finally, undermine its accuracy. Satirists always fire their best arrows at targets they can see (or once saw) the attraction of. The paradox is that the vigour and wit of Michael Young's onslaught on the meritocracy reinforces the reader's feeling of the power of what he is supposedly attacking. And looking around the shipwreck of state education in many English cities - East London included - it is clear that, of the various choices of evils, the creation of a meritocracy is the least of them.

Man of Merit
Ronald Dore

Michael Young has dazzled us so much with the inventiveness and imagination of his entrepreneurial work as freelance creator of useful organisations, that we are apt to overlook the equally inventive and imaginative contributions he has made to our understanding of the social world about us.

I was about to say 'contributions to sociology' as one might say 'contributions to microbiology' - as if the sociology departments of Europe and North America were dedicated to the careful cumulative job of building a shared body of 'knowledge' about how societies work. The fact that they are instead occupied by a diversity of people all with their own, often weird, agendas, may have something to do with why Michael has stayed out of them, but in any case the building up of a discipline is not what his sociology is about. Take, for instance, his most unexpected book, *The Metronomic Society* (1988b). I say unexpected since it is as if he were deliberately suppressing, or giving himself a compulsory 'you need it for your own refreshment' sort of holiday from, his concern for social problems, and indulging in wide-ranging, free-wheeling ruminations on what Life is about, and why in spite of all the horrors it is a Good Thing. The underlying optimism - most explicit in the chapter on social evolution -is in character; one of the reasons, I suppose, why his concern for social problems is always accompanied by a get-up-and-go impulse to do something practical about them.

But the point I was intending to make is that even in that chapter on such a well-worn theme as social evolution and whether one can reasonably talk of mankind's 'moral progress', the wide range of fascinating citations - evidence of a lifetime of voracious reading - covers hardly a single self-declared sociologist. Only Durkheim, in fact: a few lines explaining the notion of 'organic solidarity' with due acknowledgement but no mention of the term itself.

Whether or not it *was* recreation writing, the book is certainly recreation reading, full of 'insights' - observations which make one look at things in new ways. In so far as there is a dominant consistent theme, assertible in the form of a debatable proposition, I suppose it is that our most irksome and freedom-constraining tasks usually involve some form of enslavement to the clock, and there ought to be better ways of ordering things to give us greater freedom in greater harmony with nature.

> *'While at one moment after six with bent heads the clerks shuffle homeward down into the tube station, above their heads, if only they would look up, the starlings are excitably wheeling in the sky and the swifts darting about in the fading light...'*

The vision is of a piece with the *Chelsea Manifesto* of the Technician's Party in *The Rise of the Meritocracy* (1958). It ought to be possible, say the revolutionaries, to create a society in which people are valued, not for their intelligence, education, occupation and power, but for their kindliness, courage, imagination, sensitivity, sympathy, generosity.

> *'Who would be able to say that the scientist was superior to the porter with admirable qualities as a father, the civil servant with unusual skill at gaining prizes superior to the lorry-driver with unusual skill at growing roses?'*
> (p.159)

These are glimpses of what one might call the Dartington idyll. Dartington, he tells us in his book about the Elmhirsts, tried to be 'the alive rural community ... made up of people working in industries, in education, as well as agriculture', where 'people would stimulate each other, keeping their intelligence "bright and burnished", where people

> *'generate sympathy for each other instead of calling farmworkers dolts, as townspeople were liable to do from a distance, or making farmworkers jealous of industrial workers because they enjoyed much more in the way of possessions and amusements. At Dartington they were all individuals, people not type-clusters, the difference in their standard of life being to some extent justified by the obvious difference in their functions and responsibilities.'*
> (1982a, p.256)

That 'justified', though - and note the qualification, 'to some extent justified' - is the joker in the pack. *Meritocracy*, the primary subject of this note and the book of Michael Young that intersects most directly with my own interests, is, in my reading at least, a sustained argument about 'justice', against the background of a set of predictions about what was going to happen in British society in the eighty years after the book was written (that is, up to 2034, the date of the spoof PhD thesis analysing the dramatic social changes of the preceding century and the reasons for the onset of revolt).

It seems hardly credible that a work of such obvious originality, and at the same time such obvious relevance to the overt and much-discussed problems of its day, should have had the cool and uncomprehending reception from publishers which Michael describes in his preface to the 1994 reissue. (The title page tells us that the Library of Congress has it subject-catalogued under 'intellectuals' - not, note, 'intelligence' - 'progress', 'elite' and 'social status'). It seems hardly credible, too, that the book should have been read as a whole-hearted endorsement of the need for, and the virtues of, a meritocratic society.

But in his new preface, Michael is at pains to point out that he made his imaginary future apologist for meritocracy deliberately unsympathetic and in the 'Chelsea Manifesto' quoted above (significant, the choice of Chelsea rather than Hampstead?) clearly presented the alternative set of values. In the closing words of his preface:

> *'The book was, in other words, intended to present two sides of the case - the case against as well as the case for a meritocracy. It is not a simple matter and it was not intended to be. The two points of view are contrasted throughout. The imaginary author has a shadow. The decision, one way or another, was and is left to the reader, the hope being that, on the way to making up his mind on one of the great issues of modern society, he or she will also have a little fun.'*

And fun, indeed, it is. 'Compulsively enjoyable reading' as, according to the cover of the reissue *Time and Tide's* reviewer of the original edition called it. One enjoys the wit, the invention, the cleverness of the parodied prose of the solemn, public-spirited civil servant, trained in the best Ernest Gowers' *Plain Words* tradition: the sly comments-in-passing on everything from Oxbridge to British music, and the sheer playfulness of some of his flights of fancy.

I especially liked the notion that, thanks to lifelong education and the possibility of reclassification - the Open University which Michael subsequently played a large part in founding -

> *'some children have become excessively ambitious on behalf of their parents and have exerted too much pressure on them to strive for reclassification.'*

All this one *admires* without reserve, but *amused?* Yes, but with

discomfort. For the humour is black humour, a bit too close to the bone
of our modern discontents to be received in unalloyed enjoyment.

The trouble is that the book does not only offer two alternative
world-views. It bases those world views on alternative sets of empirical
propositions about the nature of human psychology and the limits
within which a technologically complex society can take shape. And
which of those sets of propositions is true and which false, while it
may actually be irrelevant to which of those two opposing sets of
values each one of us prefers, is not at all irrelevant to the question of
which set of values is likely to prevail, to get embodied in the concrete
arrangements of our society. Plausibility counts.

And whereas the empirical propositions about the conditions under
which societies can come to value generosity, etc, rather than power,
are hardly spelt out, those on which the meritocrat's values are based -
about the distribution of genetically-determined learning ability, or
about the consequences of increasing complexity for employment - are
spelt out in great detail, either explicitly, or implicitly in the form of
predictions about the future.

That future is one which, indeed, Meritocrats applaud and
Dartingtonians deplore. Deplore, but still, I take Young 1958 to be
saying, consider highly probable.

Let us look at some of the predications made and consider the
actual outcomes:

> 'The comprehensive school movement by which the Labour
> Party began, in the 1950s, to show a concern not just for
> equality of opportunity (of which it had been a major
> standard-bearer) but also for equality of condition, equality
> of outcomes, would fizzle out before comprehensive schools
> could be made the general rule.'

Why? Firstly because the English are conditioned by their aristocratic
tradition to believe in excellence; 'they assumed that some men were
better than others' and it was only the substitution of ability for birth
that was needed to preserve the principle.

Secondly, because in the event the few Labour councils which
tried comprehensive schools in the 1950s produced a half-hearted
compromise - schools which left the principle of ability-streaming
internally intact, and desperately sought to model themselves on
grammar schools (e.g., by making each school of unwieldy size in
order to have a viable sixth form, for instance).

Thirdly, because among parents, by the 1980s, the beneficiaries
of grammar school selection had become so numerous and so
articulately dominant in the middle class, and had such a stake in the

selection system that the movement fizzled out.

The original proposition was not quite right, then, in underestimating the chance of comprehensive schools becoming general policy. But it was not bad as a prediction of the operative reasons behind the dismantling of the comprehensive system in the 1990s, even though that dismantling has been ostensibly undertaken under slogans which bypass 1950s disputes about 'excellence' - greater experimental variety of more autonomous schools, greater parental choice (meaning that 'good' schools could choose their parents), publication of examination scores so that 'good' schools can be identified, and so on.

'The mechanisms which ensured the systematic distribution of educational opportunity solely according to intellectual ability (measures of the relative ability to learn - relative, that is to say, to all others of the same age group - not measures of what had already been learned, the latter being much more dependent than the former on family background) would become ever more refined, and the correlation of educational performance with position in the occupational hierarchy would become ever more perfect.'

There were two main ways in which this was expected to come about. The spread of aspirations and the diminution of poverty had already, by the 1950s, made the 11-plus very efficient as an ability-sorter independent of social class. (Floud, Halsey and Martin's findings (1956) are cited in evidence: 'The chances of children at a given level of ability entering grammar schools are no longer dependent on their social origins' in many, if not most, parts of the country.') The next step would be to make the selection stage at 15/16 equally independent of social class, to replace in the sixth forms the dumb children of the middle class with the bright children of the working class who, in the 1950s, were still leaving school in droves. This would be done with selective scholarships more generous than the wages uneducated school-leavers could earn.

The second key change was the decline to insignificance of private education. This was accomplished by throwing vast sums of money at the best grammar schools, so improving their quality (by attracting, for instance, the best teachers) that rich parents deserted Eton in droves. (A tough capital levy also helped.)

Clearly both of these 'mechanism' predictions have failed, especially the second. The reduction in upper bracket income taxes has helped greatly in the expansion of private secondary education, particularly the growth of a large tail of inferior private education for the not-so-bright, as, with a larger catchment area, the top schools have become increasingly ability-selective, bolstering their reputation for intellectual merit as well as for the social cachet, and personality training for positions of command, for which they have always been noted.

As for post-16 scholarships, it is tempting to say that the youths who used to rush out of school to get well-paid jobs in the 1950s (when the trade unions' pressure to push up apprenticeship wages - traditionally to relieve skilled adults from cheap-labour competition - were yielded to in order to compete with unskilled youth wages) are now kept in school by youth unemployment and the removal of unemployment benefits for the 16-18s. But that would ignore the fact that, apart from a few areas where its incidence is particularly heavy, youth unemployment at 16 is primarily a problem of the not-so-bright who would never have benefitted anyway from *Meritocracy's* bursary scheme.

What has led to the recent enormous expansion in post-16 and also in post-18 education is a *combination* of the diffusion of middle-class aspirations with the well-known phenomenon of qualification escalation. In the 1950s, a bright boy with good O-levels could enter banking, local government, industrial management, journalism and many other middle-class occupations and expect, by internal mobility, to get to the sort of position which university graduates normally aspired to and could reach with far less difficulty. But, as growing affluence reduced the supply of young people who deliberately chose to 'get on' the hard way, so it no longer seemed sensible for the various employing organisations to make (not costless) provision for these up-from-the-ranks careers, and eminently sensible for the various professions to raise their entry requirements as supply grew, first at A-level and then at university level, because the better they are seen to be doing in the competition for the 'pool of talent', the higher the profession's prestige and the fees it can charge or the salaries it can claim.

But predictions about the exact mechanisms are less interesting than the main prediction of outcomes, that educational opportunity gets increasingly distributed according to intellectual ability and the correlation of educational performance with position in the occupational hierarchy becomes ever more perfect.

Whether *that* has been the case over the last forty years is extremely difficult to determine, since those who concern themselves with social mobility have, as Peter Saunders has recently been complaining, been preoccupied with demonstrating the extent to which social class status is inherited.

The question *how* the transmission of top people's status to their children takes place, how far it is determined by (a) economic advantage (being able to buy them better education), (b) cultural advantage (more educative talk at the breakfast table) or (c) genetic advantage (giving them a better brain to learn things with), has aroused little interest; been pretty much taboo, in fact, because of a *generous* desire not to seem to be saying, like the psychiatrist in the New Yorker cartoon which *Meritocracy* cites: 'Has it ever occurred to you Mr Jones, that perhaps you *are* inferior?'. It puts one on the side of the underdog to assume that economic and cultural advantages are the crucial ones, and that therefore British society is far from open to the talents and hence exceedingly unfair.

Whether the system is fair or unfair according to a particular 'equality of opportunity' value criterion is, however, much less important for the future shape of our society and for an effective approach to educational policy than the question of how much of a role the genetic mechanism plays, relative to the economic or cultural mechanisms, in status transmission - taking as given the degree of homo/heterogeneity of environments found in Britain today. If the role of genes is a large one, that means what *Meritocracy* predicted - a progressive freezing of the social structure into a class system a good deal more rigid than that of the nineteenth century when it was only families, not families plus school selection, which mediated the processes of inter-generational transmission. And *Meritocracy's* predictions about the malign consequences thereof remain plausible.

Peter Saunders' recent attempts (1995) to face up to these issues, precipitating a predictable ideological war, can hardly be conclusive since the mobility studies simply have not collected independent ability measures, as opposed to crude measurements of educational level, with Oxbridge and polytechnic graduates usually lumped into a single 'graduate' category, for instance.

Saunders has however promised to look at the highly relevant data in the cohort survey of 11,000 children born in the year *Meritocracy* was published, and in the interim has produced a model which shows that *if* one assumes that in an initial generation, the x per cent of top 'service class' jobs is manned by the top x per cent of scorers on IQ tests, and the socially bottom y per cent manual working class is made up of the bottom y per cent in terms of underlying ability, then the amount of social mobility one might expect in one generation to arise from the reasonably well-known mechanisms of regression towards the mean (using an Eysenck formula), is almost exactly the amount of social mobility which Goldthorpe found between 1972 respondents and their fathers. But that is a big 'if'. The evidence that the top people of the generation centred on - 1940, would it be? -were indeed the best and the brightest is hardly overwhelming.

And in any case the question is not, surely, so much whether

Britain is and has always been a meritocracy but whether there are
signs of it becoming more completely so. The prediction about ability,
education and occupation can be broken down into the two parts (using
the initial letters of those words) as:

$$o = fe \text{ and } e = fa$$

The Saunders-Goldthorpe controversy is about the combined $o = fa$,
and it *could* possibly be that the manifest increase in the extent to
which educational achievement determines job chances has only
substituted educational competition for post-schooling 'contest'
mobility, without any change in the overall $o = fa$ function.

My own guess is that there has been a change in that function
(towards greater correlation) and that by and large the *Meritocracy*
prediction is correct. That guess is founded in the following
observations.

To start with, as the current craze for performance-related pay
indicates, the felt need for *efficiency* in all kinds of work organisations
has increased. It has been made stronger by, first of all, the national
competitiveness drive (the need to 'withstand foreign competition' in
order to 'survive as a great nation' in the words of *Meritocracy*) which
has been intensified by the hotting-up of international trade competition
brought by a vast cheapening of transport and communication.
Secondly, it has been boosted by the desperate state of national
finances faced with continuously rising levels of welfare support for a
growing underclass, and the drive for cost-cutting via 'market-testing'
over vast areas of the pace-setting public sector. Ask poor Professor
Stephen Littlechild; even to hoodwink the clever Ofregs, the managers
of what were once rather comfortable state monopolies can only defend
their new private monopolies by the even greater cleverness of the way
they massage their accounts. Thirdly, perhaps, it has been augmented
by sheer ideological change brought by the grammar school's capture
of the Conservative Party. From Baldwin to Heath, Thatcher and Major
is a long way.

Next there are changes in the nature of jobs brought by the
development both of material and organisational technology, which
have made learning ability, cognitive skills - the sort of things that IQ
tests measure - steadily more salient among the ingredients which
ensure that needed efficiency; more salient, that is, than initiative,
leadership, toughness, ability to command, submissiveness, fearlessness,
conscientiousness and all the other 'personal skills' which enter the
varying mix required for the efficient performance of different types of
jobs. I exclude from that 'other capacities' list 'the capacity for effort',
since that is an essential accompanying, catalysing, rather than a

competing or alternative, characteristic to intelligence - as *Meritocracy* recognised in the famous definition of merit as 'intelligence plus effort'.

One could equally make that the definition of 'learning ability' rather than of 'merit'. A nurse has now to learn about a much wider range of procedures and drugs than nurses twenty years ago. Bulldozer drivers have to learn how and when to punch and pull a much larger set of buttons and levers, and the damage their mistakes can do with their ever-more-powerful machines is increasing. Typists have to learn a new word processing package every two years, if not more often. *Meritocracy* has a footnote intended to drive home the effects of technological change: 'Metropolitan-Vickers had 10,000 people in 1930 of whom one fifth had some form of organised education. By 1982, 61,000 of its 74,000 work force had at least an HNC'. Had he been writing after 1982 rather than in 1958, Young might have noted instead that the lads of Kirkcaldy needed good marks in five O-level subjects to get a shop-floor job in NEC.

Thirdly, the way in which ability-streaming has spread makes it clear that there is a market for ability-labelling, in spite of the educational profession's relegation of IQ tests to its repertoire of secret rituals. In the private school sector this has shifted from streaming within schools to the more definitive form of streaming among schools, as the top schools impose stiffer admissions tests. At sixth-form level the addition of I-levels and GNVQs to S-levels and A-levels, helps to accommodate a wider ability range as well as to make for more easily identifiable ability-certification labels than the varying A to E marks of a plethora of A-level examination boards. At university level, the abolition of the much-resented dual system is accompanied by a more open hierarchisation of the whole system, accelerated by the tying of a major part of state funding to research ratings.

Oxbridge fully and joyfully accepted its modern role as the top-talent universities by substituting formal examinations for their earlier chaotic selection procedures; but Oxford, at least, has returned to chaos again in pursuit of the same objective, because the examinations were thought to be a distorted means of talent-creaming; the private schools having so much better resources for coaching their pupils than state schools. Admittedly we have not got as far as Japan where the cram schools will give you for free a ranking of the several thousand faculties of Japan's 400-odd universities according to the average standard deviation achievement score of the applicants who passed their entrance examination in the previous year. But we are on the way.

There is no space to look at the out-turn with respect to some of *Meritocracy's* other predictions - that Chinese would become our second language by the end of the century, (two or three decades too early; who could have foreseen that the century's one attempt to model society on something like the Dartington ideal - Mao's Cultural Revolution - would occur in China?); that university graduates would take over the trade union movement from the up-from-the-ranks Ernie Bevins (slowly becoming true, but too late for the unions to become entrenched as 'social partners' as they have in Germany, Sweden or Italy); that a reformed House of Lords would become a major centre of power, along with the civil service, marginalising 'amateur politicians'; that the problem of technological unemployment for those least able to learn, would be more acute for men rather than women, thanks to the renewed growth of domestic service. And so on. Spoof predictions, tongue-in-cheek? Yes, but imaginative extrapolations of what was happening in the world in the 1950s.

But it is worth a closer look at one more prediction, which is perhaps the central monitory prediction - of particular interest in the light of current controversies about board-room salaries and the lift in top civil service salaries to match them, concerning the evolution of class relations and income distribution.

> *'The family transmission of status once made rather dull people the organisational superiors of others manifestly brighter than themselves. This induced a certain modesty, a tendency to treat subordinates with a certain respect. More efficient ability-sorting removed this brake on arrogance. One result was widening income differentials as the greed of the top people who controlled the salary structure grew; pay in the ratio of 130:1 from top to bottom of the European Atomic Authority, for instance. Egalitarian objections to these differences did not disappear, however. The differentials could only eventually be preserved by the subterfuge of giving everyone a citizen's income, and providing top people with their luxury yachts and armies of domestic servants in the form of expenses deemed necessary for them to do their socially-necessary jobs.'*

One still has to go to America to find the 130:1 ratios, but our boardroom tycoons are coming along fine. What no-one, perhaps, could have foreseen in the mixed economy of the 1950s is the way in which the justification of large salaries could most effectively be made in post-Keith Joseph, post-Thatcher Britain, not in terms of 'needs for performance of crucial social functions' but under the all-justifying principle of The Market. Ian McGregor had to be borrowed at vast expense from Lazards because his talents were so extraordinarily rare, and Mrs Thatcher was naturally prepared to pay the market price. John

Major will admit that he has a political problem with these constant news stories about Chairmen's 60 per cent rises, but the only solution he can think of is a kind of Consumers' Association of shareholders to help them assess the true market value of the talent they are buying. And at the other end of the stretching spectrum, no one can think of any better solution for unemployment than cutting social security and legal wage *minima* in order to allow the unemployed to low-price themselves back into work.

Michael says in his new preface (of 1994) that of course he was not *endorsing* his predicted increase in earned income inequality, which would replace unearned income inequality, subject to more swingeing capital taxes than have in fact occurred. He comes back to that 'justified' again.

> 'Even if it could be demonstrated that ordinary people had less native ability than those selected for high position, that would not mean that they deserved to get less. Being a member of the "lucky sperm club" confers no moral right to advantage.'

(What happened to the ovum? Such insouciant lack of concern with political correctness is further proof of this sociologist's fortunate disconnection from the world of sociology.)

If it were just a question of 'ordinary people' and 'those selected for high position', one could expect the voting majority of 'ordinary people' to find some remedy. Instead, what is happening in our society is not just a pulling away of the top quarter per cent of salaries, but a general increase in the dispersion. A standard deviation above the IQ mean may still be at 115 or wherever it used to be; but one standard deviation above the income mean is steadily getting to be more pounds, and more in percentage of pounds, while conversely, a standard deviation below becomes less.

Politically it seems not to matter, as *Meritocracy* assumed it would, whether the person at one standard deviation above the income mean is or is not at one standard deviation above the IQ mean. Just as relative deprivation is what causes resentment, so relative privilege is what causes contentment, and the sixty per cent home-owning, car-owning garden-centre/DIY shoppers have good reasons for feeling glad that they do not belong to the other, insecure, inarticulate, rarely-voting forty per cent.

If our economy *is* now too complex to be run by anything but the market, then the only way of restoring some sense of community and reversing the growth of the rich-poor gap is through state taxation and redistribution, either in cash or by various forms of the 'social wage'.

That Tony Blair, with all the incompetence and unpopularity of the present government in his favour, does not dare mention increased taxation does not augur well for that prospect.

So will it be, in the end, disgruntled members of the elite, 'the shaggy young girls from Newnham and Somerville', who lead the forty per cent in an orgy of destruction? Michael's story stops on the brink of the revolution. He doesn't tell us who would become the revolution's Mirabeaus and Robespierres, or its Napoleon or Louis XVIII. But he must have known that his Chelsea Manifesto society would have trouble establishing itself, and not just because civil servants are, on the whole, better than lorry drivers at growing roses when they give their minds to it, and may even be more prone to generosity and other 'moral' impulses, by reason of their higher IQ rather than by reason of their background and more comfortable circumstances - as Barrington Moore concluded was the case when he looked into the literature for his book on social justice (1978). But it would also be because of the lowered standard of living which a society which devalued those personality characteristics which make for productive efficiency would almost certainly face. The subsequent founder of the Consumers' Association must have known that the sixty per cent would not tolerate for long the absence of goods in the shops.

And then there is also Prometheus, who disturbed the Gods' original Dartington idyll. Kurt Vonnegut, author of a somewhat similar dystopia, *Player Piano* (1952), carries the story of his cataclysmic revolt against the meritocracy (though he wrote without the benefit of Young's invention of that word to describe it) to its final collapse. The revolt's leaders, first and foremost the novel's main hero, a *male* deserter from the ranks of the IQ elite, finally give themselves up in disillusionment on the morrow of the proles' orgiastic destruction of the machines which enslaved them. This is not because the liberated masses prove finally unwilling to surrender the material comforts which the regime offered as recompense for their subordination. The leaders' final disillusionment occurs when they come across a group of the 'liberated' enthusiastically cannibalising some of the broken machines to make others work. And it is clear that they are doing so, not so much because they want the products of those machines, but from the sheer pleasure of *bricolage*, the sheer delight of clever and constructive improvisation.

So what is there to hope for as an alternative solution to the problem of callousness, the loss of a sense of fellow-citizenship, the diminishing willingness to recognise the claims of others to human dignity? The emergence, growth and eventual power of Platonic Guardians - those such as the saboteurs of *Meritocracy* who, 'like secret Catholics in a Protestant town', quietly tried to screw up the selection procedures in order to leave some able leaders for the masses?

Can we expect to see a new generation of Attlees and Cripps? Can we rely on the hope that the decent moral instincts of at least a section of the elite will prompt them to work for change in the system from within, rather than by revolution from without - some of those shaggy girls from Newnham replacing the none too shaggy Virginia Bottomleys either through the ballot box or through some extraordinary revival of the One Nation group within the Tory Party?

Michael has always been too good a democrat to have any truck with the notion of Platonic Guardians. He has too much faith in 'ordinary people'. But in fact he himself has been our foremost unofficial freelance Guardian, offering ordinary people opportunities they could not provide for themselves. And they have responded. Anyone who aspires to be the new generation of within-the-establishment Guardians, the new Attlees and Cripps, should study how and why.

Tracking the Demeter tie
Geoff Dench

The main consideration prompting Michael's decisive step away from the world of party politics into that of independent social research and commentary was his concern that the essential roots of social life were being overlooked by policy-makers. Too fascinated by the marvels of economic growth and technological innovation, they were carelessly undermining the very communities which state machines derived their ultimate legitimacy by serving. What I want to suggest briefly here is that an important aspect of this concern was an awareness that what was being neglected was the feminine aspect of society and the private realm informed by it.

Michael has attempted to conceptualise this through the idea of the Demeter tie, a special bond between mothers and daughters; but that concept has yet to make its full mark. This is something which the Labour Party in particular has continued to ignore, and it still has much to learn from his understandings if it is to cope successfully with the massive social transformations taking place in the last part of this century.

Michael's early writings on social policy show that he regarded a key function of the welfare state as compensating for the inadequacies and unreliability of men as family breadwinners, by providing direct benefits to mothers and their families. He was at one with earlier social reformers like Seebohm Rowntree in seeing the selfish behaviour of husbands as the cause of a great deal of hidden poverty, and was influenced by the wartime studies of Charles Madge (who later played a valuable role in helping set up the Institute of Community Studies), indicating that a woman's personal dependence on her husband rendered her *'the lowest paid, most exploited worker in the country, given a mere subsistence wage, with no limit on hours worked'*. (Madge, 1943, p.53.)

Michael believed that the welfare state could best liberate women from this, while supporting them in their domestic labour, by extending to them full citizenship rights in their own right. So he was an ardent supporter of Eleanor Rathbone in her campaign for family allowances payable to wives rather than husbands. On a number of occasions (e.g. 1952b, p.313) he has quoted from her decisive contribution to the famous 1945 Commons second reading, to the effect that:

177

> '*If the money is given to the mother, and if they know that
> the law regards it as the child's property, or the mother's
> property to be spent for the child, that will help them to
> realise that the State recognizes the status of motherhood.*'

In large part it was this vision of the welfare state as a vehicle for
helping virtuous mothers to become less dependent on tyrannical and
uncaring husbands which fed Michael's growing dissatisfaction with
the Labour Party. The trade unionist element was reluctant to weaken
the concept of individual male breadwinners, whose family obligations
gave moral legitimacy to their own economic demands. And the
doctrinaire radicals were so obsessed by the primacy of the public
realm, and issues like nationalisation, that they had little time to think
about families and interpersonal relationships.

The resulting narrow pre-occupation with economic issues, which
arguably produced the soil for second-wave feminism to develop in
Britain, offered little scope for Michael's more pluralist and traditional
world view - in which the link between public and private spheres
mirrored and wrote large those between men and women, with women
located at the communal hearth, nurturing children and cultivating
civilised values, while men ranged around outside as their material
supporters and agents.

Michael noted appreciatively at the end of the first Labour
administration that the welfare state, through family allowances, school
meals, milk and food supplements and the NHS had done much to
cushion women against male derelictions of obligation, and to
redistribute resources discreetly from men to women. '*In general it is
as though the taxes on tobacco and drink had been paid into a family
income equalisation pool, from which had been drawn the benefits
provided by the State.*' (1952b, p. 319.) But he was feeling that much
remained to be done, and in his penultimate policy discussion paper as
an employee of the Party he made a final plea for more to be done for
mothers.

> '*It is a remarkable fact that it was not until the election of
> a Labour Government in 1945 that anything effective was
> done to ease the strain of modern living on the ordinary,
> workaday family ... (This precedent) we should prepare to
> follow when next a Government is elected responsive to the
> needs of the people, responsive, above all, to the needs of
> the mothers in whose arms the future rests.* [Adding with
> resignation] *I herewith pass the baby to the National
> Executive Committee.*'
> (1951, p.1.)

The mother of socialism

So Michael's escape from the prison of Left thought and his journey with Peter Willmott into the East End - a region long toured by reformers and social enquirers eager to witness at first hand the effects of male moral weakness - has to be seen I think as already mapped out by an interest in the value of women's labour. But the exuberant social reporting which then followed in *Family and Kinship* suggests that even Michael was taken back by just how central women proved to be. For it was Mum who emerged as the undisputed heroine of that study. Motherhood was revealed not just as child-rearing - much as that undoubtedly was - but also as the linchpin of community itself.

Childrearing is such a relentless burden that women could not manage without mutual support and reciprocity, and the interpersonal exchanges and obligations which they arranged between themselves were the principle content of extended family networks, general neighbourliness, and an open school for learning key moral values upholding mutual aid and interdependence. The central co-operative relationship in this structure was that between mother and daughter, which combined a long-term and morally inescapable mutual indebtedness with a convenient asymmetry and compatibility of age, experience and availability. As Michael and Peter put it:

> '*And so it goes on - the daughter's labours are in a hundred little ways shared with the older woman whose days of child-bearing (but not of child-rearing) are over. When the time comes for the mother to need assistance, the daughter reciprocates, as reported elsewhere, by returning the care which she has herself received.*' (1957, p. 39).

It was through helping her daughters in this way that an older woman found herself becoming a pillar of the community, whether she wanted it or not, and a matriarch around whom the lives of younger generations revolved, and through whom people traced key relationships and placed themselves in the local community. It was Mum who slipped a fiver to the housing agent to secure a new tenancy, and whose home was the centre of the extended family, where her daughters gathered. She not only held the family together, but presided over the moral economy regulating ties with other families. There was no need to put her on a pedestal as the role she played put her there already. '*Since her status as 'Mum' is so high, it is derogatory to call her by any other name.*' (ibid. p.33)

Just as community proved to be largely a matter of extended families, these themselves turned out to be almost wholly a matter of grannies. It is perhaps surprising that this analysis did not culminate in a double equation to the effect that C = EF = Mum. Instead, and perhaps to avoid grappling directly with the paradox of why we should choose a term like fraternity to describe virtues which are characteristically taught and exemplified by women, the concept of (discreetly gendered) neighbourliness was invoked, with the formula (expressed most cogently in *Symmetrical Family*, 1973a, p. 287) that *'neighbourly socialism is the mother of political socialism'*.

That it was mainly Michael who saw civic virtue as being grounded in the private realm, among women, and community as shared motherhood, is I believe confirmed by the gender dimension present in the *Meritocracy* story, which he was writing at the same time. *Meritocracy* is notable for its ambivalence and irony: and this is why it has been read in different ways. But there is little ambiguity in its celebration of female values and activities. Thus within the clearly mixed attitudes towards family displayed in the story, it is not hard to discern that it is the male aspects of family, linked with inheritance, property and public position, which are portrayed as having anti-social implications, while the female side of nurturance and mutual support is affirmed as truly moral and socially integrative. The narrative itself can be read as a morality tale in which women are obliged to intervene in order to save the men who are supposed to be running the show from the consequences of the mistakes they are making. It suggests that women, as the guardians of the values on which social order and the legitimacy of the public domain ultimately depend, can withdraw men's licence when they lose their way.

For the emergence and rise of this meritocracy takes place as the men in charge of the state, perhaps a little like the leaders in Attlee's postwar administration, forget the varied nature of social ends or purposes and get carried away by the pursuit of specific means - in this case super-efficiency of human resource development. The open and heartlessly universalistic competitiveness of this male system then leads towards instability and social division, as ever fewer people feel they have a stake in the system. Its days are numbered after women, beginning with those shaggy young girls from Newnham and Somerville, withdraw their support for the regime.

These female leaders of revolution have sometimes been identified as harbingers of second-wave feminism. But I think that claim is invalid. The politically effective women are clearly defined in terms wholly at variance with modern feminism, which mobilises around equal participation in the public realm, and in fact they have much in common with those women vilified by Faludi (1992) as collaborators with (supposedly male) backlash. It is not that they are opposing the system because they are excluded from it. They defy it because they believe in community and its sacrificial heart, motherhood.

> '*The determination of so many of the present leaders of the movement to do all their own household work is unusual and in some ways welcome since it means the married ones have little time left over for political organisation.*
>
> *Through the women's circles, the activists have been able to assert their influence and show their menfolk, who perhaps show too little humility about the wonders with which they have furnished our estate, that they are a force to be reckoned with. In so doing they are making a protest against the standards, those of achievement, by which men assess each other.*' (1958, p.173.)

The guiding spirit of the Populists is unveiled here as Nemesis, the ancient goddess of righteous wrath.

Demeter found, and lost again

Michael's sensitivity, in the face of conventional models, to what actually goes on in society was I think a major factor behind the massive popular success of *Family and Kinship*, and possibly to some extent of *Meritocracy* too. Most people experience intimations of matriarchy at frequent intervals: but as these are not endorsed by official culture they learn to ignore them or interpret them in other ways. *Family and Kinship* held up a mirror to everyday life which ordinary people recognised instantly and which encouraged them to realise that they did after all understand how the world worked. Bethnal Green served not just as a metaphor for unrepresented common man, but also for unreconstructed common sense: for a moment sociology and folk culture sang in harmony. The appeal of the book was very similar to that of modern soap operas now which, with the exception perhaps of *Brookside*, circumvent current orthodoxy by pretending that their portrayals of female centrality are merely fiction.

Not everyone approved of it of course. For most people it breathed fresh air into corners where stuffy dogmas had lingered too long. To an anthropology student like myself, reading *Family and Kinship* a couple of years after its publication, it came as a revelation that sociology did not have to be arid or divorced from real life. I then enthusiastically spent a good deal of my final year working with Michael to establish a student Sociology Society in Cambridge to spread the word, and soon changed disciplines myself. But for radical women setting out on the long march towards strict equality, family and motherhood were not fit objects of admiration, and many said so. Michael had been warned. While *Family and Kinship* was being written he had addressed the Town Planning Institute on the importance of protecting extended families, and in the ensuing discussion the redoubtable Ruth Glass had pointed out sternly that if relatives were the most important source of support at childbirth this should be seen as indicating a failure on the part of the social services to help families in coping with their everyday lives.

> '[Moreover, she] *did not think that one could regard the extended family as a substitute for a widening of the horizon of social responsibility ... Of course, we were all capable of sharing the joys and pains of members of our own family. But in the long run it was our ability to identify ourselves with the fate of adults and children further and even far away - for instance, with the experience of a few Japanese fishermen - which would count. It was the growing sense of interdependence with ever widening groups, indeed with humanity as a whole, which signified social progress.'* (1954c p.141.)

This tone was echoed many times during the sixties, especially in the universities, by feminists (still almost entirely women) who thought that motherhood was just work like any other, and were convinced that the welfare state represented the long-awaited wand for banishing distinctions between public and private spheres. They resented what they felt to be a romanticisation by Michael and Peter of social arrangements which trapped women in domesticity. Quotations from old ladies affirming that '*With a daughter you've always got someone to ask*' (1960b p.72) were instantly translated by them into '*As a daughter you can never say no*', confirming that women lived in bondage.

What was perhaps even harder to swallow, I suspect, was that both *Family and Kinship* and *Family and Class (1960b)* revealed men as bit parters and minor characters, hardly figuring in the central action. So these studies hindered the construction of a theory of imperious patriarchy in which men could be portrayed as the arch enemy: and this made it harder to mobilise female solidarity.

During the sixties Michael explored the idea of the mother-daughter relationship as a universal and fundamental element in social relations. He started referring to it as the Demeter tie, counterposing it against the Oedipal tie which the Left were fond of dwelling on as evidence of the primordial nature of patriarchy. But he had little response, and in his next (and final) book with Peter on family and

gender, the *Symmetrical Family* (1973a), gave in I think to critiques
and pressures by choosing to explain the tie less in general terms of
elementary interpersonal reciprocity, generated spontaneously within
the private realm, and more in terms of particular changes forced onto
family life by developments in the world of economics and politics: the
'four stages' theory. It was surely no accident that this doctored model
appeared a couple of years after Jennifer Platt's *Social Research in
Bethnal Green*, which Michael and Peter reviewed, and which they
acknowledged there as 'helping to clarify' their own emerging theory.
Realism could not prevail against ideology in the longer run.

Michael withdrew from this arena as it became engulfed by sex
war. In the conclusion to *Symmetrical Family*, which failed
interestingly to repeat the popular impact of the earlier family studies,
there are suggestions made that 'women liberationists' may soon
provoke a reaction against themselves. Michael went on sniping gently
for some years, complaining that Women's Liberationists were ignoring
the problems of non-working women (1974a), and warning that:

> *'Women out at work who do not have much time to spare for
> their mothers will, when they are old themselves, suffer
> likewise when their daughters follow their example'*
> (1977, p.351).

But essentially he was shifting his major interest and activities to other
areas, such as distance education in Africa, the co-operative movement,
and the new Social Democratic Party.

So his analysis of the sexual constitution of society has been
deferred. But I believe that it would almost certainly hinge on some
fairly traditional separation of private and public domains, as spheres
of principal engagement in society of women and men. That which he
has written makes it clear that the private realm of interpersonal
relations and exchanges revolves around child-bearing and rearing,
where men cannot expect to play as full a part as women. The
corollary of this would be that men are driven to make their main
contributions and sacrifices in the public realm, as it is here that they
are best able to repay their childhood debts to mothers and
grandmothers, by labouring to exploit nature to social purposes, and
through good works to ensure that moral values originating in the
private realm are honoured and upheld in the public. Observation of
Michael's behaviour certainly suggests that his idea of male destiny or
calling focuses around the imagery of serving causes emanating from
the community, especially women, though if possible without becoming
too tied down in the process. The good knight, having fought a
decisive battle and secured a position and resources for the infant cause

and its committed carers, soon feels restless and finds himself pledging his last drop of blood to a new mission.

This pursuit of a good cause can be so enthralling for Michael that he becomes oblivious to the need for personal rewards of those serving alongside him. Not long ago I was sitting with him in a rush-hour traffic jam (*why* won't he travel by tube?) on the way to a meeting called to plot the creation of a new organisation. We were picking over some ideas to float, and I trotted out a number of suggestions that I had been peddling for several years. Michael turned towards me and said warmly, 'You know, some of your ideas seem to be catching on at last: a lot of people are starting to say the same sort of thing now.' I muttered something about how irritating it was that so few of them were giving me any credit for risking to say them before they became popular. 'Oh! come now,' he said reprovingly, without flickering, his eyes now locked firmly onto the tail of a stationary yellow Routemaster, 'that does not matter surely. What is important is that public opinion is moving in the right direction.'

Time for a new crusade

This also goes to show, I suppose, how Michael's receptivity to public mood informs his timing of action so effectively. When the current wave of feminism was at full flood he kept his head down and got on with other jobs. But since feminism has mellowed and become more divided on strategic issues and started to worry about possible unintended consequences of its own campaigns Michael has been feeling his way back towards his original causes.

Beginning with his ESRC lecture on the family (1990a) and the work on after-school clubs (1992a) which led to Education Extra, and then through the Family Covenant Association, designed to bolster parental responsibility, to his recent lobbying with Frank Field on family income and the related pamphlet with Chelly Halsey about Family Socialism, Michael has been plugging away again at his basic theme since leaving the Labour Party research department - that the central concern of social policy should lie in finding ways to support women and build families and communities around the essential work which women do, and of endorsing the Demeter tie at the heart of this.

Since Michael left its service, the Labour Party has travelled a long way down the very different road of dismantling sexual divisions of labour and complementarity of roles in favour of publicly regulated equal opportunities. It is perhaps difficult to envisage this Party now believing that there is anything to learn from Michael. But it is significant, I think, that just at the recent moment of triumph for Emily's List there should have been heard within the party the voice of a veteran campaigner for women's rights, Clare Short, warning young female careerists that it might be time to reconsider whether opening up the public realm too radically may not risk leaving men without a valued and distinctive role to fulfil. Now that feminism has worked its way through the system and the fragility and artificiality of patriarchy is becoming evident, the hostile attitudes of the last two decades are dissolving. The idea of mothers as 'friends of the enemy' (Bunting, 1993) is giving way to rediscovery of the mother-daughter bond as a source of mutual support (Billington, 1994). So maybe enough women are now ready to embrace a Demeter concept, celebrating the collective strength of women and the moral centrality of the private realm, to allow serious renegotiation of roles with men at last.

It is not only the Left (virtually synonymous these days with statist feminism) which has much to learn still from Michael. I have written a good deal lately from a different perspective (most recently in *Transforming Men*) on the collapse in male motivation precipitated by de-gendering the public realm. And my main line has been to argue that men need to have some formalised priority in this domain in order to become responsible and productive members of society. But after considering Michael's latest ideas on family wages I can see that there are always several ways of approaching a problem, and that the direct line is not necessarily the best.

So, for example, instead of explicitly pushing the notion that men should normally expect to be main breadwinners in a household, why not just juggle with the welfare system to prioritise even further the rights and benefits of women, who perform most 'community' work, while stressing the citizenship *obligations* of men? In this way social attitudes will be encouraged to shift towards acknowledging both the value of caring activities to society generally, and also the need to provide paid work in order to elicit and organise a full contribution from men. This may be a better way to re-balance the spheres.

It is also more or less what Michael has always stood for. He has never proposed obstacles to women having paid jobs, and has himself employed disproportionate numbers of them to staff his empire. But he has not encouraged this at the expense of family work, and his advocacy of the welfare state in the forties was premised on an assumption of the primacy of caring work.

'Whatever the motives of the mothers, it is clear that the temptation (sic) *for women to work outside the home will be stronger where their allowances are small'* (1952b, p.318).

These are ideas which have not been heard for years, and which some people thought not to do so again. But they will be aired increasingly, I believe, in the concluding turmoil of this millennium, as we grope our way towards a new sexual contract. Michael will be there in the thick of it all: he may at last find the opportunity in this to round out the Demeter concept. Even if he does not, his vision lights the way for others, and the reaction which it has provoked helps us to see more clearly the nature of the issues and forces that are involved.

Consumer Power as a Pillar of Democracy
Naomi Sargant

In a speech to the Fabian Centenary New Year School in January, 1984, Michael Young set up a series of evocative images about the way in which technology was changing our lives. There has, he said, already been a shift of scale in people's lives outside work. The small (and private) has replaced the big (and public). The watch has replaced the public clock, the fridge has replaced the ice-factory, the washing-machine the public laundry, the private bath-room the municipal baths; TV, the cinema; the video-cassette, the pop concert; the car, buses and trains. And even so, he suggested, might the new home-computer and teletext replace the newspaper.

This contribution attempts to track the path Michael Young took from planning for 'large and public' state provision, through its implications for individuals, relating this to people as consumers both of private and public services and to ways in which individuals and groups might be informed and empowered to deal with that 'Big World'.

His ideas made immediate connections for me in relation to my time at the Open University and at Channel 4, particularly to adult learning. In broadcasting, the 'large and public' provision of terrestrial broadcasting is increasingly being replaced by the 'small and private' provision of video, CD-Rom and satellite dish. Public service broadcasting with universality of access linked with the idea of the community's investment in cultural and educational capital is under threat. Broadcasting has, until now, always been free at the point of use.

In the same way, we have for over a century provided education free at the point of use and paid for it through the community. Increasingly, however, it is argued that education and particularly training for adults do not feed into society's capital, but into private or personal capital, and that it should therefore be selectively not universally available, increasingly provided through 'small and private' provision, often using new technologies, rather than through conventional public education institutions and, of course, to be privately paid for.

What is significant about these changes is that they stem more from developments in technology than from political ideology. In themselves, they are neither all necessarily good or all necessarily bad.

They may be good for some people and bad for others. What they have to do with is ownership, accessibility, freedom and choice. Evidently, the 'small and private' are more accessible and offer more choice to the individuals that are fortunate enough to possess them or have the money to pay from them than the 'large and public'. We cannot hold back new technologies or control access to them, though we will wish to continue to regulate them to protect the public interest. It is up to us to choose to manage them rather than letting them manage us, or than letting a small number of people manage them or manipulate them on our behalf.

The state as benevolent provider

The Welfare State, for which Michael was to assist the Labour Party in developing policies, extended 'to the many some of the sorts of privileges once reserved for the few', (Young and Willmott, 1957) the main examples being education, hospitals and medical care, access to public housing, welfare benefits and the old age pension. But they were 'large and public' in their manner of provision, with little scope for individual choice, and accountability to their users was not a matter of major concern since their provision clearly represented such an advance for most people on their previous state. Because of their scale, they were usually natural monopolies, often public utilities, hence there was little choice and no market element involved.

Michael, in a recent introduction to his 1948 Labour Party pamphlet *Small Man, Big World* (Young, 1983c), described it as an 'early reaction against the creation of so many large new organisations by a government which was at that time extending nationalisation in every direction'. The leaders of the party allowed publication because they (like the author) recognised that they were impaled on a dilemma.'

> *'There is no doubt that democracy can most easily flourish in the family and in other small groups built to the scale of the individual. All the members there meet face-to-face; if a decision is to be made, all can have a direct and personal part in making it, and all can perceive the results of their decisions. Democracy therefore seems to require smallness. But efficiency, promoted by the growth of science, often requires bigness. This is the great dilemma of modern society.'*

The idea of accountability to consumers had not yet emerged; at that stage he was making the connection with democracy rather than with the interests of consumers and users of those services.

The original ideas behind his images were described in *The Symmetrical Family* (Young and Willmott, 1973a), under the heading of *Miniaturisation of Machines*. It was suggested that the 'symmetrical family' would not have developed as it has without the aid of technology, since technology had made it possible for the family to operate within the small frame of the home, in contrast to industrial production which had needed to be organised in larger groups in a work-place. Note, of course, that the further miniaturisation of technology and telecommunications is now increasingly also allowing work to take place in the home.

The images used pre-dated even the flowering of Victorian philanthropy: water from a collective well or a tap on a tenement landing, of collective leisure activities like horse-racing and a public hanging on Tyburn Hill, of collective transport, and entertainment such as the music-hall. The mechanisation of industrial processes had enabled the development of a key invention, the fractional horse-power motor:

> *'powering home-laundries, home ice-makers, tiny cold stores, floor cleaners and cooking aids ... (similarly) machines which have brought entertainment into the home, starting with the gramophone and ending (so far) with colour television.'*

Of course the better-off had access to their own bath-houses, ice-pits, carriages and private tutors some centuries before they were made available to the general population. Victorian philanthropy and enlightened self-interest coinciding with the industrial revolution led to the development of much municipal provision in the 19th century, including the foundation of many schools, universities and hospitals. The provision of these services developed into monopolies or near-monopolies of supply locally, more because of their scale, nature and the technology involved rather than for any philosophical reason. The Victorians would not have agreed with Margaret Thatcher when she said there was no such thing as society. It was implicit in such Municipal Socialism that it should be funded by the community at large, that it should be free or very low cost at the point of use and that it should be universally available.

The negative of these benevolent structures was that they did not allow much flexibility, individuality or choice in use, particularly in relation to geographical location. What happens, to return to Michael's scenario, is that as this trend increases and public provision is reduced, those who can afford the 'small and private' maintain their personal access and choice while those who cannot are increasingly denied it or may only be provided with a lower standard of service. The obvious example of this is the increase in car ownership, which has led inevitably to a reduction in demand for public transport with the result that the standards of service of trains and buses is now lower.

Consumerism and democracy

It is current Government policy to encourage the development of market forces in all walks of life and to reduce publicly provided services. In education and training, for example, they wish to disaggregate the services for which the community pays, like student maintenance, and encourage individuals to purchase the services they or their families want. These are services which until now people have assumed are universally available and free at the point of use, and funded by payment through the community. As a matter of equity and efficiency we would wish to try to ensure equality of access, though of course it is impossible to guarantee equality of outcomes. The proposal to shift payment for such services from the community as a whole directly to individuals and their families will erect a new and significant barrier to access: that of money.

Immediately we shift away from universality of provision and close regulation to a system in which people are expected to pay at the point of use, then it is necessary to look at users as consumers and not just as citizens and learners. There is a tendency only to associate consumerism with the market and with a right-wing government. This is of course incorrect. Michael describes himself as having

> *'managed to smuggle in (to the 1950 election programme) a proposal to set up a Consumer Advisory Service to give people unbiased information about goods and services on the market ... When the Gallup Poll asked people which of all the planks in the Labour election programme they favoured most, the Consumer Advisory Service came top in popularity. From a public source, it was a little private message to me.'*
> (Young, 1988a.)

The Consumers' Association

Michael was to become closely involved with setting up the Consumers' Association (CA) in 1956, and he later chaired the National Consumer Council, set up in 1975. Eirlys Roberts has provided a charming description of the origins of CA in a text celebrating its 25th anniversary. The push came from an American post-graduate student, Dorothy Goodman, seeking a UK equivalent to

Consumer Reports. Not finding one, she enroled half-a dozen of her husband's friends, (her husband was then Director of Political and Economic Planning (PEP)) to help her start one up. She set them to work producing dummy reports on a few simple products such as razor blades and it is recorded that:

> '*unhampered by facts the reports were fresh and lively, breathing confidence and showing their author's enjoyment. The enjoyment soon came to an end. Ray Goodman got a job in the World Bank in Washington, and his wife went with him, leaving Michael Young holding the unborn and unattractive baby, supported only by the small group of the Goodman's friends, by a certain natural obstinacy, and by a love of new things.*'

Eirlys Roberts, in an 'anonymous' introduction tells the reader:

> '*Remember (or imagine) your fellow-countrymen as they were in the early 1950s: reasonably proud of themselves (they had recently won a war against considerable odds) believing that society could be made more fair and more equal.*'

There was what she described as a 'feeling in the air ...' and some other strands of similar activity at the time. Elizabeth Gundrey was editing a magazine called *Shopper's Guide* for the British Standards Institution (BSI), Marghanita Laski started consumer pieces in the *Observer*, which were continued by Eirlys Roberts, encouraged to write in time spare from her job in the Treasury.

> '*Behind all this - and indeed the material from which the threads were drawn - was the general feeling of ignorance and helplessness on the part of the nation's shoppers and the fact that after years of austerity during and just after the war, more and more goods were coming into the shops and there was more advertising, including the first television commercials ... There was money about... Many people bought with gay abandon. Many others were afraid of being swept away ...*'

> '*Finally, there was a small group of theoretical people, mainly leftish in sympathy, who seemed to be committed to something which at least the economists among them thought was necessary and the lawyers thought was not impossible.*'

Michael was able to get a small grant from the Elmgrant Trust which, combined with a grant from the US Consumers' Union, gave the group enough money to advertise for a Director and plan the first issue. Its launch amazed everybody by its success, producing 10,000 members each paying their ten-shilling subscription, and its subsequent history is well-documented. He continued to be closely involved, doing a stint as Director before permanent staff were to arrive who were to become, in turn, pillars of the consumer movement. Jeremy Mitchell, then a market researcher, had worked in the Labour Party Research Department and was later to go to the Office of Fair Trading and become Director of the National Consumer Council, and Maurice Healy, the Deputy Editor of *Which?* who was in turn to become director of the NCC, were both part of that formative time.

The Consumers' Association at its peak reached a membership of over a million but has dropped now to just over 800,000 as a result of the economic recession and subscription increases. It works to a definition of consumers as:

> *'members of the general public in their role as purchasers of goods and services, whether privately or publicly supplied.'*

The start of CA was driven by the need to inform and protect the consumers of private sector goods and services. Jeremy Mitchell picks out five main factors which, he suggests, interacted to produce the consumer revolution (Mitchell, 1976). First, the rise in personal disposable income; second, expectations of higher living standards; third, diversity of choice of goods and services; fourth, technological innovation which has made existing products more complex and introduced entirely new products; and fifth, a dearth of information to enable the taking of rational decisions. Information, Jeremy Mitchell notes, was the dominant theme of the first wave of the consumer movement. The typical consumer organisation was independent of government, a membership organisation concentrating on comparative testing of goods and services and making the results available in magazine form. He points out that:

> *'The mode used to disseminate the information (and possibly the information itself) imposes limitations on the size and character of the membership. None of the consumer organisations (in different countries) would claim to be a mass movement, but the size of membership makes them a significant minority group ... Apart from their indirect influence on the market-place, through providing better*

*information, consumer organisations have been accepted by
government and adopted with enthusiasm by the media.'*

Michael, at an early stage, discussed the relationship between being a
consumer and being a worker and identified in *The Chipped White
Cups of Dover* the critical difference between the producer interest and
the growing consumer interest (Young, 1960a). Disenchanted with the
Labour Party and its ability to act as a reforming party, he argued that
politics would become less the politics of production and more the
politics of consumption and that a 'reforming party which would appeal
this new interest almost suggests itself'. He discussed what such a new
party might be called, using the term the Consumers' Party, but said
that 'consumers' was 'here little more than another name for
individuals'.

Consumers and public services

He was also preoccupied with the way in which the public services
treated people, pointing out that people are also consumers of the
public services, where 'the need for reform was if anything even
greater' and that nothing had been done by either party to humanise
these and reduce the pressure of bureaucracy.

> *'Private enterprise cannot totally disregard what consumers
> want ... But there is no such sanction in the public sector'.*

He used education and urban planning to make his case, suggesting
that what education was currently doing was making the social
hierarchy in the UK more marked than ever.

> *'The only way to counter the new sort of inequality and open
> a more fluid communication between people is to spend far,
> far more on ordinary education ... We have, as a nation, to
> show that we can provide a first-rate education for the very
> few without providing a second-rate education for the many
> ... I believe that if the question was left to the 'consumers'
> of this service, the parents, they would willingly pay the
> taxes ...'*

It is probably not a coincidence that the early 1960s saw him
developing the first of many educational ideas and innovations
designed to help individuals and families: the start of the Advisory
Centre for Education, the prophetic article suggesting an open
university in *Where?* in autumn 1962, and setting up the National

Extension College in 1963.

In a speech in 1964, *Consumers and the quality of life*, he pursued
these issues in greater detail, focusing on three dilemmas. First, the
needs of the poor versus the needs of the rich, second, the claims of
commercial products versus public services and third, the standard of
living versus the quality of life. He described the poor as being doubly
exploited because they have less money and because generally what
they buy is worse value for money. He added a third, and critical,
disadvantage - 'that they do not get the kind of information service on
the merits of goods and services that we (the consumer organisations)
are trying to present to the public'. In reiterating the point that people
are as much consumers of public services as of private, he asked 'if we
have not the duty to try and organise people, not just in consumer
organisations, but organise people as parents, as patients, as
passengers? And have we not the duty too to scrutinise such public
services as we have to make sure that their efficiency is improved,
certainly in line with the efficiency of private business?'

It is difficult to remember that the gap between public and private
services was so great at that time. There was also a gap between the
practitioners of market research and social research. His suggestion that
'We should undertake this new function of conducting research in order
to find out not only what our members think, but also what people
generally, the consumers at large think ...' sounded almost quaint to
someone like myself who had been carrying out market and social
research studies at the Gallup Poll for ten years. The gap was not to the
benefit of social research or market research. It extended beyond it to
the teaching of social sciences: for example, when a group of us
teaching Business Studies at Enfield College of Technology in the late
1960s wished to develop a part-time degree in Public Administration
precisely to try to improve the efficiency of the public sector, we
discovered that Public Administration had traditionally always been
built on a Social Studies base, and it was with great difficulty that we
persuaded the CNAA to approve such an innovation.

A national Consumer Council

A short-lived Consumer Council was set up in 1963 by one
Conservative government and closed down by another in 1970.
Learning from this experience, the existing National Consumer Council
(NCC) was set up under statute in 1975 as an independent consumer
body by the then Labour government. It is appointed and funded by
Government and works to a definition of consumers as:

'everybody in society in one part of their life: that is, as the

purchaser or user of goods or services, whether privately or publicly supplied.'

The general criteria developed by the NCC are similar to those of CA and cover access, choice, information, redress and safety and representation. The NCC as a statutory body also includes the criterion of equity: are consumers subject to arbitrary discrimination for reasons unconnected with their characteristics as consumers?

Michael was himself able to bring work for consumers of public and private services closer together when he was appointed the first Chairman of the NCC in 1975. Jeremy Mitchell, who had a hand in Michael's appointment as Chairman, noted that during the first year of its existence it had already extended 'consumer' beyond the market place to cover users of public services, particularly the social services.

Jeremy Mitchell was also concerned that 'consumer' should be defined in a way which distinguished itself from 'citizen'. He doubted whether coalitions of individuals who 'perceive themselves as having a common interest' could be maintained if 'people's interests as consumers were submerged in their more general interests as citizens'. The suggestion that there should be a Consumer Party does indeed emerge from time to time, and indeed the short-lived emergence of the Green Party resembles this in some ways. However, it is necessary to understand that there is little long-term community of interest among consumers: they come together sharing a short-term interest in a purchase, in an activity, in some provision or in an end-use, typically in a single-issue pressure group. They do not share a long-term goal and do not normally help the democratic process. The number of local consumer groups which survive is quite small.

This lesson was taught me forcibly when as chair of the National Gas Consumers' Council and at the same time serving on the National Consumer Council, we argued strongly for a long-term national energy policy with a conservative depletion strategy in order that finite fossil fuels would last the country as long as possible. The implication of this was that prices of gas and oil could rise and that money should be invested in conservation. The policy was roundly attacked by those taking the short-term view, particularly members of the National Fuel Poverty Forum who wanted 'cheap fuel for poor consumers now' and did not care about 'future grand-children'.

Jeremy Mitchell, in discussing the political significance of the consumer movement (Mitchell, 1976) accepted that 'consumer' now has a political as well as an economic connotation but noted that the meaning of the word appeared to be developing differently in the USA and the UK. In the USA, he suggested, there was kinship between consumer affairs and issues such as citizens' rights, the quality of life and conservation. In the UK he pointed to the extension of the interests of consumers of both public and private services, discussed the necessity to distinguish the definition of citizen from that of consumer and suggested that 'the consumer movement may work towards a model of the consumer as an active participant in decisions which affect him.'

Needs and provision beyond the state

This theme is taken further and related to groups of people working together in a tract Michael Young wrote with Marianne Rigge entitled *Mutual Aid in a Selfish Society* (1979a) which argues for the development of co-operation. In a chapter entitled *The new consumerism* the State is seen as the great provider, giving immense benefit. However, the system is 'vast and complex ... too unwieldy and impersonal. In short the system has become a system'. The examples of co-operation described in this tract are designed to show the growth of self-help or mutual-aid groups 'seeking to provide for themselves what the State has been unwilling or unable to provide for them'. A key to understanding is the use of both words 'unwilling' and 'unable'. Particularly in education, the institutions he has inspired, dreamed up or started himself are designed both to complement and supplement State provision but not or rarely to replace it.

In a recent speech, *Education beyond the state*, mapping existing educational provision against a set of criteria which included whether participation was compulsory or voluntary, whether provision was complete or partial, whether there were entitlements or rights for learners, who was responsible for funding, and how was it provided, there were ten extra educational institutions described that Michael had invented or provoked into being, ranging from the National Extension College to the Open School and Education Extra.

It is obvious where these themes converge and why education, particularly of adults, is the vital key. What is necessary is both information and the knowledge and confidence to use it to make good consumer decisions. The abilities to seek information, to judge its adequacy and to act on it are the important ones. The requirements are exactly the same in a democracy. The necessary prerequisite for good decisions is enough information and education. This is where the circle links. Many adults have had inadequate educational opportunities and have inadequate capacities for good decision-making. Many of the projects Michael has started or helped to set up have been to provide additional opportunities beyond those that the state has conventionally provided. Better educated adults are going to make better decisions both about their private purchases, their public choices, their families and their political decisions.

A major concern is that increasingly the provision of education for adults is being moved into the 'small and private' domain, seen as a private good to be privately paid for and not free at the point of use. Broadcast educational programming is still free at the point of use, but this may not last. As people are asked to pay personally for education, we need to return to the issue of consumer rights and protection for education itself. More important, as we approach the information society, while the convergence of technology will break down some barriers to information and learning, other new barriers to access will be set up, the most important of which will be financial. The probable division into people and countries who are information-rich and people and countries which are information-poor will be the challenge.

My Time with MY
Tom Schuller

The Beginning

Our first meeting was in the middle of the day, in Oxford. Michael had driven up from Devon - four hours - after observing nurses on night duty in Totnes hospital. We discussed time and work, the twin themes of a research proposal which we were planning to put to the Leverhulme Trust. Then he was into the car again to get back in time to observe Nurse Bellamy's next nocturnal round, which formed the opening scene of *The Metronomic Society*. Her round begins:

> *'Soon after 10 o'clock she wheeled her mobile desk out of the office into the middle of the ward. Lights out. Except as vague shapes she could not see her patients but, with her trained ear, she could monitor them continuously ... At any falter in the rhythmic sounds coming from each bed, she jumped up noiselessly to investigate.'*

And ends:

> *'As each bed and the hump under each coverlet emerged from its night shroud and the eyelids and the veined hands became suffused with the faint glow of the new day, this was the signal for Nurse Bellamy to wheel the desk back into the office and start her first ward round. Looking as fresh as if she also had been asleep, as she moved from one bed to another she knew which of the patients had feared they might never wake, and which had lost most of the faculties and been forced back on the hearing which she told me is the last sense to go, the last stronghold of people near death.'* (1988b, p.10.)

In Oxford the impression he left, along with a fragmentary research outline and a half-finished plate of digestive biscuits, was of concentration, willpower and gentle energy. Rhythm, which he was so committed to exploring as a fundamental characteristic of life, was harder to discern.

Beforehand

In the 1930s an American sociologist, E Wight Bakke, had walked the streets of the borough of Greenwich, observing the activities of unemployed men. How did they fill the hours forcibly vacated by mass worklessness? Bakke had gone on to help Michael found the Institute of Community Studies, a few miles north across the river. With the re-emergence of widespread unemployment, a follow-up study (if such a term can be applied when the gap is of such duration) seemed appropriate, and Michael had submitted a proposal to the Leverhulme Trust. The issue itself had, and has, tremendous contemporary salience, but with a strong historical perspective. So the *longue durée* could mix with the immediate, and with a personal link to add savour - for him an irresistible combination. I had just completed a book on pension fund management and approached the Trust for support for further work on changing patterns on work and retirement. Coincidentally we both indicated a preoccupation with time and its management, at the daily or the life course level. The Trust, in the person of Ronnie Tress, made the match and we began work together on the Greenwich study in 1983.

The study covered men and women aged 50-65 who had left employment, voluntarily or not, in the last two years: how had they coped with the gift of time? Bakke, for all his careful observation, had looked at behaviour rather than the clock. We wanted to match what people did to changes in the temporal structures of their lives, and so we looked for special inspiration across to Austria and the study carried out - almost contemporaneously with Bakke's - by another friend of Michael, Marie Jahoda, in the village of Marienthal.* Marienthal men lost all sense of time; they let their watches stop, and though they had nothing to do were as often as not late for the meagre dinners which their wives - busier than ever at eking out the family's resources - had prepared. We identified only those who had left full-time employment: what would get them up in the morning, what would start or finish their week, and what would tell them when it was time to eat?

The Problem of Time

We live in a time-rich society. Fewer and fewer of us have all our waking hours occupied by keeping body and soul together in the way

---

* Jahoda must be the only scholar to have studied unemployment in both the interwar and late 20th century periods; her reflective chapter for a book edited by Michael and me, *The Rhythms of Society* (1988c), was submitted with a note of complete modesty and openness to critical comment.

people had to in earlier centuries. The harassed executives putting in ironic overtime are minuscule in number compared with those who had in the last century to work overfull time to let capitalism flourish. There is now almost an inverse relationship between temporal and material wealth, but richness is not always healthy. Excess of time corrupts its quality, and one person's valued luxury is the next's suffocation. Some of that is because time and money are so intertwined, metaphorically but also practically; it is easier to conceive of things to do if you don't have to worry about the bus fare. 'If manure be suffered to lie in idle heaps, it breeds stink and vermin. If properly diffused, it vivifies and fertilises. The same is true of capital and knowledge ... A proper diffusion of them fills a country with joy and abundance.' (*Poor Man's Guardian*, 14 June 1834). The metaphor spreads: as with manure and capital, so with time. It is surprising to me that Michael has not yet come up with a policy for diffusing working hours more effectively, as a contribution to solving the curse of unemployment. But perhaps he has; often I would draw his attention to what I considered to be someone's innovative idea only to have him refer me, with suitable modesty, to a piece of his published years before and making the very same point. 'Ahead of his time' has literal application.

Discovering the Rhythms

The French call the post-war period *'les trente glorieuses'*. The phrase signals that steady growth, more or less stable employment and prosperity which is both increasing and, however gradually, more equally distributed are not permanent, but transient features of an unusual episode in the *longue durée*. The episode may recur, perhaps closely resembling its predecessors; the great Kondratieff's cycles give us a fascinating economic rhythm. This particular 30-year cycle is epitomised by the car factory: noisy, dirty, mostly booming and in the grip of massive international technological change. One such plant was a case study for us in Greenwich. We talked to forty men before and after they took special early retirement. How strongly were their personal rhythms shaped by the rhythm of the factory, and for how long did that last after they had walked through the gates for the last time? George Parker, a buy-off inspector in quality control, couldn't leave the shiftwork behind:

> *'Since I packed up do you know the weeks I'm supposed to be doing nightwork I can't sleep. It's unbelievable. Even now I keep dozing off throughout the day every other week. It's queer the habits you get, even going to the toilet.'*

But for Eric Tanner, a skilled but underemployed toolmaker and (until
now) frustrated pianist, life had changed completely:

> *'The only things that absolutely stuns me is the galloping of
> time. I mean, it's Thursday again, isn't it? I don't know
> what's best, whether it's to stand around for all those years
> and make your life long or* (laughter) *to work hard as I'm
> doing now* (practising piano) *and get it all over quickly. I
> forget which day of the week it is. That doesn't worry me,
> provided I remember to sign on.'*
> (*Life After Work*, 1991d, pp 42, 44).

Paid time and free time are twisted together; sometimes, like ivy, paid
time chokes free time, sometimes it gives the necessary contrast for it
to be savoured.

Discerning organisational time patterns meant trawling through the
car factory's ultra-Taylorist handbook, with its prescribed actions such
as drilling cotter-pins specified to three decimal places of a minute
(1.729 in this case), and looking at the fuel bill:

> *'A kind of wave motion ran through the day's production,
> beginning slowly at the start of a shift while the men on the
> later machines waited (as if for a tide) for the first of that
> day's output to reach them. The hourly rate accelerated after
> that and reached a peak in the late morning. In the
> afternoon there was a gradual slackening till knocking-off
> time. These ups and downs over the course of the day were
> clearly shown by the fluctuations in the electricity load curve
> for the factory.'* (*Ibid.*, p.35).

Mundane detail blended with illuminating imagery are characteristic of
Michael's style, cherished as a matter almost of personal integrity.

Organisational time, fuel bills and daily lives figured largely in
some early work presented to another of Michael's creations, the
Association for the Social Studies of Time. ASSET met for the first
time in Bethnal Green, then in Cambridge, and after that has held
annual conferences in Dartington.

At the third conference Mayer Hillman first put forward his case
for bringing the UK into line with European time, saving energy costs,
extending our access to all kinds of leisure facilities and reducing
traffic deaths and injuries. It became something of a ritual for us to
receive at Dartington an annual update on the progress of this
campaign, with its near-triumph in the late eighties and its subsequent
patient progress.

Time to Finish

Sunday morning in the study at the top of Gibson Square. We are struggling to finish *Life After Work*, delayed by his efforts on *The Metronomic Society* and my moving to a new job. As part of the study we left diaries with our interviewees. Diaries as such are not unusual instruments in social science research, but we were looking not just for what people did but what regularities there were in their lives. It was not only the number of hours or minutes spent doing things, nor when or where they were done, but how often and with what regularity. Just what kind of timetables do we follow, and how far is the image of clockwork applicable to modern times? Did they do more or less the same thing at the same time every day, or every week? We were looking for a formula which would fit numerical patterns to the complexities of daily activities and also match the characters of the men and women we had interviewed. In the end we are not able to devise one adequate for the purpose, but the diaries yield powerful and often sad insights:

> 'Like T S Eliot's Mr Prufrock measuring out his life in coffee spoons, Mr Sawyer measured out his in teaspoons, cigarettes and treacle sandwiches. "I have a fag every two hours to make the time pass. It's the same with cups of tea, and at 11.30 every morning I treat myself to a treacle sandwich."' (*Ibid.*, p.117).

At least Mr Sawyer had a structure, however rickety; for others, the diaries confirmed the sheer blankness of the days and nights.

It is a notable portent for the future, with its certainty of more variegated occupational and leisure patterns, that not one of those whose time structures had collapsed was a woman. We depicted the gender difference through the images of cables and cats' cradles. Men's lives have been built round a single span of continuous work, whilst women knit together different strands. This makes the internal contrasts very different, with clock-time dominating in one sphere and task-time in the other. But since we foresaw a convergence over time of male and female patterns, in successive cohorts and within individual life courses, Mrs Bright makes a good example. She had been a single parent when that was still highly unusual, and as a result had worked a man's life - 44 years of it:

> 'Her current satisfaction came from a sense that she'd served her time and partly from the sheer novelty of being paid to do nothing. Her money dropping regularly through

*the letter box was a source of wonder. Time was not a tragic
gift but a glorious one. She was almost as glad to have no
children at home as to have no paid work. Leaving work was
"like being in the delivery room and you've just delivered -
my God it's a relief. Then it was the beginning of another
traumatic life but with this one there's no catch to it". And
about the children - "Everyone said you'll break down when
they go. But I couldn't wait to be rid of them. I had three
'glads'. 'I'll be glad when you're five and go to school; I'll
be glad when you go to work; and I'll be glad when you get
married and out of the house'." ... The rhythm with her
grandchildren was in happy contrast with what it was like
with her own children. "With my children everything was a
rush but I've got time with the grandchildren. When they're
here nothing gets done, only the cooking, because we've got
better things to do, playing silly games and having a song."'*
(*Ibid.*, p.135).

Characters like Mrs Bright are worth lingering over, but we are both
aware that the book has to be finished quickly if the research is not to
appear too dated; I more than Michael am aware of the weekends
which it has eaten up. The sessions in the study are punctuated by
phone calls; if I leave for two minutes to make a cup of coffee, the
odds are that he will be on the phone when I return - filling the
interstices of time like an obsessive plasterer. Co-authorship is
involving but sometimes disorienting, like partnering a headstrong jazz
soloist. At the end of the session comes another irony: to fix the next
date, Michael fishes out from his pocket what must be the smallest
personal diary on the market.

Personal Time

We worked on the routines and rituals of everyday lives - habit as the
'flywheel of society'. Recognisable routines have not in my experience
been a strong feature of Michael's life. Rituals are in a different
category. We unreasonably subtitled our book, 'The Arrival of the
Ageless Society', arguing against the excessive current use of
chronological age. But the need for ceremonies to mark transition
points in people's lives is something very different. We observed and
heard how people can be caught in the age trap: left in a painful limbo,
they were neither in employment nor, in their own or society's eyes,
retired. 'Early' retirement implies an established norm, but this norm
is arbitrary as well as recent, and increased longevity makes it look
increasingly so. (Bismarck's 1885 establishment of 70 as the retirement

age should be related to life expectancy at the time of 42; the same ratio today would yield a retirement age of over 120, or just over 90 if only adult life expectancy was considered.) Longevity, though, is about how long individuals live, and they deviate stubbornly from the standard. Michael was already thinking about the final frightening transition well before Sasha contracted cancer. I had little contact with him during those painful days. But the picture published in the *Guardian* of Sasha on her death bed, with Michael kneeling at her side, will mark a small turning point in many people's attitudes to that last passage. It is a beautiful, domestic image (taken by a friend) to challenge the agonising taboo which ringfences the dying.

How personal time horizons change:

And Next Week?

It would now be utmost joy
If under grey London skies
The streets spattered with litter
Gripping our arms tight
(She could still do that)
Sasha would hobble down the steps
Into the NHS wheelchair
To ride through our garden gate
Past the geraniums and the beercans
It was almost a daily outing

This week her muscles are so wasted she cannot move
She has almost hidden her pulse
Her hands are trembling.
While she is asleep,
Groaning a little now and then
Her open eyes are staring blind.
Her mouth is aghast
To suck in the gasps of air
Which is all her straining lungs can pump.
Last week, cannot I have last week again?
(1994a, p.58)

A line runs out, and yet the circle turns. In her introduction to that book of poems by Michael and Sasha, their daughter Sophie tells how her return from seclusion in a Buddhist monastery coincided with her mother's final illness. It is a synchrony which brought support to them all; family time at the last.

Time and Place
Asa Briggs

Michael Young has such a strong sense both of place and of time that what he has to say about each is strictly relevant to any assessment and appreciation of his ideas and of his actions. It is the particular that stimulates his imagination and rouses his energy. Because of this he is unusual among sociologists, a label that is in any case inadequate to describe him. He prefers associations to abstractions.

Two of the places that have mattered most to him and still matter - Bethnal Green and Dartington - contrast sharply with each other. Yet there are contrasts inside each of them. 'It's all right on this side of the canal,' says Mrs Gould who lives in Bow. 'I wouldn't like to live on the other side of the canal. It's different there.' At Dartington, where you could 'go off to the woods', for many years there were no footpaths between the new hamlets and the old. Solitude and propinquity relate to each other.

Both *Family and Kinship in East London* and *The Elmhirsts of Dartington* begin not with place but with time. 'This book is about the effect of one of the newest upon one of the oldest of our social institutions'. 'The eight richly-coloured heraldic shields on the carved angels under the hammer beams of the Hall bear the arms of the successive owners of Dartington Hall. There is a notice to say so.' The sociologist in *The Rise of the Meritocracy* is a historical sociologist. The book ends at 'the great rostrum of Peterloo' and with the footnote 'The failings of sociology are as illuminating as its successes.'

A list of the titles of Michael's many publications does not immediately focus on time and place. Dartington is a real place, not a utopia. East London is too big a concept. *The Symmetrical Family* exposes more family complexities than the title implies. Yet among the long list there is one major time book, *The Metronomic Society*, which examines not sequences but cycles, as a previous paper in *Nature* written with the physicist John Ziman. The terminology used in the paper is illuminating, but it is this preoccupation that is most significant in relation to the whole range of Michael's work, which is as much concerned with 'rhythms' as with 'processes' and with 'the passage of life' as much as with 'ways of life'. He wrote a favourable review of Phillida Salmon's *Living in Time* - 'the subject is tremendous - life itself' - while stressing rightly that the idea that life 'itself is a natural cycle is no more a metaphor, as she stated, than the circulation of the blood.' 'Our growth and decline is the source of endless metaphors: it is not in itself a metaphor.'

Michael's choice of books to review deserves attention along with his choice of what books to write, and he was obviously stimulated by time books as different as Nigel Calder's *Timescale, an Atlas of the Fourth Dimension* and Stephen Kern's *The Culture of Time and Space.* 'Scale' matters much to Michael when he turns (and nature, not contrivance, is always behind the turning) from imagination to action. *Small Man, Big World*, 'the discussion of socialist democracy', still stands out, although it was written in 1948. The volume of essays *The Rhythms of Society*, which he edited with Tom Schuller and which introduces the term 'chronosociology' should be set alongside review articles like 'Parish Councils for Cities'.

'Great Britain has the advantage of size over the two great United States of East and West,' Michael wrote in *Small Man, Big World* when many people thought the opposite. 'It is not so big that it will be impossible to form an integrated society within the ken of the individual'. And in the essay which he wrote with Edward Shils on 'The meaning of the Coronation' in 1953 he brought in the time dimension when he wrote (or perhaps Shils wrote) that 'British society combines free institutional pluralism with an underlying moral consensus.' A historian would want to place both these statements within a historical context, 'over time', that has changed irretrievably between 1948 and 1953 and 1995 at least as much as during the span of *The Rise of the Meritocracy* between 1870 and 2033 - if in very different ways.

Michael's unique capacity to spawn ideas and active social agencies has been given a natural play because while he knows about institutions he does not - and he has not - served them. Nor has he ever measured time entirely by the clock. He has also carried with him his sense for place to distant as well as familiar places. South Africa at a crucial stage in historical change has captured him in the same way as Dartington and Bethnal Green. As he reaches his birthday, a special birthday, he has his own continuing chronology and his own private map. It includes France, and it has been expressed in pictures, not charts. It was also expressed in Sasha and Michael's book of poems, *Your Head in Mine*, with its beautiful introduction by Sophie Young. The best lines about time are Sasha's:

> *'For fourteen years I moved through time like someone*
> *Walking in water, the least ripple gone*
> *To merge into the next before it was begun.*
> *So everything was now.'*

To Honour the Dead
Mary Douglas

Michael Young has often honoured anthropologists by a creative interest in the fields in which they work. For this occasion I could choose among a number of subjects to which he has contributed a vital idea, or a standard work. I have chosen one he is currently writing about so as to pay tribute to the continuing freshness of his inspiration.

The question is how the dead are treated in different places and times. As his readings show, he knows that this has always been a mainstream anthropological interest. He believes that in this day and age we should give more prominence to death in our culture, pay more respect to the dying, comfort the mourners more effectively by talking about their loss and encouraging them to talk instead of veiling the topic in silence. Generally, he admonishes us to follow foreign examples, and to compare forgetful and uncaring behaviour of modern industrial society with other places where the dead are given more honour and respect.

My argument is going to be that regard for the dead is not something that can be laid on independently, it is part of the regard for the living. This will not be an uncongenial point to make. Michael has worked all his life to protect solidarities, as between young and parents, and between young and old. His concern for the relation between living and dead is a straight continuation.

It would be out of character for him to recommend that the dead be honoured by grander monumental masonry. I am sure that he does not want us to devise more expressive public ceremonials. I think that his solution is to start by changing the conversation. However, he must know that it is difficult to transform a whole culture of embedded reticence. It is hard enough to make a deliberate speech reform; to reform a silence is a tall order. Is it possible to bring into the open topics which persons prefer to keep private? He is too sophisticated to think that talking in itself will overcome a reluctance to speak. He would like us to confront death verbally, so as emotionally not to avoid it. But he knows that some bereaved persons find it an unbearable pain to talk about their loss, and that friends who force them to talk intrude unforgivably into their privacy. He also understands that drawing a new line between what is held to be private and what is in the public sphere is not something that individuals can achieve on their own. Defining

209

what can be brought across from private to public is a collective matter.

This being so, it remains to think what else can be done, since preaching is ineffective. He is undubitably right in believing that our uncommunicative, impersonal way of death fails to do honour to the suffering of the dying and the pain of mourners. Anthropologists have no solutions, but we can try to draw comparisons. We could compare our attitudes to death with our attitudes to other matters. We could compare other things that we are reticent about. Haim Hazan, an anthropologist who has spent his youth studying old age, has a similar complaint about contemporary attitudes to aging; people do not want to talk about it, he says, and when they do, they wrap it in stereotyped disguises, so that it cannot be seen for what it is (Hazan, 1994). He suggests that not confronting old age is a way of not confronting death (p.68).

So no sooner begun we are back again at the starting point. Hazan also suggests that thinking more openly about old age and death may be an epistemological impossibility. If he is right, the subject that Michael wants us to confront may always have to be presented in cultural stereotypes. The anthropologist's craft does not help us to pierce those metaphysical veils. Instead I propose to consider how boundaries around speech are made, and then I will question the implicit idea that speech gives honour, not silence.

Sometimes reserved areas where silence reigns are absolutely necessary for friendships to continue. How can Cavalier and Roundhead, Jew and Arab, Serbian and Croat, for example, live and work together and even be friends when they know that their parents fought and perhaps killed each other? How can former enemies inhabit the same space after peace has been declared? Part of the answer is by the spontaneous creation of vast areas of silence, subjects which may not be broached at all and others which can only be mentioned with elaborate circumspection. It is necessary to say little about disagreements one may have had with the dead, or with why they died. Commemoration of one may leave others arbitrarily uncommemorated. The young Israeli soldiers who fell in the devastating Israeli War of Independence in 1948 have become the subject of a new genre of commemorative literature. The books which honour the fallen soldiers give more prominence to native born than to immigrant soldiers (Sivan, 1994). The myth arose without intention to demean the role of immigrants or to forget the role of civilians killed in the war, it supported the politics of Israel under siege, and no one who would have liked to restore the balance of memory felt free to say anything. This illustrates why it is often awkward to know what to say about the dead, to be fair to the living, to be fair to the other dead. It is all very well to tell us to speak freely about the departed, but we have to be careful.

Talking openly about the dead can be a help to mourners, but it has to be well done and it is more difficult than it might seem. A tradition would help. Christians who have lost a Jewish friend are invariably impressed by the Jewish funeral; not just by the simplicity and sincerity, but especially by the extraordinary level to which the art of the homily has been brought. Without any warning, the speaker produces from a sheaf of notes, usually written overnight, a vision of the whole person; the childhood promise, the trials of youth, the later achievements, presented movingly with wit and charm. How different from the Christian funeral service of which Michael complains. His many questions might be reduced to the one: why can Christians not bury each other with that kind of loving respect which affirms the dignity of life in general, as well as affection for the life just completed? Is it to do with Christianity? Or to do with living in an impersonal industrial society where our lives are allowed to grow separately? I doubt that the answer will be found in doctrine, but is more to do with how our lives are intertwined.

If the modern Jews do funerals well, it is not a thing that is written in the Bible. The priests were not allowed to conduct burial ceremonies (Leviticus 21) so the topic was from the outset directed to the private sphere. Biblical Judaism tried to root out spiritualist seances, conjuration, necromancy, magic of all kinds. The standard explanation is that the Bible was written against the other religions, so against the Egyptian worship of the dead, and against the divination through spirits of the dead that the people of Israel might have known through early Canaanite neighbours or through Babylon, and, above all, against polytheism. More importantly than a spirit of contrariness, the idea was that consulting spirits of the dead is close to demonism, and contrary to monotheism. Tracing how the enmity of the priestly editors to magic was enforced gives us a glimpse of how Judaic monotheism was achieved. The great word that synthesised all forms of wrongdoing was the idea of uncleanness. In the Bible any contact with a dead human body was accounted unclean, and any attempt to establish communication with the dead was regarded with disgust; hanging around tombs, touching corpses or using bones for oracles, any cult of the dead, were sins against the first commandment conveying major uncleanness.

The result is that biblical Judaism absolutely ruled out any cult of the dead. Nor is there in it any elaborate doctrine of what happens to persons in an afterlife. The dead must be buried quickly, so that the living can avoid contamination of death. If there ever was a culture that did shun the topic of death it would be biblical Judaism, but the conversation is exactly what Michael seems to have as the ideal; the dead person is respected and the mourners comforted. It would certainly comfort the bereaved and might even assuage some of the fear of dying to know that such a valediction is in store.

At a guess, I would suggest that the just and generous judgments in the Jewish homily are an example of enclave behaviour. An implicit theory of mortuary reticence needs to be brought to the surface. Living abroad, an enclaved minority could be so anxious for its boundary between the godless world outside and the fragile life of the spirit within its walls that members would be eager to take the opportunity offered by a death to reinforce solidarity. Members of a self-conscious minority group are concerned to value the person of each and every one of their number. An enclave has standardised its moral judgments, so there is less danger of putting a foot wrong than in an amorphous section of a plural society. But living at home, though the members of a less well defined community might still want to use the sad occasion to enhance solidarity, they might be inhibited. Better say nothing than say the wrong thing. Delivering a homily in a community unsure of what its boundaries are, the preacher might have to tread carefully in the criss-cross of local ties and rivalries, and speak warily among divergent moral and political views. This is the start of my anthropological approach to the question. Sometimes reticence is better.

If my guess is wrong, it can be proved so. We would only need to compare funeral orations in the dominant culture and in its dispersed minority segments; for example, do the enclaves of Irish in New York at mortuary rites conform more to Michael's ideal than the Irish in Eire? Or, how do the Hindu funerals in London compare in this respect with the much more formal funerals in India?

The Jewish example is a good beginning of comparisons, because it leads us to separate the failure to confront death in conversation, from respecting the dead, and consoling the bereaved, and choosing appropriate ceremonies. When we consider that the Bible gives the reader a religion that goes straight to God and does without the intervention of the dead we ought to realise that this is more of an achievement than it sounds. As a doctrinal policy it has its costs.

The beloved dead are irresistibly available, a category of persons and powers able to be used by the living who knew and loved them. Their availability is modified according to convention; usually the nearest kin of the dead have most to hope for from them in counsel and help. Sometimes the relation is elective: children are taught to find out which of their dead kin is most interested in them; in a spirit of enquiry they make little prayers or libations, and by trial and error can find which deceased uncle is keenest to sponsor him, then the tie between live nephew and dead ancestor becomes established. Or the choice of a living representative lies in the power of the dead, to be declared by a medium in a seance. Among the Shona in southern Rhodesia in the 1960's the spirits of the dead took an active interest in politics and chose their representatives with a keen eye to furthering the cause of independence. Invisible threads connected certain of the living to certain dead, jumping erratically across lineal and other kinship links and showing only at rituals of possession (Fry, 1976).

The variety of the possible relationships between living and dead is probably infinite. The dead of an ancestral cult may be credited with no choice but to protect their own descendants in strict lineal order. In such a system they are likely to find themselves poised one against another at appropriate levels of social segmentation. The patterns of the ancestors correspond to the patterns of the living, lineage poised against lineage, and at the apex one great creator God with final authority. Ancestors are not impartial. They decidedly favour their own followers. By avoiding cults of the dead altogether, for whatever doctrinal reason to do with monotheism, the Bible also avoided a socially divisive principle. People who pay cult to the dead usually invent some cross-cutting principle vested in the authority of another level of spiritual being, to control aggression between descent groups (Douglas, 1993, 1995). For the Bible editors such an option would have been ruled out by monotheism: God was not to be conceived as the top figure in a layered bureaucracy of divine beings.

For a very egalitarian society, God's law did well to exclude the specific internal divisions that enter with cults of the dead. That is on the plus side. On the minus side there is a disadvantage in not being able to drive division underground by laying blame on the dead. Some societies make the dead carry the burden of everything that goes wrong. Dead spirits can be ill-willed and very capricious: when they are seen in this light, we should give the community the credit for a consensus about not blaming the living. They refuse to let their community be torn apart by feuds and factions, and they agree that when there is doubt about responsibility for damage, the dead can bear it. Here again is another hunch, one that cannot be allowed the status of a fact, for the comparative work to give the idea acceptance is not in hand. My sense is that the community that can thus deflect important strife towards the absent dead has found a way of living together in harmony.

I have given these instances of how cults of the dead make a difference to the society in which they are found. This prepares the ground for approaching the question of talking about the dead from another angle. Not talking is a way of paying respect. One occasionally hears of people who do not allow the name of a dead person to be spoken. I used to wonder if this rule obliterated the deceased from living memory, or whether on the contrary it created a column of silence which would always recall the absent loved one, like the empty chair at the table or the bedroom left for ever undisturbed.

Patrick Williams in his *Nous, On N'en Parle Pas* emphatically answers Yes to the last speculation. As the title suggests, this impressive modern ethnography is about NOT speaking of the dead. The Mānuš are a gipsy community who came from Germany some two hundred years ago and have lived since then in the north of the Massif Central in France. About thirty thousand of them, living by collecting and selling scrap metal, they make a world of their own in the middle of France. Nothing shows, nothing on the surface is changed, they live discreetly and on the surface deal with other people in a normal way, but invisibly their civilisation has triumphantly appropriated the whole universe. The word superficial has no meaning in describing them, for there is no surface, everything is rooted deep in their culture.

No one and no thing that they have not stamped with their interpretation counts at all. No one from outside can gain admittance. The sign of their cultural completeness and separateness is the way they live among their own dead. One of the derogative definitions of the outsider is lack of respect for the dead. As their invisible dead are to the Mānuš among whom they live, so the life of the Mānuš is to the outsiders among whom they live. The difference largely depends on knowledge, from knowing the Romany language to knowing how to hunt hedgehogs and butcher them correctly for eating, and of course, on knowing what to do with the possessions of the dead. When someone dies, everything that belonged to him or her is taken out of circulation. Caravans or trucks may be burnt, or sold; souvenirs may be wrapped up; a ring is not worn. Other things may be on view, but there is no visible sign that things that are being kept in memory of a dead father or child are different from other things seen around. An inherited thing (if that is a fair description) will not be lent in case the dead owner is dishonoured by swearing in its presence. No one can swear at or maltreat the dog or, in the old days, the horse of the dead person. The things of the dead stop circulating and no one can profit from them. Any cash realised from the sale of such a dedicated possession, for example the dead man's truck, will be devoted to the care of the graves.

This form of memorialising by making an empty space is taken to a more developed point in the habits of speech. The rules are that the name of the dead person is not mentioned by his or her close kin; at the same time, those who are not kin are under obligation to talk about him and use his name. In a cross section of time, the refusal to name the dead would show up as pillars of silence surrounded by acclamations and naming. But over time the roles are exchanged, close kin gradually drop the practice of silence and start carefully, affectionately and respectfully to speak of their dead, while the others begin to feel less obliged to keep remembering stories about them. Meanwhile, new deaths are occurring, and the same process is being constantly renewed, so that every member of the community is bound tight in the shifting web of rules about naming and not naming the ever present dead.

Imagine a stranger trying to enter a conversation where all this was going on. There could not be a more exclusionary device. It falls halfway between never speaking about the dead and speaking of them casually as if they had never gone: here respect requires naming of the dead in precisely regulated ways.

This beautiful example suggests something for Michael's concern that we should care more about death, dying and the dead. For one thing, it suggests that we need to know each other well in life, if we are to know how to honour each other afterwards. When the Christian pastor or Jewish rabbi who is conducting the service chooses to say a few words about the occasion, he is completely at a loss if he has never met the bereaved family till the evening before the ceremony. He does his best, but in doing it his words only betray the distance created by mutual ignoring in the past.

For another thing, the case confirms what I hinted about living and dying in a minority enclave. The members make it their business to know each other, they dread losing their members to the outside, sorrowfully they count the mixed marriages and dropouts. The death of a member gives them a chance to revive the life of the fellowship. Fundamentalism may have its drawbacks for outsiders. Fundamentalists do not hesitate to tell us where we are going wrong. But we should not overlook the blessings of the good death and the good funeral that they can promise to their fellowship, even in modern industrial society.

Chapter References

(A bibliography of Michael's own main writings follows this section. These notes refer only to *other* materials, grouped according to the chapter of reference).

Resolving the Dilemma of Bigness (pp.1-7)

Peter Marris (1958) *Widows and Their Families*, Routledge and Kegan Paul.

Peter Marris (1961) *Family and Social Change in an African City: a Study of Rehousing in Lagos*, Routledge and Kegan Paul.

Peter Marris & Martin Rein (1967) *Dilemmas of Social Reform: Poverty and Community Action in the United States*, Routledge and Kegan Paul.

Peter Marris (1982) *Community Planning and Conceptions of Change*, Routledge and Kegan Paul.

Plowden Report (Central Advisory Council for Education) (1967) *Children and Their Primary Schools*, HMSO.

E Shils (1985) 'On the eve: a prospect in retrospect' in M Bulmer (editor) *Essays on the History of British Sociological Research*, Cambridge University Press.

Peter Townsend (1957) *The Family Life of Old People: an Enquiry in East London*, Routledge and Kegan Paul.

Peter Willmott (1966) *Adolescent Boys of East London*, Routledge and Kegan Paul.

Knowledge and Persuasion: Research at ICS (pp.75-83)

Note: This paper discusses the early work of ICS, and does not attempt to do justice to the Institute's work as a whole, and the contribution of those who joined it later. Some of the books referred to in the text are already listed in the notes (above) to Resolving the dilemmas of bigness. The other references are:

Alvin W Gouldner (1970) *The Coming Crisis of Western Sociology*, New York.

Jennifer Platt (1971) *Social Research in Bethnal Green* Macmillan, London.

Hearing what they say, knowing what they mean (pp.85-92)

Robert Aunger (1995) 'On Ethnography. Storytelling or Science?' *Current Anthropology* XXXVI, 1.

Mark Clapson (1992) 'Playing the system. The world of organised street betting in Manchester, Salford and Bolton, c.1880 to 1939' in Andrew Davies & Steven Fielding, eds., *Workers' Worlds*. Manchester, Manchester University Press.

Helen Forrester (1979) *Twopence to Cross the Mersey*. London, Bodley Head.

Hannah Gavron (1966) *The Captive Wife*. London, Routledge.

Peter Hiller (1975) 'Continuities and Variations in Everyday Conceptual Components of Social Class' *Sociology* IX, 2.

Mark Hudson (1994) *Coming Back Brockens*. London, Cape.

M E Loane (1908) *From their Point of View*. London, Edward Arnold.

David Lockwood (1992) *Solidarity and Schism*. Oxford, Clarendon Press.

Gordon Marshall *et al.* (1988) *Social Class in Modern Britain*. London, Hutchinson.

Ross McKibbin (1990) *The Ideologies of Class*. Oxford, Clarendon Press.

W G Runciman (1966) *Relative Deprivation and Social Justice*. London, Routledge.

"   (1983) *A Treatise on Social Theory*. Volume I. Cambridge, Cambridge University Press.

"   (1991) 'Are there any irrational beliefs?' *Archives Européennes de Sociologie* XXXII, 2.

Practicing What You Preach (pp.93-96)

Noel Annan (1990) *Our Age: portrait of a generation*. London: Weidenfeld & Nicholson.

V Carasov (1971) *Two Gentlemen to See You, Sir: the autobiography of a villain*. London: Gollancz.

The Sociologist as Man of Action (pp.123-128)

Note: This chapter is an updated version of the Introduction written by Daniel Bell to Young (1983a).

Ronald Blythe (1969) *Akenfield*. London, Allen Lane.

Charles Booth (1889-1902) *Life and Labour in London* (18 vols.) London, MacMillan.

William Morris (1892) *News From Nowhere*. London, Kelmscott Press.

R H Tawney (1920) *The Acquisitive Society*. New York.

"   (1931) *Equality*. New York.

H G Wells (1933) *The Shape of Things to Come*. New York.

The Ups and Downs of the Meritocracy (pp.153-162)

Paul Barker (1968) 'Michael Young' *New Society*, vol 12 No. 304, 8 August, reprinted from *Interplay* [New York].

Zelda Cheatle and Michael Mack (eds) (1993) *The Street Photographs of Roger Mayne*, Zelda Cheatle Press.

Bernard Crick (1980) *George Orwell: A Life*, Secker & Warburg.

Susan Crosland (1982) *Tony Crosland*, Jonathan Cape.

Geoffrey Crowther (chairman) (1959) *15 to 18*, HMSO for the Central Advisory Council (England).

H C Dent (1954) *Growth in English Education, 1946-1952*, Routledge & Kegan Paul, cited in Peter Hennessy, *Never Again: Britain 1945-51* (Jonathan Cape, 1992).

David Donnison (1967) 'Education and opinion' *New Society*, vol 10 No. 265, 26 October.

Margaret Drabble (ed) (1985) *The Oxford Companion to English Literature*, fifth edn., Oxford University Press.

Robert Hewison (1988) *Too Much: Art and Society in the Sixties, 1960-75*, Methuen.

Richard Hoggart (1957) *The Uses of Literacy*, Chatto & Windus.

Nicholas Lemann (1994) '2034' - review of new American edition of 'The Rise of the Meritocracy' *Atlantic Monthly*, vol 273 No. 6, June.

Colin MacInnes (1959) *Absolute Beginners*, MacGibbon & Kee.

Magnus Magnusson (ed) (1990) *Chambers Biographical Dictionary*, fifth edn., Edinburgh: Chambers.

Charles Murray and Richard Herrnstein (1994) *The Bell Curve: Intelligence and Class Structure in American Life*, New York: The Free Press.

Iona and Peter Opie (1959) *The Lore and Language of Schoolchildren*, Oxford: The Clarendon Press.

Paul Rock and Stanley Cohen (1970) 'The Teddy Boy', in Vernon Bogdanor and Robert Skidelsky, *The Age of Affluence, 1951-1964*, Macmillan.

Raphael Samuel (1994) *Theatres of Memory*, Verso.

Edward Shils and Michael Young (1953) 'The meaning of the Coronation' *The Sociological Review*, new series, vol 1 No. 2, December.

Herbert Spencer (1864-7) *The Principles of Biology*, Williams & Norgate, 2 vols.

Jonathan Swift (1729) *A Modest Proposal for preventing the Children of poor people in Ireland, from being a Burden to their Parents or Country; and for making them beneficial to the Public*, Dublin: S. Harding; reprinted in 'Macmillan Anthologies of English Literature', vol 3, Ian MacGowan (ed), *The Restoration and 18th Century*, Macmillan, 1989.

Raymond Williams (1958) *Culture and Society*, Chatto & Windus.

Note: At Thames & Hudson, Helen Scott-Lidgett kindly gave access to the publisher file of newspaper and magazine reviews of the first British and US editions of *The Rise of the Meritocracy*.

Man of Merit (pp.163-175)

J E Floud, A H Halsey and F M Martin (1956) *Social Class and Educational Opportunity*.

Barrington Moore Jr. (1978) *Injustice; The Social Bases of Obedience and Revolt*, London, Macmillan, p.107-8.

Peter Saunders (1995) "Might Britain be a Meritocracy?", *Sociology*, 29,i, Feb.

Kurt Vonnegut Jr. (1952) *Player Piano*, London, Macmillan.

Tracking the Demeter Tie (pp.177-186)

Madeleine Bunting (1993) 'The lost generation' *Guardian*, 7th September.

Rachel Billington (1994) *The Great Umbilical: mothers, daughters, mothers*, London, Hutchinson.

Geoff Dench (1995) *Transforming Men*, New Brunswick, Transaction publishers.

Susan Faludi (1992) *Backlash*, London, Chatto & Windus.

Charles Madge (1943) *War-time Patterns of Saving and Spending*, Cambridge, NIESR.

Jennifer Platt (1971) *Social Research in Bethnal Green*, London, MacMillan.

Consumer Power as a Pillar of Democracy (pp.187-197)

HMSO (1991) *The Citizen's Charter: Raising the Standard*, Cm 1599.

Jeremy Mitchell (1976) 'Management and the consumer movement', Vol 3 no 4 *Journal of General Management.*

Eirlys Roberts (1983) *Which? 25 - Consumers' Association 1957-1982.* London, Consumers' Association

Naomi Sargant (1994) 'Education beyond the state', in *Conference Proceedings of British Comparative and International Education Society.*

To Honour the Dead (pp.209-215)

Mary Douglas (1993) *In the Wilderness, the Doctrine of Defilement in the Book of Numbers*, Sheffield Academic Press.

Mary Douglas (1995) 'Demonology in William Robertson Smith's theory of religious belief', William Johnstone, editor, *Essays in Reassessment*, Sheffield Academic Press.

Peter Fry (1976) *Spirits of Protest, Spirit Mediums and the Articulation of Consensus amongst the Zezuru of Southern Rhodesia*, Cambridge University Press.

Haim Hazan (1994) *Old Age, Constructions and Deconstructions*, Cambridge University Press.

Emmanuel Sivan (1994) 'The Life of the Dead: Sabras and Immigrants', editor Jonathan Frankel, *Reshaping the Past: Jewish History and the Historians*, Studies in Contemporary Jewry, The Avraham Harman Institute of Contemporary Jewry, The Hebrew University of Jerusalem.

Patrick Williams (1993) *Nous, On N'en Parle Pas, Les Vivants et les Morts chez les Manouches*, Paris, Collection Éthnologie de la France, Éditions de la Maison des Sciences de l'Homme.

Main Publications and Writings of Michael Young

This is not a complete list of Michael's writings, as that would be a volume in itself. It covers books and pamphlets, plus his main articles, reports and key lectures. What it leaves out is a multitude of reviews, speeches and conference papers, press releases and manifestos, obituaries, minor articles or book contributions, and shorter or less significant research and institutional reports. Not all editions and versions of publications are listed; but those subsequent editions which *are* included here are placed with the first edition rather than under the year of their own publication.

1938   *Manpower Policy*, Political and Economic Planning Broadsheet no.133.

1940   *Paying for the War*, PEP Broadsheet no.160.

1941   *London under Bombing*, PEP Broadsheet no.169.

1943a   *Financial Mysticism*, PEP Broadsheet no.188.

1943b   *Will the War make us Poorer?* With Henry N Bunbury, OUP. (Oxford Pamphlets on Home Affairs, No. H5).

1943c   *Employment for All*, PEP Broadsheet no. 206.

1944   *Civil Aviation*, Pilot Press.

1945   *Let us Face the Future*, Labour Party Election Manifesto.

1947   *Labour's Plan for Plenty*, Gollancz: Left Book Club.

1948a   *What is a Socialised Industry?* Fabian Society.

1948b   *The Social Sciences*, Labour Party Research Document 118.

1948c   *Scientific Policy Committee: the Social Sciences: Proposal for the Establishment of a Social Science Research Council,* Labour Party Research Document 172.

1948d   'Industrial Democracy', *Towards Tomorrow* no.1 (Labour Party discussion document).

1948e   'Public Ownership, the Next Step', *Towards Tomorrow* no.2.

1948f   'Small Man, Big World: A discussion of socialist democracy', *Towards Tomorrow* no.4.

1950   *The Future of Industrial Assurance: Labour's proposals for mutual ownership by the policyholders,* Labour Party Discussion Pamphlet.

1951   *For Richer for Poorer,* Report to Labour Party Research Departrment.

1952a   *Fifty Million Unemployed,* Labour Party Discussion Pamphlet.

1952b   'Distribution of income within the family', *British Journal of Sociology,* vol.III. no.4.

1953a   'The meaning of the coronation', (With Edward Shils) *Sociological Review,* vol.1, no. 2 (New series).

1953b   *Draft Proposal for the Establishment of a London Institute of Community Studies,* (unpublished).

1954a   'Kinship and Family in East London', *Man,* vol. LIV no.5.

1954b   'The role of the extended family in a disaster', *Human Relations,* vol.VII no.3.

1954c   'The planners and the planned: the family', *Journal of Town Planning Institute,* vol.XL no.6.

1954d   'Social grading by manual workers', (with Peter Willmott) *British Journal of Sociology,* vol.VII no.4.

1955   *Seven Million Bathrooms,* Report to Labour Party NEC.

1957   *Family and Kinship in East London*, (With Peter Willmott)
         Routledge & Kegan Paul. Penguin paperback edition, 1961.
         Revised Routledge edition, 1986.

1958   *The Rise of the Meritocracy*, Thames & Hudson. Random
         House, New York, 1959. Penguin paperback edition, 1961.
         Transaction Publishers, New Brunswick, New Jersey, 1994
         (with new introduction). Also translated into *French, German,
         Italian, Dutch, Danish, Norwegian, Swedish, Finnish, Japanese
         and Spanish.*

1960a   *The Chipped White Cups of Dover: a discussion of the
         possibility of a new progressive party*, Unit 2.

1960b   *Family and Class in a London suburb*, (With Peter Willmott)
         Routledge & Kegan Paul. Nel Mentor paperback, 1967.

1961a   'Old age in London and San Francisco,' (With Hildred Geertz)
         British Journal of Sociology, June.

1961b   'The Institute of Community Studies, Bethnal Green', (With
         Peter Willmott) *The Sociological Review*, July.

1962a   'Is your child in the unlucky generation?' *Where?* no.10.

1962b   'Education, regression and mobility', (With Chris Wallis)
         Paper to *5th World Congress of Sociology*, Washington DC,
         Sept.

1963a   *Note on a Possible Reform League*, (With Edward Shils, Peter
         Willmott, Peter Marris) Sent to Anthony Crosland.

1963b   'In search of an explanation of social mobility', (With John
         Gibson) *The British Journal of Statistical Psychology*, vol XVI
         part 1.

1963c   'Announcing the National Extension College' ,*Where?* no. 14.

1963d   'Who uses correspondence colleges?' (With Christine Farrell)
         Where? no.14.

1963e   'The mortality of widowers', (With Bernard Benjamin & Chris
         Wallis) *The Lancet*, 31 August.

1963f   'Family life in 1984', *New Scientist,* November.

1964a   *The Future of Independent Schools,* For Fabian Society.

1964b   *New Look at Comprehensive Schools*, (With Michael Armstrong) Fabian Society Research Series 237.

1965a   *Innovation and Research in Education,* Routledge & Kegan Paul.

1965b   'The flexible school: the next step for comprehensives', (With Michael Armstrong) *Where? Supplement 5.*

1967   'Give us back the Thames' and 'The next 17,000 tides' (Both with Peter Willmott) *Observer*, 16 July.

1968a   *The Story of the National Extension College*, (With Brian Jackson) Sent to Open University Planning Committee.

1968b   *Learning Begins at Home: a study of a junior school and its parents,* (With Patrick McGeeney) Routledge & Kegan Paul.

1968c   'The liberal approach; its weaknesses and its strengths', *Daedalus*, vol 97 no.4.

1968d   *Forecasting and the Social Sciences,* (ed) Heinemann.

1969a   'Social reform in the centrifugal society', (Michael as member of 'The Open Group') *New Society Pamphlet.*

1969b   *Why our Susan? Comprehensive Schools: the case for parental choice*, Harringey Parents Group.

1970a   'Parish schools for cities', *New Society*, 29 January.

1970b   'Up schools' *New Society*, 2 April.

1970c   'How urgent are London's motorways?' (With Peter Willmott) *New Society*, 10 December.

1971a   'Cycles in social behaviour', (With John Ziman) *Nature*, vol 229 no. 5280.

1971b 'The increasing obsolescence of childhood education', *The Times Saturday Review*, 9 January.

1971c 'On the air: the end of a phase', (With Brian Jackson & Peter Laslett) *Where?* no.53.

1971d *The Hornsey Plan: a role for neighbourhood councils,* (With John Baker) Association of Neighbourhood Councils.

1971e *The Young-Chesworth report,* (With Donald Chesworth) Mauritius College of the Air.

1971f 'Foreword' (in V Carasov, *Two Gentlemen To See You, Sir: the autobiography of a villain,* Gollancz).

1972a *One Year's Work,* (With Tony Dodds & Hilary Perraton) IEC

1972b 'Historical changes in social cycles', *Journal of Interdisciplinary Cycle Research*, vol 3 no.2.

1972c *Lifeline Telephone Services for the Elderly,* (With Peter Gregory) National Innovations Centre.

1972d 'Is equality a dream?' 1st *Rita Hinden Memorial Lecture*, at Bedford College, 18 November.

1972e 'What might have been?' *New Society*, 2 November.

1972f *Sport in the London region,* (with Peter Willmott) Report to Sports Council.

1972g 'Dilemmas in a new Europe', (in *The Future is Tomorrow: 17 prospective studies,* European Cultural Foundation, Martinus Nijhoff, The Hague).

1973a *The Symmetrical Family: a study of work and leisure in the London region,* (With Peter Willmott) Routledge & Kegan Paul Penguin paperback 1975.

1973b *Multi-media Education in Swaziland,* International Extension College.

1973c *The International Extension College, 1972-73,* (With Hilary Perraton & Tony Dodds) IEC.

1973d 'A day in the kitchen', *New Society*, 15 November.

1974a 'Women - the new poor' (With Lucy Syson) *Observer*, 17 January.

1974b 'The unacquisitive society,' (With Tony Lynes) *Observer*, 17 March.

1974c 'The shortening of childhood and the lengthening of education', Opening address at Centenary Seminar, *Universities in a Rich and Poor World*, University of Adelaide, August.

1974d *Poverty Report 1974*, (ed + Intr. + chapters) Maurice Temple Smith.

1975a 'Poverty in a West German town', (With Jorg Munstermann & Konrad Schacht) *New Society*, 6 March.

1975b *Poverty Report 1975*, (ed + Intr. + chapters) Maurice Temple Smith.

1975c *For Richer, for Poorer: some problems of low income consumers*, (ed) HMSO (National Consumer Council).

1976   'Education on the defensive' (With S. Duncan) in Peter Willmott (ed.) *Poverty Report 1976* Maurice Temple Smith.

1977   'Towards a new concordance', *New Society*, 17 November.

1979a *Mutual Aid in a Selfish Society*, (With Marianne Rigge) Mutual Aid Press.

1979b 'A manifesto for co-ops: a return to an older definition of socialism?' (With Marianne Rigge) *New Society*, 26 April.

1979c 'China's co-op shops', *New Society*, 1 November.

1979d 'Hackney survey: support for alternatives,' *Where?* July/August.

1980   *Distance Teaching for the Third World: the lion and the clockwork mouse*, (With Hilary Perraton, Tony Dodds & Janet Jenkins) Routledge & Kegan Paul. Revised edition, 1991, IEC.

1981a   'Never go out after dark', *New Society*, 15 January.

1981b   *Prospects for Workers' Co-operatives in Europe*, (With Marianne Rigge) Commission of EC.

1981c   *Report from Hackney*, (With H Young, E Shuttleworth & Wyn Tucker) Policy Studies Institute.

1981d   *Bigness is the Enemy of Humanity*, SDP Open Forum.

1982a   *The Elmhirsts of Dartington - the creation of a utopian community*, Routledge & Kegan Paul.

1982b   *Inflation, Unemployment and the Remoralisation of Society*, Tawney Society Pamphlet no.2.

1982c   *The Middle of the Night*, (ed., with Peter Hall) Tawney Society Pamphlet no.4.

1983a   *Revolution From Within - co-operatives and co-operation in British industry*, (With Marianne Rigge) Weidenfeld & Nicholson.

1983b   'The round of time: A sociologist's view' 7th *Barnett Shine Memorial Lecture*, Queen Mary College, May.

1983c   *Social Scientist as Innovator*, (collected papers) Abt books, Cambridge Massachusetts.

1984a   'Progressive education at Dartington, 1930s to 1980s' 8th *W B Curry Lecture*, University of Exeter, 7 June.

1984b   'The mutual aid/self-help movement' in *Mutual Aid Universities*, (ed. E Midwinter) Croom Helm.

1985   'How to cultivate Martians on an old Scottish island', *Guardian*, 3 August.

1986   'Coping strategies used by nurses on night duty,' (With Jeffrey Adams & Simon Folkard) *Ergonomics*, v.29 no.2.

1987   *The Chipped White Cups of Steel*, Unit 2.

1988a   'Education for the New Work' in *Open Learning in Transition,* (ed. N Paine) NEC.

1988b   *The Metronomic Society,* Harvard University Press and Thames & Hudson.

1988c   *The Rhythms of Society,* (ed. with Tom Schuller) Routledge.

1988d   'My hero: Michael Young on FDR', *The Independent Magazine,* 15 October.

1988e   'Choice from cradle to grave', *Samizdat* no. 1.

1989a   'Social Democratic Party and co-ops', *Journal of Comparative Studies,* no.64.

1989b   'Will Keir Hardie get wet in the rainforest?' *Samizdat* no.7.

1990a   *Death and Modern Culture,* Lecture given at University of California at Santa Barbara, 25 February.

1990b   'Planetary ethics and planetary politics', (With Geoffrey Thomas) *Samizdat* no.10.

1990c   'The future of education' 1st *Dartington Annual Lecture,* 22 June.

1990d   'Liberating the old and the young: the case for an ageless society' *Presidential Address to British Association for Advancement of Science,* August 23.

1990e   '25 years of the ESRC', (MY et al.) *Social Sciences,* issue 7, HMSO.

1990f   'From nation-state to world society', (in *The Alternative: politics for a change,* Eds. Ben Pimlott, Anthony Wright & Tony Flower. W H Allen & Co.).

1991a   'A haven in a heartless world: the future of the family' 1st *ESRC Annual Lecture:* delivered 6th December 1990, published 1991.

1991b   'Slaves of time', *New Statesman & Society,* 12 July.

1991c   *The Development of Adult Basic and Secondary Adult Education in South Africa*, (With Tony Dodds & Greville Rumble) IEC.

1991d   *Life After Work: the arrival of the ageless society*, (With Tom Schuller) Harper Collins.

1992a   *Campaign for Children's After-school Clubs: the case for action*, (With Matthew Owen) ICS.

1992b   'Change, British society and the family', Lecture given to National Commission on Education, and published in their *Insights into Education and Training*, Heinemann, 1994.

1992c   'Death', (Contribution to *Encyclopedia of Time*, ed. Sam Macey, Garland Publishing Inc.).

1993   *The Relevance of Community*, Address at Funerals Conference at Mansfield College, Oxford, 18 April.

1994a   *Your Head in Mine*, (With Sasha Moorsom) Carcanet Press.

1994b   *The Dead Citizen's Charter*, Speech to launch National Funerals College, 11 June.

1994c   'The prospects for Open Learning', Lecture given on the 25th Anniversary of the Open University, and published in *Open Learning* vol.10 no.1.

1995a   'Obituary: Edward Shils', *Guardian*, 8 February.

1995b   'Robben Island calling', *Guardian*, 15 March.

1995c   *Family and Community Socialism*, (With A H Halsey) IPPR.

1995d   *A Good Death*, (With Lesley Cullen) Routledge (forthcoming).

Biographical Outline for Michael Young

1915	Born August 9th, Manchester.
1929-35	Dartington Hall School, Totnes, Devon.
1938	BSc., London School of Economics.
1939	Called to Bar, Gray's Inn.
1939-41	Political & Economic Planning (PEP).
1941-45	Director, PEP.
1942-92	Trustee, Dartington Hall.
1945-51	Secretary to Research Department, Labour Party.
1953	Founding Director, Institute of Community Studies.*
1953	PhD, London School of Economics.
1956	Founding Chairman, Consumers' Association.*
1959	Founding Chairman, Advisory Centre for Education.*
1961-66	Fellow, Churchill College, Cambridge.
1962	Founding Chairman, National Extension College.*
1963-66	Member, Central Advisory Council for Education.
1965	Hon. LittD, Sheffield University.
1965-68	First Chairman, Social Science Research Council.
1967	Founding Chairman, Dartington Amenity Research Trust.
1970	Founding Director, International Extension College.*
1972	Director, Mauritius College of the Air.*
1973	Hon. Doc., Open University.
1974	Visiting Professor, Ahmadu Bello University, Nigeria.
1974	Hon. DLitt, University of Adelaide.
1975-77	First Chairman, National Consumer Council.
1975-78	Member, National Economic Development Council.
1977	Founding Chairman, Mutual Aid Centre.*
1978	Life Peer: Baron Young of Dartington.
1978	Hon. Fellow, London School of Economics.
1980	Hon. Fellow, Plymouth Polytechnic.
1981-83	Member, Policy Committee, Social Democratic Party.
1982	Founding Chairman, Tawney Society.*
1982	Hon. LLD, Exeter University.
1983	Founding Chairman, College of Health.*
1983	Hon. Fellow, Queen Mary College.
1984	Founding Chairman, Argo Venture.*
1985	Regents' Lecturer, University of California, Los Angeles.

1987	Founding Chairman, Open College of the Arts.*
1987	Founding Chairman, Health Information Trust.*
1989-92	President, Birkbeck College.
1989	Founding Chairman, Open School.*
1989	Founding Chairman, *Samizdat* magazine.*
1991	Hon. DLitt, Keele University.
1992	Founding Chairman, Education Extra.*
1993	Founding Chairman, National Association for Education of Sick Children.*
1994	Founding Chairman, National Funerals' College.*
1994	Hon. Doc. University of East London.
1994	Founding Chairman, Family Covenant Association.*
1995	Hon. Fellow, Churchill College, Cambridge.
1995	Hon. Fellow, British Academy.

*   See the following Directory of Organisations linked to ICS for details.

Directory of Main Organisations
Linked to or Founded through the ICS

The Institute of Community Studies

ICS was set up during 1953-4 in Bethnal Green to carry out social research. But in the event its actual role for much of its existence has been as a fast-breeder and first home for new ideas and the organisations needed to put them into practice. Most of the other bodies listed here have at some point, usually at their formation, operated from within the ICS building; and many of those which have moved out still have a close connection with ICS and their sister bodies, often mediated by Michael's continuing participation and overlapping of boards of trustees.

Michael has been Director of ICS from its foundation to the present day, with Peter Willmott as Co-Director for many years. The other early members were Peter Marris and Peter Townsend. The current trustees of ICS are Peter Willmott (Chairman), Michael Young (Director), Tony Flower, Roger Warren Evans, Paul Barker and Kate Gavron.

NB. Linked organisations are listed here alphabetically, with dates when first initiated (and terminated, where known) given in parentheses. Note that this is not an exhaustive listing, and does not cover all organisations referred to in the text. Many small or short-lived ventures, or those in which Michael has not been greatly involved himself, are not included.

Advisory Centre for Education (ACE) (1959-)

ACE was founded as a follow-up to CA, to provide information to parents and other interested parties on educational matters. The publishers of *Where?* magazine, for many years ACE occupied the basement at ICS, until moving to Highbury Grove in the mid-Eighties. Michael was Chairman until 1976, and has been President since then.

Argo Venture (1984-95)

The aims of this shifted (see Tony Flower's contribution) from the setting up of simulated space colonies to the establishment of the National Space Museum in London. It published *Britain's Future in Space*, by Martin Rees. Michael was Chairman, with Tony the Director.

Association of Neighbourhood Councils (1969-)

ANC was set up to press for the establishment of 'neighbourhood' or 'urban parish' councils as part of the restructuring of local government. It was based in Bethnal Green for some years before moving out. (See the chapter by Andrew McIntosh).

Association for the Social Study of Time (ASSET) (1983-)

Has a more academic focus than the other organisations, and promotes conferences and research. Co-founded by Michael, now Chairman, and Tom Schuller (whose discussion in the text gives more information), who is now Secretary. Still run from ICS.

Bethnal Green Exports Ltd (1964-66)

This company was formed after the balance of payments crisis of the early sixties to promote exports from Bethnal Green and East London generally, by providing services to businesses too small to have their own export department. Also known as Bethex.

Brass Tacks Workshops

An offshoot of the Mutual Aid Centre, this was an employment-creating scheme giving work to young people in refurbishing household appliances and furniture from which Michael and MAC eventually withdrew in the mid-eighties.

Centre for Educational Choice (1988-)

Established to study and promote small non-fee-paying schools started by parents groups and others, with Tony Flower as its initial Director. It's first publication was *Save Our Schools*.

Centre for Electoral Choice (1987-)

Promoted tactical voting in elections, with Michael as Chairman and Tony Flower as Director. Produced the *Consumers' Guide to Tactical Voting*, written by Iain McLean.

College of Health (CH) (1983-)

The purpose of CH is to apply mutual aid strategies to the promotion of patients' interests in the NHS. Its journal evolved into *Which way to Health?* now published by CA. Co-founded by Michael, who was Chairman until 1990, with Marianne Rigge, now Director. Currently occupies premises down the road from ICS. (See contribution by Marianne Rigge)

Commuter Study Clubs (1980-)

Also known as the Brain Train. Created to organise study clubs on British Rail commuter trains into London. Directed by Pamela Le Pelley.

Consumers' Association (CA) (1956-)

Founded to promote the consumer interest through its magazine *Which?* The Association was set up in garage in Bethnal Green next door to ICS, effectively from 1956 but formally not until 1957. Michael was Chairman until 1965, then President until 1993. His link is now as non-active 'Founding President'. (See Naomi Sargant's and Jeremy Mitchell's contributions.)

Education Extra (EE) (1992-)

This is the operating title of the *Foundation for Children's After School Activities Ltd* (1991-), set up to encourage and enable schools to offer children after hours activities, in order to enrich their lives and extend their learning. Michael was Chairman 1992-94, and is now 'Founder and patron', with Kay Andrews as Director and Mike Walton Deputy Director.

Family Covenant Association (FCA) (1994-)

Established to promote alternative forms of baptism or 'welcoming ceremonies' for children. Produced guidebook *How to make a family covenant* by Tony Flower with Michael. Director is Rosie Styles.

Health Information Trust (1987-)

This was created to administer Healthline and a number of other related information services. Initial Director, Tony Flower.

Healthline (1986-)

A pioneering telephone information service on health matters set up by Michael with Marianne Rigge, and then run by Tony Flower. Now part of the College of Health.

Institute for Social Studies in Medical Care (ISSMC) (1970-94)

Developed by Ann Cartwright as Medical Care Research Unit within ICS, becoming autonomous as ISSMC in 1970. (See her contribution in main text).

International Alert (1981-)

Founded by Michael with Leo Kuper and others, as an international forum on ethnic conflict, genocide and human rights, to protect threatened peoples and promote reconciliation and peace. Martin Ennals was the first Secretary-General, and the present incumbant is Kumar Rupesinghe.

International Extension College (IEC) (1970-)

This was created in order to carry new methods of open learning to Africa and Asia, and has close links with many institutions which it has helped to set up, such as Mauritius College of the Air, which was the first IEC college, and had Michael Young as its first director. It has always been based in Cambridge, but has shared some administration with ICS. Michael is still Chairman of IEC. Tony Dodds is Executive Director; see his chapter in the text.

Language Line (1990-)

A telephone interpreting service, initially for local minority groups, but later a national (and now international) service. Michael still chairman. Director Tom Pointon. Currently housed within ICS.

LinkAge (1988-95)

Intended to bring together people of grandparent age without grandchildren, and of grandchild age without grandparents. Michael chairman until 1990, when it moved out and became part of Community Service Volunteers, with Tricia Adams as Director.

Milton Keynes OK Service Station Ltd (1978-)

A community garage which provides professional hands-on training in car maintenance, and produces training videos. Managing Director Bill Dredge; other directors Roger Warren Evans and Tony Flower.

Mutual Aid Centre (MAC) (1977-)

Has a general brief to promote schemes operating on the basis of mutual aid. It has become the vehicle for creating a number of offshoots including the Commuter Study Club, Milton Keynes OK Service Station Ltd, College of Health, Healthline and Language Line. Michael is currently chairman, with Tony Flower as Secretary and a trustee. Other trustees are Roger Warren Evans and Paul Barker. Based at ICS still.

National Association for the Education of Sick Children (NAESC) (1993-)

Developed from within Open School (See contribution by Kirsteen Tait) to secure educational provision for hospitalised children. Still at ICS.

National Extension College (NEC) (1962-)

This was the first open learning institution in Britain, and the pilot project for the Open University. Based always in Cambridge. Michael was Chairman until 1971, and has been President since. Director Ros Morpeth. (See commentary by Peter Laslett in this volume).

National Funerals College (1994-)

Founded by Michael with Revd. Peter Jupp to promote training for officiants at funeral services. Peter Jupp is Director and Michael the Chairman. Administration split between Bethnal Green and Peterborough.

National Innovations Centre (1968-74)

In the CA mould, and lineal successor to the *National Suggestions Centre* (1967-8), and publisher of *What?* magazine. Director Richard Luce and Editor Rudolf Klein.

Open College of the Arts (OCA) (1987-)

First-in-the-world open learning institution for teaching the practical skills of a wide range of the arts. Current Chairman Bob Gavron and Director David Davies, whose chapters here should be consulted.

Open School (1989-)

Founded to adapt Open University methods for the school level. Concentrating on teacher-shortage subjects which are highlighted by the national curriculum. See the discussion in main text by Kirsteen Tait. Michael still Chairman.

Open University

See National Extension College.

Samizdat (1988-90)

A centre-left political magazine promoting 'the popular front of the mind'. Michael Chairman, Ben Pimlott the initial Editor and Tony Flower Managing Editor and producer (later Editor).

Social Audit (1972-)

Set up in 1972, to develop and apply mechanisms for ensuring the disclosure of information and social accountability in major centres of power. (Current chairman Christopher Zealley, and Directors Charles Medawar, Andrew Phillip, Elaine Rassaby and Anthony Sampson. Secretary Maurice Frankel.) Link loose since 1980.

Tawney Society (1982-88)

The SDP's equivalent of the Fabian Society. Produced regular pamphlets and newsletters; seminars, workshops, lectures and summer schools. Tony Flower general secretary.

Thameside Research and Development Group (1967-9)

Formed to promote the development of London's riverside areas and active in initiating revival of St. Katharine's Dock. Director Nigel Spearing.

University of the Third Age (U3A) (1982-)

Founded by Michael with Peter Laslett, Eric Midwinter and Dianne Norton to promote and encourage mutual education among older people. Now over one hundred local U3As operating. Michael the first chairman but not now formally involved.

Contributors

Paul Barker is a writer and broadcaster, and a senior fellow and trustee of the Institute of Community Studies. He was the Editor of *New Society* from 1968 to 1986.

Daniel Bell is Henry Ford ll Professor Emeritus of Social Sciences at Harvard University, and scholar-in-residence at the American Academy of Arts and Sciences. His books include *The End of Ideology* and *The Coming of Post-Industrial Society*.

Tessa Blackstone is Master of Birkbeck College and frontbench opposition spokesman on foreign affairs in the House of Lords. She has been a member of the Central Policy Review Staff in the Cabinet Office (a recent book is *Inside the Think Tank: Advising the Cabinet*), was chairman of the BBC's General Advisory Council from 1987-91 and is currently chairman of the trustees of the Institute for Public Policy Research and a trustee of the Natural History Museum.

Asa Briggs was Chancellor of the Open University from 1978 to 1994 and Provost of Worcester College, Oxford, from 1976 to 1991. His many books include *The Age of Improvement, Victorian Cities, A Social History of England*, and a five-volume *History of Broadcasting in the United Kingdom*.

Vincent Brome is an author, feature writer and broadcaster, who has written numerous novels, biographies, plays and essays. His books include *Jung, Man and Myth, The Problem of Progress, The Day of the Fifth Moon*, and *J B Priestley*.

Ann Cartwright worked at ICS from 1960 to 1970, running the Medical Care Research Unit, and was then Director of the Institute for Social Studies of Medical Care until 1994. Her recent books include *Parents and Family Planning Services* and *Health Surveys in Practice and potential*.

Sue Chisholm has been personal secretary to Michael at the Institute of Community Studies since 1971, and in that capacity has worked for or with many of the organisations referred to in this collection.

David Davies has been a research oceanographer, Editor of the science journal *Nature*, Director of the Dartington North Devon Trust and, since 1989, Director of the Open College of the Arts. Through all of this he has also done much communal music-making.

Malcolm Dean has worked on the *Guardian* for 26 years and is social policy leader writer and Editor of the Wednesday 'Society' section. Over the years he has collaborated with Michael in launching a number of ventures and campaigns.

Geoff Dench is a professor of sociology at Middlesex University. Two recent books are *Minorities in the Open Society* (short-listed for the Amalfi European Prize for Sociology) and *The Frog, the Prince, and the Problem of Men.*

Tony Dodds is Executive Director of the International Extension College, which he has worked with (as its first full time employee) since its foundation in 1971. Before that he worked in adult and distance education in Africa, on which he has written extensively.

Ronald Dore is senior research fellow at the Centre for Economic Performance at LSE, where he has formerly been a professor of sociology. He has spent most of his life studying and writing about Japanese society and economy.

Mary Douglas trained as an anthropologist at Oxford and in Central Africa. She is currently an honorary fellow of University College, London University, and has written numerous books including *Purity and Danger*, *Natural Symbols* and *Risk and Blame.*

Tony Flower is a deputy director of the Institute of Community Studies, a director of the Mutual Aid Centre, and a consultant to or trustee of many organisations including the Joseph Rowntree Reform Trust Ltd., Gaia, Education Extra, and the Museum of the Earth.

Kate Gavron has worked extensively in publishing, and is currently Chairman of Carcanet Press and Virago Press. She is also a research associate and trustee of the Institute of Community Studies.

Robert Gavron was the founder (and Chairman 1964-93) of St Ives plc, and a director of Octopus Books plc. He is Chairman of the Open College of Arts and of the Folio Society, a director of the Royal Opera House and a trustee of the National Gallery.

A H Halsey is Emeritus Professor of Social and Administrative Studies in the University of Oxford and an emeritus fellow of Nuffield College. His books include *Origins and Destinations*, *Change in British Society* and *The Decline of Donnish Dominion*.

Peter Laslett has been a fellow of Trinity College, Cambridge, since 1953, and Director of the Cambridge Group for the History of Population and Social Structure since 1964. His books include *The World we have Lost* and *A Fresh Map of Life*.

Peter Marris was at ICS from 1955 until 1973, when he joined the Centre for Environmental Studies. In 1976 he became professor of social policy planning at the University of California in Los Angeles. For the last four years he has been teaching at Yale University and writing novels. His books include *Loss and Change* and *Meaning and Action*.

Andrew McIntosh is Deputy Leader of the Labour Opposition in the House of Lords. He has been chairman of the Market Research Society, of the Association for Neighbourhood Councils and of the Fabian Society.

Jeremy Mitchell works independently as consumer policy adviser to governments and public bodies and has written and edited several books on consumer protection. He has been Deputy Research Director at the Consumers' Association, Secretary of the SSRC, Director of Consumer Affairs at the Office of Fair Trading and Director of the National Consumer Council.

Marianne Rigge has been Director of the College of Health since 1983. Her books include *Prospects for Worker Co-operatives in Europe* and (with Michael) *Mutual Aid in a Selfish Society*.

W G Runciman is a fellow of Trinity College, Cambridge, and was recently chairman of the Royal Commission on Criminal Justice. His books include *Relative Deprivation and Social Justice* and *A Treatise on Social Theory*.

Naomi Sargant is currently honorary senior research fellow at the National Institute of Adult Continuing Education. She was on the National Consumer Council and chaired the National Gas Consumers Council, and has been professor of applied social research and a Pro-Vice Chancellor at the Open University. Her books include *Learning and Leisure* and *Adult Learners, Broadcasting and Channel 4*.

Tom Schuller is Director of the Centre for Continuing Education at the University of Edinburgh. He was with the ICS from 1983 to 1985 and, with Michael, co-authored *Life after work* and co-edited *The Rhythms of Society*.

Trevor Smith is Vice-Chancellor of the University of Ulster and Chairman of the Joseph Rowntree Reform Trust Ltd. He is a past president of the Political Studies Association. Recent books are *The Politics of the Corporate Economy*, and *British Politics in the Post-Keynesian Era*.

Kirsteen Tait is Director of the National Association for the Education of Sick Children, and London director of the Open School. Previously she has been private secretary to Shirley Williams at the Department of Education and Science, and more recently head of the British section of the Abu Dhabi Department of Historical Records.

Patricia Thomas is Deputy Director of the Nuffield Foundation and the author of *Aims and Outcomes of Social Policy Research.*

Wyn Tucker is a deputy director of the Institute of Community Studies, where she has worked continuously since 1961. She is the joint author of *The Hackney Report.*

Roger Warren Evans has served with Michael as a trustee of the Institute of Community Studies since 1974, also as a director of the Mutual Aid Centre. A historian and barrister by training, and a property developer by occupation, he is now Property Director of Estates and Agency Holdings plc.

Peter Willmott was with Michael Young at the Institute of Community Studies from its foundation and for many years thereafter, most of them as Co-Director, and is now chairman of ICS trustees. Since 1983 he has been a senior fellow at the Policy Studies Institute, where his books include *Friendship Networks and Social Support* and *Community Initiatives*.

Alison Young (no relation to Michael) has worked at Chatham House, the Acton Society Trust and the Center for International Affairs at Harvard University. In addition to co-authoring *The Fixers* with Trevor Smith, she assisted him with *Anti-politics* and has also written *The Reselection of MPs*.

INDEX

247